P9-CMV-680

THE COOKBOOK

MICHAEL MINA

M

THE COOKBOOK

MICHAEL MINA

M

MICHAEL MINA

WITH JOANN CIANCIULLI

BULFINCH PRESS

NEW YORK BOSTON LONDON

Bulfinch Press

Hachette Book Group USA
237 Park Avenue, New York, NY 10169
Visit our Web site at www.bulfinchpress.com

First Edition: November 2006
Second Printing, 2007

Library of Congress Cataloging-in-Publication Data

Mina, Michael
    Michael Mina : the cookbook / Michael Mina.—1st ed.
        p. cm.
    Includes index.
    ISBN 978-0-8212-5753-1
    1. Cookery, American. 2. Restaurant Michael Mina. I. Title.

TX715.M668 2006
641.5973—dc22   2006002124

Printed in Singapore

M

For my wife, partner, and best friend, Diane,
and my two beautiful children, Sammy and Anthony,
and to my mother and father
for their encouragement and unwavering love

CONTENTS

01

M

02

03

FOREWORD

I first met Michael several years ago at Aqua in San Francisco. I had just finished one of the most amazing meals of my life, and he came to the table—as he did with every customer in the restaurant—to be sure that the experience lived up to his standards. He was executive chef of the restaurant at the time and clearly driven by the desire to deliver not just exceptional food, but extraordinary experiences.

Being new to the area, and with New Year's Eve just five days away, during his stop at my table I asked him to recommend a chef to cater a gathering of friends at my home. (Based on the exceptional experience I had just had, it was easy to trust his judgment.) To my surprise, he said he would be happy to do it himself. I enjoyed an unforgettable meal with friends, and a new friendship was formed.

When Michael established the Mina Group in 2002, we became business partners in his venture because I believe a talent like his is rare. Designing his own concept restaurants gave Michael the ability to infuse the atmosphere with the same vision and detail that he brings to his cuisine. We have since opened restaurants in my own backyard with SeaBlue, Michael Mina Bellagio, and Nobhill, which continue to raise the level of culinary excellence in Las Vegas and keep me from traveling to San Francisco for dinner.

I not only celebrate Michael's passion, but I admire his gift. When you experience the best in any field, you quickly develop an appreciation for how good the best can be. Michael combines his extraordinary talent with an appreciation for life's finer details, and the results are found in every one of his creations.

We are blessed that Michael is sharing his creativity and talents in this new book. He is truly as good as it gets.

—ANDRE AGASSI

INTRODUCTION

Opening Restaurant Michael Mina in the legendary Westin St. Francis Hotel in the heart of San Francisco's Union Square has been a dream come true. The St. Francis is so much a part of the city's past that it truly *is* San Francisco. I felt that the landscape of the hotel and its historical value and location made it a perfect setting for my namesake restaurant. My goal was to create a timeless space that would become a landmark in the city I live in and love. I wanted to establish a sense of permanence, to make an impact with a restaurant that would be an enduring part of the city.

I have been in love with San Francisco since I was a boy. I will always remember my first visit to the city as a thirteen-year-old on vacation with my family. From that moment, I knew that I belonged here. All through school, I had posters of the Golden Gate Bridge and Fisherman's Wharf on my bedroom walls. I guess I was biding my time until I was old enough to make the move.

My first exposure to the culinary profession also came from San Francisco. As a teenager, watching *Lifestyles of the Rich and Famous,* I saw Robin Leach feature Jeremiah Tower, the chef/owner of the city's famed Stars Restaurant. The restaurant's walls were covered with photographs of movie stars, and celebrities filled the tables, sipping champagne and eating caviar. I thought to myself, "I want to be a chef in San Francisco." I was very fortunate to know at an early age where I wanted to live and what I wanted to be when I grew up. The fact that the two were simpatico was a happy accident.

Chefs from all over the world view San Francisco as one of the great restaurant towns. It is arguably one of the best epicurean cities in the country and is frequently hailed as the culinary capital of the West Coast. Like New York City and New Orleans, it is virtually impossible to disconnect the place from its cuisine; food is a vital part of the city's magnetism. From artisanal breads to seasonal produce and seafood, San Francisco is a gourmet's paradise. The people who grow the products, prepare the food, and make the wine are our rock stars.

Developing and cultivating relationships with local purveyors is a special privilege of being a chef in San Francisco. I have a profound admiration for the hand-crafted artistry that goes into creating products with individual character and relevance. I cannot think of too many other places that can match the accessibility to such ingredients as we have in the Bay Area. Over the years, I have seen a maturing of the California style that has allowed us to develop a distinctive cuisine, one driven by seasonal ingredients. It feels organic, not forced, and, more important, it is right for the climate and the population.

The unqualified joy of being a chef in San Francisco comes from our diners. Dining is a big deal—people are food savvy with educated palates and an appreciation of great food and wine. Even people who aren't in the food industry read the *Chronicle* food section, follow the latest culinary trends, and take an interest in restaurant openings. It is an enormous luxury to have a built-in clientele so passionate and well versed.

I am also lucky to have three restaurants, Nobhill, SeaBlue, and Michael Mina Bellagio, in Las Vegas. It is a city that has undergone an incredible transformation in recent years as it has become the fastest-growing urban community in the nation. When it comes to food, Las Vegas promises unparalleled dining experiences. Visitors are treated to some of the most noteworthy restaurants in the world. The very concept of Las Vegas dining has changed remarkably in the past decade. A town built on gambling, it was infamous for mediocre food. Today, the culinary arena has grown to become one of the country's most competitive and exciting. Many renowned chefs have opened first-rate restaurants in the lavish hotels that dot the famous Strip. Joël Robuchon, one of the greatest French chefs of the last century, now has a restaurant in Las Vegas, evidence that the city has truly evolved to a food lover's destination. Las Vegas was invented for celebration; a refuge for people to escape to and leave stress behind. Visitors come to have fun, especially in the evening hours. I get enormous pleasure from running restaurants with a convivial energy that reminds me of being at a great party. Everyone is there for the same reason—to laugh, relax, enjoy a drink, and along the way partake in a fine meal.

I believe that a restaurant should paint a strong portrait of its owner. Everything you're trying to distinguish about yourself is found in the details. All of the elements should be carefully conceived and integrated, adding up to one grand gesture. I take great pride in seeking out the best of everything as I go the extra distance to create a special environment for my guests. I examine the dining experience from every angle, not just in terms of food and service, but from the décor perspective as well. This has opened my eyes to the beauty and intricacy of each facet of building a great restaurant. When I got into this business, I had no idea how important it is to have every layer fit seamlessly together. You never know which specifics are going to blow people away, so the safest thing to do is to make sure every detail is covered and that the overall style of the restaurant comes together as a complete package. The highest compliment paid is that people can't identify exactly what it is that strikes them.

A driving force throughout my career is the intense energy I get in learning something new. Each step along the way to becoming a chef was a totally fresh experience. While my love of cooking always comes first, I am now excited about being a restaurateur, devising new and different dining concepts, overseeing multiple restaurants, and working with designers. As I have expanded my restaurant group, I have been privileged to collaborate with four of the most prominent designers and architects in the world, Barbara Barry, Tony Chi, Adam Tihany, and Wendy Tsuju. In fact, the only people I have come across in my career who seemed to share the same concentrated exuberance as chefs have been designers. The relationship between the chef and the restaurant designer has an immediate impact on the interior style of a space. Working as a team, we sculpted the restaurants' atmosphere to balance the food concept, location, and clientele. Celebrating the unique tapestry of the particular locale, each restaurant has its own ambience and authenticity based on our distinct vision. All of my restaurants are within hotels and are characterized by their strong sense of place. It's important to make sure the restaurant doesn't feel like a hotel dining room while also taking into consideration the fact that it must blend in with the rest of the building. The environment that is realized defines the cuisine, allowing dining and décor to come together in a transcendent combination.

Although I have wanted to write a cookbook for some time, I felt that it was important to wait until I could create a book that would truly reflect my culinary journey. This seems to be that time. With the help of my extraordinary wife, Diane, I am more focused on my goals. The responsibility of parenting has both mellowed my personality and motivated me to grow and expand. I so enjoy having my boys involved in what I do every day. I bring one child to work on Friday night and the other one on Saturday to keep them as engaged in the restaurant as possible. I know how lucky I am to be able to do this. In fact, my seven-year-old, Sammy, now sits down to dinner and announces, "Daddy, I want a tasting menu." How many kids even know what a tasting menu is?

My life's ambition is about the most universal of desires: to follow a dream you've had since you were young, obsess about it, get colleagues as excited about it as you are, adjust it, and turn it into reality. More than a decade of living and cooking in San Francisco has influenced my culinary sensibilities. What I do is a reflection of my life and my passions. I now know what it takes to master a craft and that the intensity, discipline, rigors, and constant search for excellence on all levels do have their rewards. But in the end, being in the kitchen remains a labor of love. I hope that it is expressed on every page.

O I

TRIOS

The philosophy at most of my restaurants celebrates a twist on refined American cuisine in one form or another. At the forefront is merging peak seasonal ingredients with modern cooking techniques to produce pure flavors that can be presented in an innovative fashion. Seasonal trio selections define the elevated food concept that I crafted especially for MICHAEL MINA. The trio concept highlights a primary ingredient that is accessorized with a trilogy of accompaniments; each of the three presentations offers an intricate array of taste sensations. I often describe the trio idea as complex simplicity. The three variations seem complicated when assembled on one plate, but when broken down individually, each is fairly straightforward to prepare. One example is Potato-Crusted Dover Sole (see page 50), which is the master recipe and centerpiece of the plate. The fish is then served with side components of differing vegetables, sauces, and garnishes. The method for preparing the sole remains constant throughout the variations.

In the first preparation, the sole is matched with Cauliflower Purée, Champagne Beurre Blanc, and Champagne Aïoli; cauliflower and champagne are the go-to ingredients in the classic medley. The second variation consists of Roasted Sweet Onion Purée, Malt Vinegar Beurre Blanc, and Classic Tartar Sauce; onion and malt are the flavor vehicles that drive it forward. The final presentation is Truffle Salsify, Beurre Rouge, and Truffle Aïoli; earthy salsify and truffles work together to provide the unifying line that runs through it.

In each interpretation, two or three choice ingredients are featured in a variety of ways to create layers of flavor in the final dish. I most regularly like to fuse one main flavor with a seasonal grouping of vegetables or fruits. The ingredients are utilized in multiple forms—roasted, juiced, or puréed, for instance—to bring the greatest range to their inherent flavor. I try to maintain the purity of the dish by isolating a specific flavor and then concentrating it through changing the way the ingredient has been prepared. Sampling several approaches to the same ingredients I feel teaches you something about your own taste. There isn't so much of any single item as to bore your palate.

When I first suggested this innovative way of presentation to my staff, they were confused; admittedly, I too was unsure of how to successfully pull my ideas together. As challenging as the trio concept has been to execute, I now cannot imagine any other menu for the restaurant. To my knowledge, this concept is unique and it has been great fun to devise an original approach to fine dining.

Prior to committing to the trio concept as a full-time menu idea, I experimented with the notion of eating in triplicate throughout my career. Often it was something as simple as running a foie gras trio as a special or as a course on a tasting menu, which always seemed to be a hit at the table. Over the years, I realized that two variations on a theme didn't have enough impact and four was too many. Three seemed to be the perfect number to make the flavor point.

Since I try to use locally grown, seasonal ingredients in all of my dishes, San Francisco is the perfect venue, as it gives me access to some of the world's best purveyors. There is such a wonderful variety of products available locally and we can quickly access exotic items from around the world. This is most advantageous when putting together the trio dishes, as all of this bounty allows us the freedom to create broad strokes on the plate.

When developing trio dishes it is important to define the flavors individually. Restraint is essential; I follow the old adage that the best ingredient is often the one the chef left out. I take one product, usually a protein, and then let it shine in a trinity of dishes. My goal is to keep the flavors in each variation simple and uncompromised. Each preparation has its own distinct identity, yet envelops an overall fluidity.

Not everyone wants to commit the better part of an evening to dining, so sampling all of the trio variations in a single course compresses an hours-long tasting menu to a reasonable dining period. MICHAEL MINA is located in San Francisco's downtown theater district so we have to acknowledge the time constraints of our theater-going diners. On the other hand, a night at the restaurant could be the high point of the dining-out year with the celebration of a birthday, engagement, or anniversary. So we have to make the dining experience as memorable as possible for both requirements, and the innovative trios do the trick in the most elegant way.

Once I established the trio concept, it was necessary to devise a method of serving the dishes. I knew that without the proper china, the trios would not succeed, since an integral part of fine dining is how the food is showcased on the plate. The china must set the tone of the dish. The trios were more elaborate than a traditional menu so we had to make certain that the finished dishes were impressive, not a group of components spread out across a plate. Consequently, I spent more than a year designing and perfecting a custom line of china that would allow the trios to star. Bernadaud worked with me to manufacture our brand of plateware to display the trio assortment together yet keep the preparations separate so they don't run into each other. Premium china companies commonly work with chefs to produce a table line that matches their singular style. This instance is unique because the china is tailor-made to model a particular menu concept, making it a focal point of the dining experience. I believe that the final plateware displays each dish in its best possible light.

Each trio is presented on a large, tray-like square plate, fitted with three small dish inserts of various shapes and sizes, the star and the teardrop being my favorites. The three variations are lined up in rows, in the same progressive order as the recipes are written. For optimal effect, we encourage guests to flow through the series of tastings from left to right, front to back, with the idea that the finish is the strongest flavor. Obviously, this is not something to worry about when serving these dishes at home, unless you want to make an evening of it.

There are those who eat to live and those who live to eat. I am lucky because so many diners at my restaurants fit into the latter group. It is a challenge and a great deal of fun to cook for them. I believe that a meal is an intimate exchange, a dialogue among the chef, the dish, and the diner. With the trio concept, I have produced a contemporary dining experience that my guests find memorable. There is nothing more rewarding for a chef.

HOW TO MAKE THE TRIOS

I decided to make the trio concept the focus of my first cookbook because I believe that it translates so well to the home kitchen. All cooks have foods that they love to prepare and often get so comfortable doing so that they cook the same thing over and over. I know that I often find myself doing this when cooking at home. Such repetition may provide comfort, but it can also be boring—both for the cook and for diners. And that's just what makes the trio concept so useful. Once you get the hang of any master recipe, you have three different ways to enjoy it.

Each trio preparation stands on its own and is equally creative and delicious. You can present one variation one day and introduce the master recipe in another arrangement later on. You will still be using the identical pots and pans and going through the same general routine. I think it is really liberating for home cooks to play with the variations; it frees you up to think on your feet. Once the blueprint of the dish is learned, the trio format is clear-cut.

The structure of each trio is built on a solid foundation; the master recipes are supported by a cluster of components that fit together in tone and content. The fundamentals and focus stay the same, only the flavor combinations revolve. For instance, the marmalades on the Seared Squab Breast (see pages 114–19) require the same process to complete but the fruit in each is the element that alters the outcome.

The trio recipes also encourage versatility by showing how to take each master dish down three avenues of taste simply by adjusting a few techniques and ingredients. The wide range of selections gives each cook the flexibility and freedom to alternate menus with ease, and the ability to master basic recipes, particularly when given insight on how to elaborate on them, builds confidence in the kitchen.

My trio recipes are constructed as fully realized dishes, each serving four standard portions. I suggest that you begin by considering each of the three variations and preparing the one that is most appealing to you. More often than not, most home cooks (including me) will not have the time to prepare all the groupings at once. However, if you are feeling adventurous, make the three variations in unison and present the trios just as I do in the restaurant. It is a clever and interactive way to have a dinner party.

I realize that often, as you flip through the pages of a cookbook, a recipe might pique your interest but you don't have all the ingredients on hand, or a particular component is not a favorite flavor, or everything is not available locally. The trios eliminate these issues because there is enough variety that you are sure to find at least one that you can make without omitting or substituting ingredients.

Although the variations are meant to be prepared and enjoyed together, each dish can be plated individually, as described in the recipe method, or served family-style on platters for more casual dining. Each variation is meant to be prepared and enjoyed together; it is not recommended to mix and match items from one variation to another, unless you are undertaking the whole trio. The formula should always stay the same; three variations of one main ingredient.

While all of the recipes have been written and tested with the home cook in mind, they are not watered-down versions of those we use in the restaurant. They are designed to be prepared in the home kitchen by a single cook. Particularly helpful at home is the fact that many of the components of the trios can be prepared in advance. The main point to remember about the trio concept is that each one is a variation on a theme, not a random selection. So, enjoy learning a master recipe and have fun testing your skill and your palate with the variations.

CHAPTER ONE

FIRST COURSE TRIOS

When I go out to eat, I usually do what most chefs do—order as many different dishes as I think I just might possibly be able to eat. This is in part because all chefs relish the experience of dining in another's restaurant. For me, it is also for the thrill I feel when I indulge in a profusion of flavors and textures. Sometimes I savor just a bite or two and sometimes my empty plate leaves me wanting more, but I never regret my choices.

So that diners at MICHAEL MINA can enjoy this same experience, my first course trios are based on two variations of one main ingredient on each presentation. I offset them with techniques and seasonal accompaniments to create six different, but interrelated, dishes to complete the course. The interplay created by the complementary and contrasting ingredients and cooking techniques balances the entire plate with the progression of hot and cold variations, designed to be eaten from the front of the plate to the back. For example, the hot seared scallops with caviar, corn, and roasted beets have three corresponding chilled ceviches that echo the nearly identical flavor combinations. The same philosophy applies to the parallel portraits of soup and salad. The preparation of these different dishes is, without a doubt, labor intensive, even for a restaurant kitchen. For this reason, I have made sure that each dish can stand on its own when required. However, if you do decide to go the distance, I suggest that you keep the same set of trios that I have put together, as the flavor profiles have been designed to work together as a whole.

At home, just as in the restaurant, hors d'oeuvres or appetizers are your first chance to excite your guests and give them a hint of the meal to follow. It is important that all of the components of a meal have a corresponding relationship so that the intensity of the dining experience results from a perfect marriage. The first course should simply be the seduction.

M

SEARED DIVER SCALLOPS

O I
CORN, TRUFFLE
SCALLOP CEVICHE WITH CORN GARNISH, YELLOW CORN PUDDING

O 2
BEET, LOBSTER
SCALLOP CEVICHE WITH BEET GARNISH, SCARLET BEET BEURRE ROUGE

O 3
LEMON, CAVIAR
SCALLOP CEVICHE WITH LEMON, LEMON BEURRE BLANC WITH CAVIAR

MEATY SCALLOPS PERCHED ON CRISPY POTATO CAKES IS ONE OF THE BEST COMBINATIONS ON THE PLANET. I ADORE SCALLOPS BECAUSE THEIR TRANSLUCENT TEXTURE HOLDS UP TO A MULTITUDE OF COOKING METHODS. YOU CAN STEAM, POACH, GRILL, SAUTÉ, OR SIMPLY EAT THEM RAW, SASHIMI-STYLE. THEIR STRONG, SUPPLE FLAVOR STANDS UP BEAUTIFULLY TO OTHER STRONGLY FLAVORED ACCOMPANIMENTS. THE HOT SCALLOP PREPARATION REQUIRES VELVETY SAUCES, WHILE THE CHILLED CALLS FOR SOMETHING PUNGENT AND ACIDIC. THE SAVORY, SEARED SCALLOPS WITH THE RICH, BUTTERY SAUCE ARE FOLLOWED BY THE BRIGHT, REFRESHING CEVICHE, WHICH CLEANS THE PALATE AND GETS YOU READY FOR THE NEXT ROUND. TOGETHER, THIS TRINITY IS A NEAR-PERFECT DISH: IT EXEMPLIFIES THE BALANCE OF TEXTURE, FLAVOR, AND VISUAL APPEAL. IF CAVIAR, TRUFFLES, AND LOBSTER ARE OUT OF REACH, THE SCALLOPS ARE SIMPLE TO EXECUTE AND STILL WORTH TRYING.

WINE SUGGESTION

PRAGER RIESLING 'STEINRIEGEL' FEDERSPIEL, WACHAU, AUSTRIA 2001

A rich wine is needed to balance the sweetness of the scallops and the high acidity of the dish. A dry Riesling can encompass all the flavors of the meal and give a different experience with every bite. A Sauvignon Blanc can also be served.

SEARED DIVER SCALLOPS
MASTER RECIPE

SERVES 4

12 POTATO CAKES (PAGE 176)
12 LARGE DIVER SCALLOPS (ABOUT 1 POUND)
  KOSHER SALT AND FRESHLY GROUND BLACK PEPPER
1/4 CUP CANOLA OIL

TO PREPARE THE Potato Cakes: Follow the directions in the Caviar Parfait (page 176), up to the point of frying, except use a small 1 1/2-inch ring mold so the Potato Cakes are about the same size as the seared scallops.

LINE A PLATTER with a double layer of paper towels and set aside. Season the scallops generously with salt and pepper. Place a large sauté pan over medium heat. When hot, drizzle 2 tablespoons of the oil into the pan and when it just gets hazy, add 6 of the scallops. Sear the scallops for 1 minute, without moving them around, until the bottoms are nicely browned. Turn and sear the other side for 30 seconds. (The scallops should be medium-rare.) Transfer the scallops to the prepared platter.

COAT THE PAN with the remaining 2 tablespoons of oil and sear the remaining scallops. Transfer to the platter and cover to keep warm.

FRY THE POTATO Cakes as directed in the recipe on page 176.

FOLLOW THE ASSEMBLY and serving directions for the variation you are making.

O1
CORN, TRUFFLE

SCALLOP CEVICHE WITH CORN GARNISH

SCALLOP CEVICHE

4 RAW DIVER SCALLOPS
  KOSHER SALT AND FRESHLY GROUND BLACK PEPPER
1/4 CUP BLACK TRUFFLE VINEGAR (USE WHITE BALSAMIC VINEGAR
  FOR VARIATION 2, FRESH LEMON JUICE FOR VARIATION 3)
2 TEASPOONS EXTRA-VIRGIN OLIVE OIL, FOR DRIZZLING

GARNISH

  KERNELS FROM 1 EAR SWEET YELLOW CORN (ABOUT 1 CUP),
  BLANCHED
1/2 TABLESPOON BLACK TRUFFLE VINEGAR
2 TABLESPOONS EXTRA-VIRGIN OLIVE OIL
1 TABLESPOON WHITE TRUFFLE OIL
1 TEASPOON MINCED FRESH CHIVES
  KOSHER SALT AND FRESHLY GROUND BLACK PEPPER

TO PREPARE THE ceviche: Using a very sharp thin-bladed knife, slice each scallop horizontally into 4 disks. Place the scallops in a nonreactive bowl and season with salt and pepper. Add the vinegar and toss to combine. Cover and refrigerate for 30 minutes or up to 1 hour.

TO PREPARE THE garnish: Combine the blanched corn, vinegar, olive oil, truffle oil, and chives in a mixing bowl. Season well with salt and pepper. Set aside for 5 minutes to let the flavors marry.

REMOVE THE CHILLED scallops from the vinegar and fan 4 slices on each of 4 small bowls or plates. Lightly season the scallops with salt and a little drizzle of olive oil. Garnish each plate with a generous tablespoon of the corn mixture.

YELLOW CORN PUDDING

This impressive and easy sauce, called a pudding because of its thickness, is also great on crab cakes, grilled shrimp, or as a dip for blanched asparagus.

MAKES 1 CUP

2	EARS SWEET YELLOW CORN
2	TABLESPOONS TRUFFLE BUTTER (SEE SOURCES)
	KOSHER SALT AND FRESHLY GROUND BLACK PEPPER

GARNISH

4	SLICES FRESH BLACK TRUFFLE

USING A SHARP knife, cut the kernels from the cob and put them through a vegetable juicer. (Alternatively, combine the corn and 1/4 cup water in a blender and purée until completely smooth.) Pass the corn juice through a fine-mesh strainer into a small saucepan, pushing firmly with a spatula to release the juice, and discard the solids.

PLACE THE CORN juice over low heat and cook, whisking constantly until the natural corn starch thickens the juice into a bright yellow sauce, about 5 minutes. Stir in the truffle butter and season lightly with salt and pepper. Cover and keep warm until ready to serve.

TO ASSEMBLE AND serve: Pool about 2 tablespoons of the Corn Pudding in the center of 4 small plates. Set 3 Potato Cakes on the sauce and place a hot Seared Scallop on top of each. Garnish with sliced truffles. Serve with the chilled Scallop Ceviche with Corn Garnish.

O 2

BEET, LOBSTER

SCALLOP CEVICHE WITH BEET GARNISH

It is a good idea to wear plastic gloves when working with beets to avoid staining your hands. When roasting beets, I line a sheet pan with rock salt to make a salt-bed. Not only does this impart a subtle flavor to the beets, but the crystals help insulate them so they cook more evenly; it also prevents burning on the bottom where they rest on the pan. Roast all the beets for the garnish and beurre rouge at once.

SCALLOP CEVICHE

4	RAW DIVER SCALLOPS
	KOSHER SALT AND FRESHLY GROUND BLACK PEPPER
1/4	CUP WHITE BALSAMIC VINEGAR
2	TEASPOONS EXTRA-VIRGIN OLIVE OIL, FOR DRIZZLING

BEET GARNISH

1	RED BABY BEET, SCRUBBED
1	YELLOW BABY BEET, SCRUBBED

2   TABLESPOONS CANOLA OIL
     KOSHER SALT AND FRESHLY GROUND BLACK PEPPER

MAKE THE SCALLOP Ceviche as directed in the recipe, substituting the white balsamic vinegar for the truffle vinegar.

TO PREPARE THE beet garnish: Preheat the oven to 375°F.

RUB THE BEETS with the oil and season with salt and pepper. Wrap each beet individually in aluminum foil and place on a baking pan. Roast the beets until a knife can pierce the beets without meeting any resistance, 30 to 40 minutes.

CAREFULLY UNWRAP THE beets and set aside to cool. When cool enough to handle, rub off the skins with paper towels. Quarter the beets and reserve each type separately so the red doesn't bleed onto the yellow.

REMOVE THE CHILLED scallops from the vinegar and fan 4 slices on each of 4 small bowls or plates. Lightly season the scallops with salt and a little drizzle of olive oil. Garnish each plate with a wedge of red and yellow beet.

SCARLET BEET BEURRE ROUGE

MAKES 1 CUP

2   RED BABY BEETS, ROASTED AND COOLED (AS ABOVE)
2   TABLESPOONS CANOLA OIL
     KOSHER SALT AND FRESHLY GROUND BLACK PEPPER
     BEURRE ROUGE (PAGE 220)
1/2 CUP DRY RED WINE, SUCH AS CABERNET SAUVIGNON
1/4 CUP RED WINE VINEGAR

COARSELY CHOP THE roasted beets and place in a blender with 1 tablespoon of water. Purée until completely smooth.

FOLLOW THE DIRECTIONS for Beurre Rouge on page 220, using the red wine and red wine vinegar. Add the beet purée to the shallot mixture and proceed as instructed.

GARNISH

     BEURRE MONTÉ (SEE PAGE 220)
4   OUNCES COOKED LOBSTER MEAT, CUT INTO MEDALLIONS
     KOSHER SALT AND FRESH GROUND BLACK PEPPER

PREPARE A BEURRE Monté (page 220) as directed in the recipe. Place the Beurre Monté in a small sauté pan over medium-low heat. Add the lobster and heat for 1 to 2 minutes to warm through. Season lightly with salt and pepper.

TO ASSEMBLE AND serve: Pool 2 tablespoons of the Scarlet Beet Beurre Rouge in the center of 4 small plates. Set 3 Potato Cakes on the sauce and place a hot Seared Scallop on top of each. Garnish with the lobster mixture. Serve with the Scallop Ceviche with Beet Garnish.

O 3

LEMON, CAVIAR

SCALLOP CEVICHE WITH CAVIAR

SCALLOP CEVICHE

4	RAW DIVER SCALLOPS
	KOSHER SALT AND FRESHLY GROUND BLACK PEPPER
1/4	CUP FRESHLY SQUEEZED LEMON JUICE
2	TEASPOONS EXTRA-VIRGIN OLIVE OIL, FOR DRIZZLING

GARNISH

1/2	OUNCE CAVIAR, PREFERABLY OSETRA
1	TEASPOON BLANCHED LEMON ZEST OR MEYER LEMON CONFIT
	(SEE PAGE 59)
1	TEASPOON MINCED FRESH CHIVES

MAKE THE SCALLOP Ceviche as directed in the recipe, substituting the lemon juice for the truffle vinegar.

REMOVE THE CHILLED scallops from the lemon juice and fan 4 slices on each of 4 small bowls or plates. Lightly season the scallops with salt and a little drizzle of olive oil. Garnish each serving with a tiny bit of caviar (about 1/8 ounce on each), a few pieces of lemon zest, and a sprinkle of chives.

LEMON BEURRE BLANC WITH CAVIAR

MAKES 1 CUP

	BEURRE BLANC (PAGE 220)
1/2	CUP DRY WHITE WINE, SUCH AS SAUVIGNON BLANC
1/4	CUP CHAMPAGNE VINEGAR
	JUICE AND ZEST OF 1/2 LEMON

GARNISH

1 1/2	OUNCES CAVIAR, PREFERABLY OSETRA
1	TABLESPOON MINCED FRESH CHIVES

TO MAKE THE Lemon Beurre Blanc: Prepare the Beurre Blanc as directed in the recipe, using the white wine and champagne vinegar. Add the lemon juice and zest to the shallot mixture and proceed as instructed.

TO ASSEMBLE AND serve: Mix the Lemon Beurre Blanc with 1/2 ounce of the caviar and the minced chives. Pool about 2 tablespoons of the sauce in the center of 4 small plates. Set 3 Potato Cakes on the sauce and place a hot Seared Scallop on top of each. Garnish with the remaining caviar. Serve with the Scallop Ceviche with Caviar.

SESAME-CRUSTED SOFT-SHELL CRAB
WITH DUNGENESS CRAB FALAFEL

O 1
LEMON, CUMIN
MARINATED ENGLISH PEA SALAD, CREAMY LEMON VINAIGRETTE

O 2
SAFFRON, GARLIC
CHICKPEA SALAD, CREAMY SAFFRON VINAIGRETTE

O 3
TOMATO, LIME
FAVA BEAN SALAD, CREAMY TOMATO-LIME VINAIGRETTE

I DRAW INSPIRATION FROM MY ETHNIC ROOTS AND REFINE THE IDEAS BY UTILIZING MY FORMAL FRENCH TRAINING AND EXPERIENCE. THE BIRTH OF THIS DISH STEMS FROM THE FALAFEL; IT IS GENERALLY ACCEPTED THAT THE FALAFEL ORIGINATED AS STREET FOOD IN EGYPT, WHERE THESE HEAVILY SPICED FRIED FRITTERS HAVE BECOME A NATIONAL DISH. WHEN I WAS GROWING UP, MY MOM WOULD MAKE HOMEMADE FALAFEL FOR MY BROTHER AND ME AS AN AFTER-SCHOOL SNACK, AND THE MEMORY HOLDS DEEP MEANING FOR ME. THE EGYPTIAN VARIATION USES EXCLUSIVELY FAVA BEANS, WHILE OTHER MIDDLE EASTERN COUNTRIES INCORPORATE CHICKPEAS. I PUT MY OWN TWIST ON MY FAMILY'S TRADI-TIONAL RECIPE BY GRINDING ENGLISH PEAS INTO THE FAVA MIXTURE. TAHINI, A THICK PASTE MADE OF GROUND SESAME SEEDS, IS CLASSICALLY SERVED WITH FALAFEL. FROM THAT STARTING POINT, I GOT THE NOTION TO BASE THE VINAIGRETTES ON THE SMOOTH NUTTINESS OF TAHINI. TO FURTHER INTENSIFY THE FLAVOR AND KEEP IT INTERESTING, I ADDED BLACK SESAME SEEDS TO THE CRAB TEMPURA BATTER.

I AM A FIRM BELIEVER IN COOKING SEASONALLY AND EATING WHAT IS GOOD WHEN IT IS GOOD. SWEET SOFT-SHELL CRABS AND EARTHY FAVA BEANS ARE A WELCOME SIGN OF SPRING AND THEIR FLAVORS COMPLEMENT ONE ANOTHER ESPECIALLY WELL. IT IS IMPORTANT TO PURCHASE THE SOFT-SHELL CRABS LIVE AND USE THEM SHORTLY AFTER CLEANING.

WINE SUGGESTION
LEITZ RIESLING 'MAGDALENENKREUZ' SPATLESE, RHEINGAU, GERMANY 2003

Fried fish and German Riesling are a perfect pairing. Once you add spicy Asian flavors the combination gets better. The sweetness in the wine will balance the sweet and sour flavors of the vinaigrettes. Any wine you serve must also be low in alcohol so the spice is not amplified.

M

SESAME-CRUSTED SOFT-SHELL CRAB
MASTER RECIPE

SERVES 4

4	LIVE SOFT-SHELL CRABS, PRIME SIZE (ABOUT 3 OUNCES EACH)
	APPROXIMATELY 1 GALLON CANOLA OIL, FOR DEEP-FRYING
1 3/4	CUPS ALL-PURPOSE FLOUR
3/4	CUP CORNSTARCH
2	TABLESPOONS BAKING POWDER
2	TABLESPOONS SUGAR
1 1/2	TEASPOONS KOSHER SALT, PLUS ADDITIONAL FOR SEASONING
1 1/2	TABLESPOONS BLACK SESAME SEEDS
1 1/2	TABLESPOONS WHITE SESAME SEEDS
2 1/2	TO 3 CUPS ICE WATER
	FRESHLY GROUND BLACK PEPPER

TO CLEAN THE crabs: Hold the crab from the back end and, using kitchen shears, quickly cut off about 1/4 inch from the front of the crab, just behind the eyes and mouth. Squeeze gently to clean out the contents. Unfold the pointed sides of the top shell and remove the feathery gills. Turn the crab over and cut off the bottom tail flap, known as the apron. Repeat with the remaining crabs. Place the crabs in a resealable plastic bag and transfer to the refrigerator.

FILL A LARGE heavy pot or deep fryer three-quarters of the way with oil and heat to 360°F on a frying thermometer. While the oil is heating up, make the tempura batter.

MIX THE FLOUR, cornstarch, baking powder, sugar, salt, and sesame seeds in a large bowl. Whisk in 2 cups of the ice water until a pancake batter consistency is achieved and there are few lumps. Add more water if needed. Transfer the batter to the refrigerator if you are going to hold it longer than 10 minutes; it is important that it stay cold.

LINE A PLATE with a double layer of paper towels and set aside. Season the crabs well on all sides with salt and pepper. Dip each crab into the batter a couple of times to coat it completely, letting the excess drip back into the bowl. Holding the crabs by the leg, carefully and gently lower them into the hot oil 2 at a time, so as not to overcrowd the pot. The crabs should sort of fizz when they hit the hot oil and will puff up fairly quickly. Fry the crabs for 3 minutes, turning with tongs or chopsticks so they cook evenly. When the coating is light golden brown and crisp, carefully remove the crabs to the prepared plate. While they are still hot, lightly season with salt. Cut the fried soft-shell crabs in half through the center of the body before serving.

FOLLOW THE ASSEMBLY and serving directions for the variation you are making.

DUNGENESS CRAB FALAFEL
MASTER RECIPE

MAKES 12 FALAFEL

2	CUPS SHELLED, BLANCHED, AND PEELED FRESH FAVA BEANS
1/2	CUP SHELLED AND BLANCHED ENGLISH PEAS
1/4	CUP FINELY CHOPPED FRESH FLAT-LEAF PARSLEY LEAVES
1/4	CUP FINELY CHOPPED FRESH DILL SPRIGS
1/4	CUP FINELY CHOPPED FRESH CILANTRO LEAVES
3	SCALLIONS, GREEN PARTS ONLY, FINELY CHOPPED
1	CLOVE GARLIC, MINCED
1/2	TABLESPOON GROUND CUMIN, TOASTED
1/2	TEASPOON GROUND CORIANDER, TOASTED
1/4	TEASPOON RED PEPPER FLAKES
	KOSHER SALT AND FRESHLY GROUND BLACK PEPPER
1/4	POUND DUNGENESS CRABMEAT, PICKED THROUGH FOR SHELLS AND CARTILAGE, LARGE PIECES OF LEG MEAT RESERVED FOR GARNISH
1/4	CUP WONDRA FLOUR
	CANOLA OIL, FOR FRYING
	BEURRE MONTÉ (PAGE 220)

TOSS THE FAVA beans, peas, parsley, dill, cilantro, scallions, and garlic together in a large bowl. Place the mixture in a food processor fitted with a metal blade and pulse until coarsely ground, scraping down the sides of the bowl as needed. Transfer the mixture to a large bowl. Stir in the cumin, coriander, and red pepper flakes and season generously with salt and pepper. Using a spatula, fold the crabmeat into the falafel mixture to incorporate. (May be made a day ahead and stored covered and refrigerated.)

WITH MOISTENED HANDS, form the falafel mixture into 12 patties about 2 inches in diameter. You will need 2 falafel per person; freeze the remaining 4 for another use. Refrigerate the falafel until ready to use.

SPREAD THE WONDRA flour out on a platter. Dredge the falafel to lightly cover on both sides, and shake off the excess.

HEAT 1/4 INCH of oil in a large sauté pan over medium heat. Gently lay the falafel in the hot oil, taking care not to crowd the pan (you may need to do this in batches). Fry until nicely browned, turning often, 2 to 3 minutes. Transfer to a platter lined with paper towels. Season the falafel lightly with salt.

TO PREPARE THE crabmeat garnish: Prepare a beurre monté (page 220). Place the beurre monté in a small sauté pan over medium-low heat. Add the reserved crabmeat and heat for 1 to 2 minutes to warm through. Season lightly with salt and pepper.

FOLLOW THE ASSEMBLY and serving directions for the variation you are making.

O 1

LEMON, CUMIN

MARINATED ENGLISH PEA SALAD

1	CUP SHELLED AND BLANCHED ENGLISH PEAS
1	LEMON, CUT INTO SEGMENTS (SEE SEGMENTING CITRUS, PAGE 225)
1/2	TEASPOON FINELY GRATED LEMON ZEST
2	TABLESPOONS EXTRA-VIRGIN OLIVE OIL, PREFERABLY LEMON-INFUSED
1/4	TEASPOON GROUND CUMIN, TOASTED
	KOSHER SALT AND FRESHLY GROUND BLACK PEPPER

COMBINE THE PEAS, lemon segments, lemon zest, oil, and cumin together in a small bowl. Season generously with salt and pepper. Reserve at room temperature for 15 minutes to allow the flavors to marry.

CREAMY LEMON VINAIGRETTE

MAKES 1 CUP

1	TABLESPOON TAHINI
1	LARGE EGG YOLK
1/4	CUP FRESH LEMON JUICE
3/4	CUP CANOLA OIL
1 1/2	TEASPOONS GROUND CUMIN, TOASTED
	KOSHER SALT AND FRESHLY GROUND BLACK PEPPER

COMBINE THE TAHINI, yolk, and lemon juice in a blender, processing until smooth. With the motor running, slowly drizzle in the oil. The dressing will be fairly thick and creamy. Stir in the cumin and season well with salt and pepper.

TO ASSEMBLE AND serve: Pool a tablespoon of the Lemon Vinaigrette on opposite ends of each of 4 rectangular plates. Drag another tablespoon of vinaigrette diagonally across the center of each plate to make a stripe. (Any leftover vinaigrette can be stored, covered and refrigerated, for up to 3 days.)

SET A CRAB Falafel on each vinaigrette pool and place a piece of crabmeat garnish on top. Divide the Pea Salad among the plates, mounding it in the center stripe of vinaigrette. Place a soft-shell half on either side of the salad, standing them up on the cut side.

O 2

SAFFRON, GARLIC

CHICKPEA SALAD

Fresh chickpeas—also known as garbanzo beans—are a beautiful light-green hue and have started to pop up from early May to September at farmers' markets and specialty stores across the country. If you cannot find fresh chickpeas, it is perfectly fine to substitute dried. (Soak the dried chickpeas in a large bowl covered with cool water to cover by 2 inches in the refrigerator for at least 18 hours or up to 24; the chickpeas will rehydrate and swell to triple their original size. Drain and rinse thoroughly in a colander before using.)

5	SPRIGS FRESH THYME
2	SHALLOTS, SLICED
2	CLOVES GARLIC, SMASHED

1	BAY LEAF, PREFERABLY FRESH
1	TEASPOON WHOLE BLACK PEPPERCORNS
1	CUP FRESH CHICKPEAS, PICKED THROUGH AND RINSED
1 1/2	CUPS CHICKEN STOCK (PAGE 222)
1/2	TEASPOON KOSHER SALT, PLUS ADDITIONAL FOR SEASONING
2	TABLESPOONS EXTRA-VIRGIN OLIVE OIL
	PINCH OF RED PEPPER FLAKES
	FRESHLY GROUND BLACK PEPPER
4	CLOVES GARLIC, HALVED LENGTHWISE
	PINCH OF SAFFRON

MAKE A SACHET/BOUQUET garni by placing the thyme, shallots, garlic, bay leaf, and peppercorns in a piece of cheesecloth and tying closed with kitchen string. Toss the bouquet garni into a large saucepan.

ADD THE CHICKPEAS and stock and bring to a simmer over medium-low heat. Simmer for 20 to 25 minutes or until the beans are tender, skimming foam off the top if necessary. When the beans are cooked through and tender, season with the 1/2 teaspoon salt.

DRAIN THE CHICKPEAS and place in a large bowl. While they are still warm, add the olive oil and toss to coat. Season with the red pepper flakes and a pinch of salt and pepper. Set aside to cool to room temperature.

IN THE MEANTIME, combine the halved garlic, saffron, and a pinch of salt in a separate saucepan. Add 1 cup of water and place over medium heat. Bring to a simmer and cook gently until the garlic is soft and takes on the vibrant yellow color of the saffron, about 10 minutes. Drain the garlic and let cool. Gently stir the garlic into the chickpea mixture, taking care not to mash it.

CREAMY SAFFRON VINAIGRETTE

MAKES 1 CUP

	PINCH OF SAFFRON
3/4	CUP CANOLA OIL
2	CLOVES GARLIC, MINCED
1	LARGE EGG YOLK
2	TABLESPOONS CHAMPAGNE VINEGAR
1	TABLESPOON TAHINI
	KOSHER SALT AND FRESHLY GROUND BLACK PEPPER

COMBINE THE SAFFRON with a tablespoon of hot water in a small bowl. Steep for 1 minute to bleed the color out.

HEAT 2 TABLESPOONS of the oil in a small sauté pan over low heat. Add the garlic and sauté for a minute or two until lightly toasted. Do not allow it to burn. Remove from the heat and cool to room temperature.

COMBINE THE YOLK, vinegar, tahini, and saffron, along with its water, in a blender and purée until smooth. With the motor running, slowly drizzle in the remaining oil. The dressing will be fairly thick and creamy. Add the sautéed garlic and oil and blend. Season well with salt and pepper.

TO ASSEMBLE AND serve: Pool a tablespoon of the Saffron Vinaigrette on opposite ends of each of 4 rectangular plates. Drag another tablespoon of vinaigrette diagonally across the center of each plate to make a stripe. (Any left-over vinaigrette can be stored, covered and refrigerated, for up to 3 days.)

SET A CRAB Falafel on each vinaigrette pool and place a piece of the crabmeat garnish on top. Divide the Chickpea Salad among the plates, mounding it in the center of the vinaigrette. Place a soft-shell half on either side of the salad, standing them up on the cut side.

O 3

TOMATO, LIME

FAVA BEAN SALAD

8	SWEET 100 TOMATOES, HALVED LENGTHWISE
1	LIME, CUT INTO SEGMENTS (SEE SEGMENTING CITRUS, PAGE 225)
1	CUP SHELLED, BLANCHED, AND PEELED FRESH FAVA BEANS
2	TABLESPOONS EXTRA-VIRGIN OLIVE OIL
1	TEASPOON FINELY GRATED LIME ZEST
	KOSHER SALT AND FRESHLY GROUND BLACK PEPPER

MIX THE TOMATOES, lime segments, fava beans, oil, and lime zest together in a small bowl. Season well with salt and pepper. Set aside at room temperature for 15 minutes to allow the flavors to marry.

CREAMY TOMATO-LIME VINAIGRETTE

MAKES 1 1/4 CUPS

6	SUN-DRIED TOMATOES IN OIL, DRAINED AND CHOPPED
1	LARGE EGG YOLK
6	TABLESPOONS TOMATO WATER (PAGE 224)
1/4	CUP FRESH LIME JUICE
1	TABLESPOON TAHINI
3/4	CUP CANOLA OIL
	KOSHER SALT AND FRESHLY GROUND BLACK PEPPER

COMBINE THE SUN-DRIED tomatoes, yolk, tomato water, lime juice, and tahini in a blender and purée until smooth. With the motor running, slowly drizzle in the oil to emulsify. The dressing will be fairly thick and creamy. Taste and season well with salt and pepper.

TO SERVE: On rectangular plates, pool a tablespoon of the Tomato-Lime Vinaigrette on opposite ends of each plate. Drag another tablespoon of vinaigrette diagonally across the center of the plates to make a stripe. (Any leftover vinaigrette can be stored, covered and refrigerated, for up to 3 days.)

SET A CRAB Falafel on each vinaigrette pool and place a piece of the crabmeat garnish on top. Divide the Fava Bean Salad among the plates, mounding it in the center stripe of vinaigrette. Place a soft-shell half on either side of the salad, standing them up on the cut side.

TORCHON OF FOIE GRAS
WITH FOIE GRAS GASTRIQUE

O 1
PLUM, GINGER
ROASTED PLUMS, PLUM GASTRIQUE, PLUM CONSOMMÉ,
PLUM GELÉE, GINGER SALT

O 2
PINEAPPLE, VANILLA
ROASTED PINEAPPLE, PINEAPPLE GASTRIQUE, PINEAPPLE CONSOMMÉ,
PINEAPPLE GELÉE, VANILLA SALT

O 3
RHUBARB, LIME
RHUBARB COMPOTE, RHUBARB GASTRIQUE, RHUBARB CONSOMMÉ,
RHUBARB GELÉE, LIME SALT

FOIE GRAS IS THE ULTIMATE DELICACY, FULL OF LUXURY AND ROMANCE. CHEFS HAVE LONG BEEN ARDENT FANS OF ITS VERSATILITY, SENSUAL FLAVOR, AND CREAMY TEXTURE, AND THE LURING PROMISE OF INDULGENCE INVARIABLY SEDUCES DINERS TO EXCESS. COOKING FOIE GRAS REQUIRES SOME FINESSE AND VIGILANCE, AS IT IS COMPOSED ALMOST ENTIRELY OF FAT. ITS ETHEREAL TEXTURE IS AS MELTINGLY SOFT AS A WARM PIECE OF BUTTER. TO BALANCE IT, A BRACING ACCOMPANIMENT IS NEEDED TO CUT ITS DENSE RICHNESS. PLUM, PINEAPPLE, AND RHUBARB ARE TART FRUITS WITH UNDERLYING SWEETNESS, WHICH PROVIDE THE PERFECT COUNTERPOINT FOR BOTH HOT AND COLD FOIE GRAS VARIATIONS. EITHER ONE OF THESE FOIE GRAS PREPARATIONS CAN STAND ON ITS OWN AND IS A LOVELY WAY TO BEGIN A SPECIAL MEAL. *TORCHON* IS A CLASSIC FRENCH RECIPE IN WHICH A LOBE OF FOIE GRAS IS WRAPPED IN CHEESECLOTH (*TORCHON* MEANS "DISHTOWEL" IN FRENCH) AND THEN QUICKLY POACHED TO GENTLY COOK IT. MAKING THE *TORCHON* IS A TWO-DAY PROCESS, SO PLAN AHEAD. DEVEINING AND CLEANING THE LIVER TO REMOVE ANY IMPURITIES ARE OF THE UTMOST IMPORTANCE. YOU WILL NEED KITCHEN TWINE AND CHEESECLOTH TO FORM THE *TORCHON*. TO KEEP IT SIMPLE, SERVE THE *TORCHON* WITH YOUR FAVORITE FRUIT JAM AND TOAST POINTS. IN PLACE OF THE *TORCHON*, SUBSTITUTE A FOIE GRAS TERRINE OR PÂTÉ, WHICH ARE AVAILABLE AT GOURMET MARKETS.

WINE SUGGESTION
DOMAINE DES BAUMARD QUARTS DE CHAUME, LOIRE, FRANCE 2002
A late harvest Chenin Blanc will uphold the fresh fruit flavors and balance the sweetness. It is also very important to balance the acidity (that cuts through the fat in the foie gras). Any sweet wine works as long as it has high sugar content and lots of acidity.

TORCHON OF FOIE GRAS
MASTER RECIPE

SERVES 4

1	GRADE A DUCK FOIE GRAS (ABOUT 1 1/4 POUNDS)
2	TABLESPOONS KOSHER SALT
2	TEASPOONS SALTPETER (SEE NOTE)
2	TEASPOONS SUGAR
1/4	TEASPOON GROUND WHITE PEPPER

BRING THE FOIE gras to room temperature (in its Cryovac bag), 1 to 2 hours. Gently remove the foie gras from the package and carefully separate the two lobes with your hands; it should feel like soft clay. Pull out the connective tissue between the lobes and rinse the foie gras under cold water. Reserve the small lobe for the hot foie gras variation or for another use. To store, wrap the lobe in parchment paper and then tightly in plastic wrap. May be refrigerated for up to 3 days or frozen for up to 1 month.

COVER A CUTTING board with a piece of plastic wrap. Place the large lobe on the plastic, rounded side down. Using a butter knife, neatly make an incision in the shape of a "y" on the underside of the lobe. Spread the foie gras open to expose the main vein. Scrape carefully to pull the vein out, using fish tweezers if you have them to avoid tearing. Don't be afraid to make more cuts to open up the lobe as needed or to mash the flesh in search of veins. It is important that anything red be removed. Spread the foie gras into a uniform piece of even thickness, about 1/2 inch, without any holes. It should be butter-soft at this point.

TO MAKE THE cure, combine the salt, saltpeter, sugar, and white pepper in a small bowl. Liberally sprinkle the surface of the foie gras with half of the curing mixture. Place a piece of plastic wrap on top and flip the foie gras over. Lift the plastic wrap and season the bottom of the foie gras with the remaining cure mix. Again, flip the foie gras back over and roll it up tightly in the plastic wrap. Refrigerate 8 hours or overnight.

CUT A 2-FOOT-LONG piece of cheesecloth and fold it in half, making a doubled 1-foot piece. Remove the large lobe of foie gras from the refrigerator. Carefully cut it in half lengthwise and lay the pieces end to end across the cheesecloth. Use your fingers to press the foie gras into a log approximately 1 inch wide. Roll very tightly into a cylinder, keeping tension on the cheesecloth in order to ensure a compact roll. Tightly twist together the ends of the cheesecloth, and tie them securely with kitchen twine. Refrigerate for 15 to 30 minutes so that the foie gras is not too soft to cook properly.

FILL A BAKING pan large enough to fit the *torchon* halfway with water and bring to a simmer over medium heat. Have an equally large ice bath set up on the side. Place the *torchon* in the simmering water and hold it down with tongs or a spoon to keep it submerged. Cook for 1 to 2 minutes, until fat begins to seep out of the cheesecloth and the *torchon* is soft throughout. Immediately transfer to the ice bath. Let the *torchon* chill for at least 5 minutes to ensure that it has cooled completely; it should be firm to the touch.

REMOVE THE *TORCHON* from the ice bath and hold by one end. Squeeze to force the foie gras to one end, reforming the tight tube shape with no air pockets. When done properly and with enough pressure, some of it will seep out of the cheesecloth. Twist the end of the cheesecloth to ensure that the mixture is compact, and tie as close to the foie gras as possible. Put the *torchon* on a plate and refrigerate until firm, about 2 hours. May be refrigerated up to 3 days or frozen for up to a week.

WORKING WITH A sharp knife that has been dipped in hot water, cut the *torchon* into 1/4-inch medallions. Use a 1-inch cookie cutter or ring to punch out the foie gras slices from the cheesecloth. If not serving immediately, place the medallions on a plate, cover, and put in the refrigerator to stay chilled.

FOLLOW THE ASSEMBLY and serving directions for the variation you are making.

Note: Saltpeter

Saltpeter, also referred to as pink curing salt or sel rose, is used in many types of sausage curing; it works particularly well in the foie gras torchon. The cotton candy–colored salt contains a small amount of sodium nitrite which reacts with the liver to form a more stable protein complex, making it especially resistant to oxidizing. This helps maintain the rosy tinge of the foie gras.

SEARED FOIE GRAS
MASTER RECIPE

4 FOIE GRAS MEDALLIONS (ABOUT 3 OUNCES EACH)
KOSHER SALT AND FRESHLY GROUND BLACK PEPPER
1/4 CUP MICRO GREENS, FOR GARNISH
4 SLICES BRIOCHE, TOASTED, FOR SERVING
(PAGE 144 OR STORE-BOUGHT)

SCORE THE TOP of each medallion in a diamond pattern and season generously on all sides with salt and pepper.

HEAT A SAUTÉ pan over medium-high heat. Lay the medallions in the pan, scored side down. Sear for 30 seconds on each side, until golden brown. The seared foie gras should have no resistance when pressed. Transfer to a plate.

FOLLOW THE ASSEMBLY and serving directions for the variation you are making.

FOIE GRAS GASTRIQUE BASE
MASTER RECIPE

MAKES 3/4 CUP

4 OUNCES GRADE A OR B DUCK FOIE GRAS
1/4 CUP PLUS 1/2 TABLESPOON WATER
1/2 CUP SUGAR
6 TABLESPOONS BALSAMIC VINEGAR

COARSELY CHOP THE foie gras and put it in a saucepan with the 1/4 cup water. Place over medium heat and cook until the duck fat has completely melted and only little rubbery pieces of foie gras remain. Strain the duck fat into a plastic container and transfer to the refrigerator. Discard the solids. The rendered fat will rise to the top and solidify as it cools. Discard the water and reserve the rendered fat. You should have 1/4 cup.

COMBINE THE FOIE gras fat with the remaining 1/2 tablespoon of water and the sugar in a small saucepan (it should look like wet sand) over medium heat. Cook, whisking constantly, until the sugar is bubbling and the mixture looks like taffy, about 5 minutes.

WHISK IN THE balsamic vinegar (the sauce will bubble up). Simmer until reduced by half, about 3 to 5 minutes. Remove from the heat and set aside to cool.

FOLLOW THE ASSEMBLY and serving directions for the variation you are making.

O I

PLUM, GINGER

FOR THE HOT VARIATION: ROASTED PLUMS

1/4	CUP SIMPLE SYRUP (PAGE 225)
1-INCH	PIECE FRESH GINGER, THINLY SLICED
4	PLUMS, HALVED AND PITTED (PREFERABLY PLUOT OR ELEPHANT HEART)
	KOSHER SALT AND FRESHLY GROUND BLACK PEPPER

PREHEAT THE OVEN to 350°F.

COMBINE THE SIMPLE Syrup and ginger in a baking dish. Add the plums, cut side down, and roast until they are very soft, about 15 minutes. Let cool slightly. When cool enough to handle, carefully peel off the skin. Cover to keep warm.

PLUM GASTRIQUE

| 2 | PLUMS, PITTED AND CHOPPED (PREFERABLY PLUOT OR ELEPHANT HEART) |
| 2 | TABLESPOONS FOIE GRAS GASTRIQUE BASE (FROM MASTER RECIPE) |

COMBINE THE PLUMS and the Gastrique Base in a small saucepan over low heat. Using a wooden spoon, smash the plums to release the flavor and color. Simmer until thick, about 10 minutes.

FOR THE COLD VARIATION: PLUM CONSOMMÉ

5	PLUMS, HALVED AND PITTED (PREFERABLY PLUOT OR ELEPHANT HEART)
2	SLICES FRESH GINGER, ABOUT 1/4 INCH THICK
1	SHALLOT, SLICED
1 1/2	CUPS WATER
6	TABLESPOONS SIMPLE SYRUP (PAGE 225)
2	TABLESPOONS PLUM WINE
	PINCH OF KOSHER SALT

COMBINE THE PLUMS, ginger, shallot, water, Simple Syrup, plum wine, and salt in a pan over low heat. Stir and press the plums lightly with a spoon to release the juices. Cook for about 15 minutes. Do not let the mixture bubble or it will turn cloudy. Remove from the heat and let the plums steep until cool, about 10 minutes. Strain the mixture through a coffee filter into another bowl; you should have at least 1 cup. You need 3/4 cup for the Plum Gelée and the remaining 1/4 cup for serving.

PLUM GELÉE

| 4 | SHEETS GELATIN OR 1 (1/4-OUNCE) ENVELOPE POWDERED GELATIN |
| 3/4 | CUP PLUM CONSOMMÉ |

SOAK THE GELATIN sheets in cool water for 5 minutes to soften, then remove and squeeze out the excess water (if using powdered gelatin, soak the gelatin in 3 tablespoons cool water for 2 minutes).

PLACE THE CONSOMMÉ in a small saucepan over medium heat. Bring to a boil. Add the bloomed gelatin, and whisk to combine. Pour the liquid into a small container, so it is about 1/4 inch deep. Chill until completely set. Once firm, cut the gelée into 1/4-inch cubes.

GINGER SALT

1   TEASPOON MINCED CANDIED GINGER
1   TABLESPOON PINK HAWAIIAN SALT

MIX THE CANDIED ginger and salt together until well combined.

GARNISH

2   TABLESPOONS DICED FRESH PLUM

TO ASSEMBLE AND serve: For the chilled presentation, lay several cubes of the Plum Gelée on each of 4 small dishes to create a platform for the *Torchon*. Set 3 slices of *Torchon* on top of the gelée, season lightly with the Ginger Salt and garnish with diced plums. Spoon a tablespoon of the Plum Consommé around the bottom of each dish.

FOR THE HOT presentation, divide the Roasted Plum halves among 4 plates. Top each with a Seared Foie Gras medallion. Drizzle about 1 1/2 tablespoons of Plum Gastrique over and around the plate. Garnish with micro greens and serve with toasted brioche.

0 2

PINEAPPLE, VANILLA

ROASTED PINEAPPLE

2   CUPS PINEAPPLE JUICE
2   TABLESPOONS SIMPLE SYRUP (PAGE 225)
1/2   VANILLA BEAN, SCRAPED
1/4   PINEAPPLE (PREFERABLY MAUI GOLD), PEELED
      KOSHER SALT AND FRESHLY GROUND BLACK PEPPER

PREHEAT THE OVEN to 400°F.

COMBINE THE PINEAPPLE juice, Simple Syrup, and vanilla seeds in a baking dish, mixing with a fork to evenly distribute. Add the pineapple and season with salt and pepper. Cover the dish with aluminum foil and transfer to the oven. Roast until tender, about 30 to 35 minutes. Remove the pineapple from the liquid and let it cool a bit, then cut crosswise into slices. Pour the liquid into a small saucepan and simmer over medium heat until reduced slightly, about 3 minutes. Set the pineapple and the reduced liquid aside for the gastrique.

PINEAPPLE GASTRIQUE

1/4   CUP REDUCED PINEAPPLE COOKING LIQUID
2   TABLESPOONS FOIE GRAS GASTRIQUE BASE (FROM MASTER RECIPE)

COMBINE THE PINEAPPLE liquid and the Gastrique Base in a small saucepan over low heat. Simmer for 5 minutes until thick.

PINEAPPLE CONSOMMÉ

1   CUP CHOPPED FRESH PINEAPPLE (PREFERABLY MAUI GOLD)
1   SHALLOT, SLICED
1   CUP PINEAPPLE JUICE
3   TABLESPOONS SIMPLE SYRUP (PAGE 225)
1/2   CUP WATER

1/2   VANILLA BEAN, SCRAPED

PINCH OF KOSHER SALT

COMBINE THE PINEAPPLE, shallot, pineapple juice, Simple Syrup, water, vanilla bean, and salt in a saucepan over low heat. Stir and press the pineapple lightly with a spoon to release the juices. Cook for about 15 minutes. Do not let the mixture bubble or it will turn cloudy. Remove from the heat and let the pineapple steep until cool, about 10 minutes. Strain the mixture through a coffee filter into a bowl; you should have at least 1 cup. You will need 3/4 cup for the Pineapple Gelée and the remaining 1/4 cup for serving.

PINEAPPLE GELÉE

3   SHEETS GELATIN OR 1 (1/4-OUNCE) ENVELOPE POWDERED GELATIN

3/4   CUP PINEAPPLE CONSOMMÉ

SOAK THE GELATIN sheets in cool water for 5 minutes to soften, then remove and squeeze out the excess water (if using powdered gelatin, soak the gelatin in 3 tablespoons cool water for 2 minutes).

PLACE THE PINEAPPLE Consommé in a small saucepan over medium heat. Bring to a boil. Add the bloomed gelatin, and whisk to combine. Pour the liquid into a small container, so it is about 1/4 inch deep. Chill until completely set. Once firm, cut the gelée into 1/4-inch cubes.

VANILLA SALT

1/4   VANILLA BEAN, SCRAPED

1   TABLESPOON GRAY FLEUR DE SEL

MIX THE VANILLA bean and salt together until well combined.

GARNISH

2   TABLESPOONS DICED FRESH PINEAPPLE

(PREFERABLY MAUI GOLD)

TO ASSEMBLE AND serve: For the chilled presentation, lay several cubes of the Pineapple Gelée on each of 4 small dishes to create a platform for the *Torchon*. Set 3 slices of *Torchon* on top of the gelée, season lightly with the Vanilla Salt and garnish with diced pineapple. Spoon a tablespoon of the Pineapple Consommé around the bottom of each dish.

FOR THE HOT presentation, divide the Roasted Pineapple among 4 plates. Top each with a Seared Foie Gras medallion. Drizzle about 1 1/2 tablespoons of Pineapple Gastrique over and around the plate. Garnish with micro greens and serve with toasted brioche.

03
RHUBARB, LIME

RHUBARB COMPOTE

6	TABLESPOONS FRESH LIME JUICE
1/4	CUP SUGAR
1	SHALLOT, MINCED
1/2	RHUBARB STALK, SLICED (ABOUT 1/2 CUP)
2	TABLESPOONS HONEY
2	TABLESPOONS GRENADINE
	PINCH OF KOSHER SALT

COMBINE THE LIME juice and sugar in a small saucepan over medium heat and cook until the sugar begins to melt and bubble, about 2 minutes. Stir in the shallot, rhubarb, honey, and grenadine. Lightly season with salt and cook until the rhubarb is just tender, about 2 minutes. Using a slotted spoon, transfer the rhubarb to a side plate to cool. Continue to simmer the rhubarb cooking liquid until reduced slightly. Reserve the liquid for the Rhubarb Gastrique.

RHUBARB GASTRIQUE

1/4	CUP REDUCED RHUBARB COOKING LIQUID
2	TABLESPOONS FOIE GRAS GASTRIQUE BASE (FROM MASTER RECIPE)

COMBINE THE RHUBARB liquid and Gastrique Base in a small saucepan over low heat. Simmer for 5 minutes, until thick.

RHUBARB CONSOMMÉ

4	STRAWBERRIES, QUARTERED
1	RHUBARB STALK, SLICED (ABOUT 1 CUP)
1	SHALLOT, SLICED
1	TABLESPOON FINELY GRATED LIME ZEST
1	TEASPOON WHOLE BLACK PEPPERCORNS
1 1/2	CUPS WATER
1/4	CUP SIMPLE SYRUP (PAGE 225)
2	TABLESPOONS WHITE PORT
2	TABLESPOONS GRENADINE
	PINCH OF KOSHER SALT

COMBINE THE STRAWBERRIES, rhubarb, shallot, lime zest, peppercorns, water, Simple Syrup, port, grenadine, and salt in a pan over low heat. Stir and press the strawberries lightly with a spoon to release the juices. Cook for about 15 minutes. Do not let the mixture bubble or it will turn cloudy. Remove from the heat and let the rhubarb steep until cool, about 10 minutes. Strain the mixture through a coffee filter into a bowl; you should have at least 1 cup. You will need 3/4 cup for the Rhubarb Gelée and the remaining 1/4 cup for serving.

RHUBARB GELÉE

3   SHEETS GELATIN OR 1 (1/4-OUNCE) ENVELOPE POWDERED GELATIN
1   CUP RHUBARB CONSOMMÉ

SOAK THE GELATIN sheets in cool water for 5 minutes to soften, then remove and squeeze out the excess water (if using powdered gelatin, soak the gelatin in 3 tablespoons cool water for 2 minutes).

PLACE THE RHUBARB Consommé in a small saucepan over medium heat. Bring to a boil. Add the bloomed gelatin, and whisk to combine. Pour the liquid into a small container, so it is about 1/4 inch deep. Chill until completely set. Once firm, cut the gelée into 1/4-inch cubes.

LIME SALT

1   TEASPOON FINELY GRATED LIME ZEST
1   TABLESPOON MALDON SEA SALT

MIX THE LIME zest and salt together until well combined.

RHUBARB GARNISH

2   TABLESPOONS JULIENNED RHUBARB
1   TABLESPOON SIMPLE SYRUP (PAGE 225)
1   TEASPOON LIME JUICE

MACERATE THE RHUBARB in the Simple Syrup and lime juice for at least 15 minutes.

TO ASSEMBLE AND serve: For the chilled presentation, lay several cubes of the Rhubarb Gelée on each of 4 small dishes to create a platform for the *Torchon*. Set 3 slices of *Torchon* on top of the gelée, season lightly with the Lime Salt and Rhubarb Garnish. Spoon a tablespoon of the Rhubarb Consommé around the bottom of each dish.

FOR THE HOT presentation, divide the Rhubarb Compote among 4 plates. Top each with a Seared Foie Gras medallion. Drizzle about 1 1/2 tablespoons of Rhubarb Gastrique over and around the plate. Garnish with micro greens and serve with toasted brioche.

LOBSTER SOUP AND SALAD

01
MUSHROOM, FENNEL

WILD MUSHROOM SOUP, ROASTED FENNEL AND CHANTERELLE SALAD,
LEMON CRÈME FRAÎCHE

02
TOMATO, BASIL

CIOPPINO, HEIRLOOM TOMATO SALAD, AVOCADO MOUSSE

03
CORN, COCONUT

THAI COCONUT AND WHITE CORN SOUP,
GRILLED CORN AND COCONUT SALAD, RED PEPPER CREAM

A SIMPLE SOUP AND SALAD COMBO INSTANTLY BECOMES ELEGANT BY INVITING SUC-CULENT LOBSTER TO THE PARTY. THE STRAIGHTFORWARD THEME OF COOL REFRESHING SALADS AND HOT HEARTY SOUPS TAKES ON DIFFERENT GUISES IN THIS TRIO. THE CREAMY, COMFORTING MUSHROOM SOUP MARRIES MUSKY MUSHROOMS WITH THE LICORICE ESSENCE OF FENNEL FOR A CLASSIC EUROPEAN PAIRING. CIOPPINO IS A BELOVED TOMATO-LACED FISH SOUP THAT ORIGINATED IN THE NORTH BEACH SECTION OF SAN FRANCISCO AND IS A FAVORITE AT MY RESTAURANT NOBHILL. THE THAI-INSPIRED CORN AND COCONUT SOUP IS REDOLENT OF EXOTIC AROMATICS SUCH AS GALANGAL AND LEMONGRASS. THESE SOUL-SATISFYING SOUPS CAN BE MADE A DAY AHEAD, AS THE FLAVORS WILL DEEPEN WITH TIME. ANY ONE OF THE SOUP AND SALAD VARIATIONS CAN STAND SECURELY ON ITS OWN BUT IF YOU'RE ENTERTAINING, SERVE THE TRIO TOGETHER FAMILY STYLE TO SAMPLE A GATHERING OF TASTES THAT IS BOTH SOPHISTICATED AND CASUAL.

WINE SUGGESTION

CRAGGY RANGE SAUVIGNON BLANC 'TE MUNA,' MARTINBOROUGH, NEW ZEALAND 2004

To pair one wine with all these soups may seem like a challenge, but it is not. The core flavor is lobster and vegetables. A ripe and round Sauvignon Blanc will bring out the complexity in each component. The secret to a successful pairing is to match the acidity, and this New Zealand Sauvignon Blanc has the ripeness and the herbaceousness to balance the dishes.

GRILLED LOBSTER TAILS
MASTER RECIPE

SERVES 4

2 (1 1/4-POUND) COOKED LOBSTERS
1/4 CUP EXTRA-VIRGIN OLIVE OIL
     KOSHER SALT AND FRESHLY GROUND BLACK PEPPER

TO COOK THE lobsters: Follow the procedure as directed in the Maine Lobster Potpie (page 189), reserving the body for the Lobster Stock. Split the lobster tails in half lengthwise, keeping them in the shell, and set aside for the salad. Chop the claw and knuckle meat into large pieces and reserve for the soup. You should have about 1 cup.

PREHEAT THE BROILER or preheat and oil a grill.

RUB THE LOBSTER tails with the oil and season well with salt and pepper. Place them on a baking sheet, flesh side up, and broil for about 5 minutes, until the meat is slightly charred on the edges. Alternatively, place the lobster tails flesh side down on an outdoor grill and grill for 3 minutes. Turn the lobster tails over, using tongs, and cook the shell side for 2 minutes.

IMMEDIATELY TRANSFER THE lobster tails to the refrigerator or freezer to stop the cooking process. Once the tails are cool, pull the meat from the shell. Cover and chill until ready to use for the salad.

FOLLOW THE ASSEMBLY and serving directions for the variation you are making.

O I

MAKES 2 QUARTS

1/4	CUP CANOLA OIL
1	POUND CHANTERELLE MUSHROOMS, WIPED OF GRIT AND CHOPPED
1/2	POUND CREMINI MUSHROOMS, WIPED OF GRIT AND CHOPPED
2	CLOVES GARLIC, SMASHED
2	STALKS CELERY, CHOPPED
1	YELLOW ONION, PEELED AND CHOPPED
1	LEEK, WHITE AND LIGHT GREEN PARTS ONLY, WELL RINSED AND CHOPPED
1	BULB FENNEL, HALVED AND CHOPPED
	KOSHER SALT AND FRESHLY GROUND BLACK PEPPER
10	SPRIGS FLAT-LEAF PARSLEY
4	SPRIGS TARRAGON
2	BAY LEAVES, PREFERABLY FRESH
1	TEASPOON WHOLE BLACK PEPPERCORNS
1/2	TEASPOON FENNEL SEEDS
1	CUP DRY SHERRY
1 1/2	QUARTS LOBSTER STOCK (PAGE 223)
1	CUP HEAVY CREAM
1	CUP CLAW AND KNUCKLE LOBSTER MEAT (FROM MASTER RECIPE)
2	TABLESPOONS EXTRA-VIRGIN OLIVE OIL, PREFERABLY LEMON-INFUSED, FOR SERVING
1	TEASPOON FENNEL POLLEN (OPTIONAL), FOR GARNISH
1/4	CUP LEMON CRÈME FRAÎCHE (RECIPE FOLLOWS)

HEAT A LARGE saucepan over medium heat and coat with the oil. Once the oil gets hazy, add the mushrooms, garlic, celery, onion, leek, and fennel. Cook, stirring constantly for 10 to 15 minutes, until the vegetable mixture caramelizes and the flavors meld. Season with salt and pepper.

ADD THE PARSLEY, tarragon, bay leaves, peppercorns, and fennel seeds and sauté until fragrant, about 1 minute.

ADD THE SHERRY and stir to deglaze the pan, scraping up the bits from the bottom with a wooden spoon. Simmer until the liquid is almost totally evaporated, about 3 minutes.

ADD THE LOBSTER Stock and bring to a boil. Reduce the heat to low and simmer until slightly thickened, 20 to 25 minutes.

STIR IN THE cream and cook until slightly thickened and reduced, 5 to 7 minutes. Remove from the heat. Using a standard or immersion blender, purée until the soup is smooth and thick.

CAREFULLY POUR THE soup through a strainer into a clean saucepan and return to medium heat. Taste and adjust the seasoning with salt and pepper. Bring to a simmer and fold in the lobster meat. Cook to heat through, about 5 minutes.

ROASTED FENNEL AND CHANTERELLE SALAD

1	SHALLOT, MINCED
	JUICE AND FINELY GRATED ZEST OF 1 LEMON
1	BULB FENNEL, TRIMMED AND HALVED, FRONDS RESERVED
1/2	CUP CANOLA OIL
	KOSHER SALT AND FRESHLY GROUND BLACK PEPPER

1   POUND CHANTERELLE MUSHROOMS, WIPED OF GRIT, HALVED

1   TEASPOON MINCED FRESH TARRAGON,
    PLUS WHOLE LEAVES FOR GARNISH

1/2   CUP DRY SHERRY

1/4   CUP LEMON CRÈME FRAÎCHE (RECIPE FOLLOWS)

2   GRILLED LOBSTER TAILS, HALVED (FROM MASTER RECIPE), CHILLED

2   CUPS FRISÉE, CURLY ENDIVE, OR CHICORY LETTUCE,
    WASHED AND DRIED

COMBINE THE SHALLOT, lemon juice, and zest in a small bowl. Let sit at room temperature for at least 15 minutes to soften the shallot slightly and mellow the flavor of the dressing.

PLACE A GRILL pan over medium-high heat or oil and preheat an outdoor grill to very hot.

RUB THE FENNEL with 2 tablespoons of the oil and season well with salt and pepper. Lay the fennel on the hot grill, rotating to char all sides. Remove from the grill. Cut out and discard the core. Slice the fennel crosswise into strips.

PLACE A SAUTÉ pan over medium-high heat and coat with 2 tablespoons of the oil. Add the mushrooms and tarragon, tossing to coat. Sauté until the mushrooms release their moisture and begin to brown, about 5 minutes. Season with salt and pepper.

ADD THE SHERRY and stir to deglaze the pan, scraping up the browned bits from the bottom with a wooden spoon. Simmer until the liquid is almost totally evaporated, about 2 minutes.

REMOVE FROM THE heat and set aside to cool completely. Taste and adjust the seasoning if necessary (generally cold food needs more seasoning than hot food). When cool, fold in the fennel slices and reserved fennel fronds.

WHISK THE REMAINING 1/4 cup of oil into the lemon shallot mixture. Pour the vinaigrette over the salad and marinate at room temperature for at least 15 minutes before serving.

LEMON CRÈME FRAÎCHE

MAKES 1/2 CUP

1/2   CUP CRÈME FRAÎCHE

1   TABLESPOON FINELY GRATED LEMON ZEST

1   TEASPOON MINCED TARRAGON
    KOSHER SALT AND FRESHLY GROUND BLACK PEPPER

COMBINE THE CRÈME fraîche, zest, and tarragon in a small bowl. Season generously with salt and pepper. Cover and refrigerate. May be made up to 1 hour in advance.

TO ASSEMBLE AND serve: For the salad, spoon 1 tablespoon of the Lemon Crème Fraîche onto each of 4 plates and spread it into a circle with the back of a spoon. Set a 3-inch ring mold in the center of the cream and spoon one-quarter of the Roasted Fennel and Chanterelle Salad into it. Press down gently with the back of a spoon to pack it in well. Carefully remove the ring, so the salad keeps its shape. Place half of a Grilled Lobster Tail across each salad and pile 1/2 cup of frisée on top. Garnish with a few tarragon leaves. Spoon any leftover vinaigrette from the salad over the greens. Ladle the soup into 4 heated bowls, garnish with a drizzle of olive oil and a light dusting of fennel pollen. Top with a dollop of Lemon Crème Fraîche.

O 2

CIOPPINO

MAKES 2 QUARTS

1/4	CUP CANOLA OIL
4	RED BELL PEPPERS, CORED, SEEDED, AND COARSELY CHOPPED, PLUS 1/2 CUP DICED FOR GARNISH
4	CLOVES GARLIC, SMASHED
1	LARGE YELLOW ONION, COARSELY CHOPPED, PLUS 1/2 CUP DICED FOR GARNISH
1	JALAPEÑO, SEEDED AND CHOPPED
1/4	BUNCH BASIL, STEMS AND LEAVES SEPARATED
1	BAY LEAF, PREFERABLY FRESH
1	TEASPOON WHOLE BLACK PEPPERCORNS
1/2	TEASPOON CORIANDER SEEDS
	KOSHER SALT AND FRESHLY GROUND BLACK PEPPER
8	ROMA TOMATOES (ABOUT 2 POUNDS), COARSELY CHOPPED, PLUS 1/2 CUP DICED FOR GARNISH
1	CUP DRY WHITE WINE, SUCH AS SAUVIGNON BLANC
1 1/2	QUARTS LOBSTER STOCK (PAGE 223)
1	CUP CLAW AND KNUCKLE LOBSTER MEAT (FROM MASTER RECIPE)
1/4	CUP AVOCADO MOUSSE (RECIPE FOLLOWS)

HEAT A LARGE saucepan over medium heat and coat with the oil. Once the oil gets hazy, add the red peppers, garlic, onion, and jalapeño. Cook, stirring constantly, until the vegetable mixture caramelizes and the flavors meld, about 5 minutes. Season with salt and pepper. Add the basil stems, bay leaf, peppercorns, and coriander seeds and sauté until fragrant, about 2 minutes.

STIR IN THE tomatoes and continue to cook until they begin to break down and the moisture begins to evaporate, 5 to 10 minutes.

ADD THE WINE and simmer for a couple of minutes to burn off some of the alcohol. The mixture should not be totally dry. Add the stock and bring to a boil. Reduce the heat to low and simmer until slightly thickened, about 20 minutes.

TASTE AND ADJUST the seasonings if necessary. Put the hot soup through a food mill or purée with a standard or immersion blender until the soup is smooth and thick.

RETURN THE SOUP to a clean saucepan. Place over medium-low heat and add the remaining diced onion, peppers, tomatoes, and lobster meat. Cook to heat through, about 5 minutes.

HEIRLOOM TOMATO SALAD

1	SHALLOT, MINCED
2	TABLESPOONS WHITE BALSAMIC VINEGAR
1/4	CUP EXTRA-VIRGIN OLIVE OIL
	KOSHER SALT AND FRESHLY GROUND BLACK PEPPER
3	ASSORTED RIPE HEIRLOOM TOMATOES, SUCH AS BRANDYWINE, GREEN ZEBRA, AND SUNGOLD
1/4	CUP AVOCADO MOUSSE (RECIPE FOLLOWS)
2	GRILLED LOBSTER TAILS, HALVED (FROM MASTER RECIPE), CHILLED
2	CUPS BABY ARUGULA, STEMS TRIMMED
	FRESH BASIL LEAVES, FOR GARNISH

COMBINE THE SHALLOT and vinegar in a small bowl. Let sit at room temperature for at least 15 minutes to soften the shallot slightly and mellow the flavor. Whisk in the oil and season with salt and pepper. Set the vinaigrette aside.

CUT THE TOMATOES crosswise into 1/4-inch-thick slices. (For a great presentation, use a cookie cutter to punch out uniform circles and remove the skin.) Lay the slices in a single layer in a baking dish and season well with salt and pepper. Pour the vinaigrette over the tomatoes and marinate at room temperature for at least 15 minutes before serving.

AVOCADO MOUSSE

MAKES ABOUT 1 CUP

1/4	CUP TOMATO WATER (PAGE 224)
	JUICE OF 1 LIME
1/2	JALAPEÑO, COARSELY CHOPPED
1	SMALL RIPE HASS AVOCADO, PITTED, PEELED, AND COARSELY CHOPPED
	KOSHER SALT AND FRESHLY GROUND BLACK PEPPER
2	TABLESPOONS CRÈME FRAÎCHE

COMBINE THE TOMATO Water, lime juice, and jalapeño in a blender and purée until smooth. Add the avocado and blend until creamy and thick. Scrape the mixture into a small bowl and season well with salt and pepper. Stir in the crème fraîche until well combined. Cover and refrigerate until ready to serve. May be made up to 1 hour in advance.

TO ASSEMBLE AND serve: Spoon 1 tablespoon of the Avocado Mousse onto each of 4 plates and spread it into a circle with the back of a spoon. Lay 1 slice of each type of tomato from the Heirloom Tomato Salad on top, placing the slices next to each other in a triangle shape. Place half a Grilled Lobster Tail across each salad and pile 1/2 cup of arugula on top. Garnish with a few basil leaves. Spoon any of the leftover vinaigrette from the salad over the greens.

LADLE THE CIOPPINO into 4 heated bowls, garnish with a few basil leaves, and top with a dollop of Avocado Mousse.

O 3

CORN, COCONUT

THAI COCONUT AND WHITE CORN SOUP

MAKES 2 QUARTS

1/4	CUP CANOLA OIL
8	SHALLOTS, SLICED
8	CLOVES GARLIC
4	EARS SWEET WHITE CORN, KERNELS CUT FROM THE COB (ABOUT 4 CUPS), AND COBS CUT UP
4	STALKS LEMONGRASS, WHITE BULB ONLY, HALVED LENGTHWISE
4	KAFFIR LIME LEAVES
4-INCH	PIECE FRESH GINGER, PEELED AND SLICED
4-INCH	PIECE FRESH GALANGAL, PEELED AND SLICED
	KOSHER SALT AND FRESHLY GROUND BLACK PEPPER
1	TABLESPOON THAI RED CURRY PASTE
1/2	CUP MIRIN
1/2	CUP SAKE
TWO	14-OUNCE CANS UNSWEETENED COCONUT MILK
1 1/2	QUARTS LOBSTER STOCK (PAGE 223)
1	TABLESPOON CORIANDER SEEDS
1/2	BUNCH FRESH CILANTRO, STEMS AND LEAVES SEPARATED
1/2	BUNCH FRESH THAI BASIL, STEMS AND LEAVES SEPARATED
1	TEASPOON WHOLE BLACK PEPPERCORNS
1	CUP CLAW AND KNUCKLE LOBSTER MEAT (FROM MASTER RECIPE)
2	THAI BIRD CHILIES, SLICED, FOR GARNISH
1/4	CUP RED PEPPER CREAM (RECIPE FOLLOWS)

PLACE A LARGE saucepan over medium heat and coat with the oil. Once the oil gets hazy, add the shallots, garlic, lime leaves, corn cobs, lemongrass, ginger, and galangal. Sauté until the aromatics are soft and very fragrant, 5 to 8 minutes. Season with salt and pepper. Stir in the curry paste and cook for 1 minute to combine. Add the mirin and sake and stir to deglaze the pan. Cook until the liquid is evaporated, about 2 minutes.

ADD THE COCONUT milk, stock, coriander seeds, cilantro stems, basil stems, and peppercorns. Bring to a boil and reduce the heat to low. Simmer for about 20 minutes to allow the flavors to intensify.

CAREFULLY POUR THE soup through a strainer into a clean saucepan, discard the solids, and return the soup to medium heat. Taste and adjust the seasoning if necessary with salt and pepper. Bring the soup to a simmer. Add half of the corn kernels. Remove the soup from heat and purée with an immersion blender to thicken the soup and deepen the corn flavor. Add the remaining 2 cups of corn kernels and the lobster meat. Cook to heat through, about 5 minutes.

GRILLED CORN AND COCONUT SALAD

1	SHALLOT, MINCED
2	THAI BIRD CHILIES, STEMMED AND SLICED
2	TABLESPOONS FRESH LIME JUICE
1/4	TEASPOON FISH SAUCE (NAM PLA), SUCH AS THREE CRABS BRAND
1/4	CUP PLUS 2 TABLESPOONS CANOLA OIL
1	EAR SWEET YELLOW CORN, HUSKED
1	EAR SWEET WHITE CORN, HUSKED
	KOSHER SALT AND FRESHLY GROUND BLACK PEPPER
1/4	CUP FRESH CILANTRO LEAVES, PLUS MORE FOR GARNISH
2	SCALLIONS, WHITE AND GREEN PARTS, SLICED

1/2	SMALL COCONUT (PREFERABLY MACAPUNO), SHAVED (ABOUT 1 CUP)
1/4	CUP RED PEPPER CREAM (RECIPE FOLLOWS)
2	GRILLED LOBSTER TAILS, HALVED (FROM MASTER RECIPE)
2	CUPS WATERCRESS, STEMS TRIMMED

COMBINE THE SHALLOT, chilies, lime juice, and fish sauce in a small bowl. Let sit at room temperature for at least 15 minutes to soften the shallot and chilies slightly and mellow their flavor. Set aside.

PLACE A GRILL pan over medium-high heat or preheat an outdoor grill to very hot.

RUB THE EARS of corn with 2 tablespoons of the oil and season well with salt and pepper. Lay the corn on the hot grill, rotating frequently until all sides are charred. Let cool.

USING A SHARP knife and holding the cobs upright, cut off the kernels and place the corn in a large bowl. Add the cilantro leaves, scallions, and coconut. Season with salt and pepper and toss to combine.

WHISK THE REMAINING 1/4 cup of oil into the reserved shallot mixture. Pour the vinaigrette over the corn mixture and marinate at room temperature for at least 15 minutes to absorb the flavor.

RED PEPPER CREAM

MAKES ABOUT 1/2 CUP

2	RED BELL PEPPERS
1	TEASPOON FRESH LIME JUICE
1/2	CUP CRÈME FRAÎCHE
	KOSHER SALT

PASS THE PEPPERS through a juicer; you should have about 1 1/2 cups of liquid. Combine the bell pepper juice and lime juice in a small saucepan. Place over low heat and simmer until the juice cooks down into a dark thick syrup, about 30 minutes.

TRANSFER THE SYRUP to a small bowl and let cool. Stir in the crème fraîche and season with a pinch of salt. Cover and refrigerate until ready to serve.

TO ASSEMBLE AND serve: For the salad, spoon 1 tablespoon of the Red Pepper Cream onto each of the 4 plates and spread into a circle with the back of a spoon. Set a 3-inch ring mold in the center of the cream and spoon one-quarter of the Grilled Corn and Coconut Salad into it to fill the ring. Press down gently with the back of a spoon to pack it in well. Carefully remove the ring, so the salad keeps its shape. Place half a Grilled Lobster Tail across each salad and then pile 1/2 cup of watercress on top. Garnish with a few cilantro leaves. Spoon any leftover vinaigrette from the salad over the greens.

FOR THE SOUP, divide the cilantro leaves, basil leaves, and chilies among 4 heated bowls. Ladle the soup on top and garnish with a dollop of Red Pepper Cream.

CHAPTER TWO

FISH ENTRÉE TRIOS

All successful cooking lies in using quality ingredients, but never is this maxim more true than when working with fish. Seafood must be absolutely pristine—glistening, sweet smelling, ocean fresh—or it will not be flavorful when cooked. The good news in this department is that neighborhood supermarkets, in response to consumers' demands, are stepping up the quality and selection in their seafood sections.

Because much of my career in the kitchen has focused on the preparation of fish, I have worked hard to cultivate relationships with individual purveyors of quality seafood so that I might offer diners the best and brightest of the world's oceans and lakes.

Cooking fish well is, to me, one of the most challenging tasks in the kitchen. And some of the dishes in this section do require some skill to master. I know that not many home cooks have had experience preparing a delicate piece of Dover sole crusted with potato scales or egg-battered abalone (which will toughen when cooked too long). If you are in this category, do not let these recipes intimidate you. These are not all that difficult, but they do require some thought and care.

If you cannot get the type of fish called for in the recipe, check the substitution I have noted. Then think about the type of fish called for—is it flaky? Oily? Meaty? Do not be too concerned about starting with the exact fish called for in the recipe but *do* be concerned with starting with the correct type of fish. Learn to improvise with and take advantage of the best your fish market has to offer.

Once you have the perfect piece of fish, great care must be taken when cooking it. In the restaurant, all fish is cooked to order, which I realize is not so easy to do at home. However, there is no other way I know to serve a perfectly cooked piece of fish without preparing it just before serving. Although this often requires very little time and preparation, it is absolutely essential that, no matter how it is cooked, it not be overcooked. When pan-searing, move the fish as little as possible to minimize sticking and to avoid tearing the flesh.

Seafood is an integral part of my repertoire and, in truth, I love working with every type. I have found that every species of finfish and shellfish has its own personality and unique traits which, over the years, I have learned to finesse. The four fish trios in this chapter offer a great range in texture, flavor, and preparation. I hope they present a challenge that you will enjoy.

POTATO-CRUSTED DOVER SOLE

O 1
CAULIFLOWER, CHAMPAGNE

CAULIFLOWER PURÉE, CHAMPAGNE BEURRE BLANC, CHAMPAGNE AÏOLI

O 2
ONION, MALT

ROASTED SWEET ONION PURÉE, MALT VINEGAR BEURRE BLANC,
CLASSIC TARTAR SAUCE

O 3
SALSIFY, TRUFFLE

TRUFFLE SALSIFY, BEURRE ROUGE, TRUFFLE AÏOLI

THIS IS MY DRESSED-UP VERSION OF THE FINE BRITISH DISH FISH AND CHIPS. ON A WINDY DAY, PIPING-HOT FRIED FISH AND POTATOES SMOTHERED IN TARTAR SAUCE AND DOUSED WITH MALT VINEGAR SIMPLY CANNOT BE BEAT. I HAD A LITTLE FUN PLAYING WITH THE CONCEPT BY SHINGLING THE POTATO CHIPS RIGHT ON THE FISH TO REPLICATE SCALES. I NAMED THE ORIGINAL INCARNATION CHIPS ON FISH. FOR THE VARIATIONS, CAULIFLOWER, ONION, AND SALSIFY ARE LUSH VEGETABLES THAT ADD AN EARTHY BACKDROP TO THE WHIMSICAL THEME. THE AÏOLIS AND TARTAR SAUCE MAY BE PREPARED A DAY IN ADVANCE, COVERED AND REFRIGERATED.

WINE SUGGESTION

DOMAINE ROULOT MEURSAULT 'CHARMES' 1ER CRU, BURGUNDY, FRANCE 2002
A great Burgundy will uplift the individual flavors and enhance the texture of this dish. Domaine Roulot is one of the stellar producers of Chardonnay in the world. Their electrifying wines are extremely rich and have a crisp acidic balance. Any Chardonnay can be substituted as long as it is rich and crisp.

POTATO-CRUSTED DOVER SOLE
MASTER RECIPE

SERVES 4

Dover sole is definitely a king among fish; it is the most delectable of the flatfish family, boasting a subtle flavor and a fine creamy texture that is just firm enough to hold together when you cut into it. Imported from England, Dover sole may be difficult to find, but domestic flounders such as petrale sole, lemon sole, and sand dab are good alternatives.

8	RUSSET POTATOES, PEELED
2 1/2	CUPS WARM CLARIFIED BUTTER (PAGE 221)
2	TABLESPOONS POTATO STARCH SOLE (POTATO FLOUR)
FOUR	6-OUNCE DOVER SOLE OR PETRALE SOLE FILLETS, SKIN REMOVED
	KOSHER SALT AND FRESHLY GROUND BLACK PEPPER

USING A 1-INCH ring mold or round cookie cutter, cut the potatoes lengthwise into perfectly rounded logs. Place the potato logs in a saucepan of salted cold water to cover by 1 inch. Place over low heat and cook for 15 minutes. Do not fully cook or boil, or the potatoes may become mushy. They should be completely translucent when sliced.

DRAIN THE POTATOES and cool completely. Using a mandoline or very sharp knife, slice the potatoes into paper-thin rounds, about the thickness of potato chips.

IN A LARGE bowl, combine 1 1/2 cups of the Clarified Butter with the potato starch; it should look a bit soupy. Add the sliced potatoes, stirring gently to coat in the butter mixture. Do this in a timely manner before the butter cools and begins to solidify.

LINE A SHEET pan or cookie sheet with parchment paper. Lay the fish fillets, skin side up, on the pan. Shingle the potato slices along the top of each fillet, overlapping slightly to resemble fish scales. When completely covered, place the fish in the refrigerator for at least 30 minutes to set. (Once cooled, the butter and starch mixture will act as the glue to hold the potatoes together.)

PLACE A LARGE sauté pan over medium heat, add 1/2 cup of the Clarified Butter and swirl it around the pan to coat. When the butter is hot, carefully lay 2 fillets in the pan, potato side down. Season the fish lightly with salt and pepper. Do not move the fish at all until the crust has a chance to crisp and brown, about 5 minutes. Carefully flip the fillets over and cook until the fish is cooked through, 2 to 3 minutes. Transfer the fish to a side plate and season the top with salt and pepper. Cover to keep warm. Repeat with the remaining 2 fillets, adding more Clarified Butter as necessary to keep the fish from sticking.

FOLLOW THE ASSEMBLY and serving directions for the variation you are making.

O I

CAULIFLOWER, CHAMPAGNE

CAULIFLOWER PURÉE

MAKES 2 CUPS

1/2	HEAD CAULIFLOWER COARSELY CHOPPED (APPROXIMATELY 3 CUPS)
2	CUPS HEAVY CREAM
2	CUPS WHOLE MILK
1/4	CUP (1/2 STICK) PLUS 2 TABLESPOONS UNSALTED BUTTER
	KOSHER SALT AND FRESHLY GROUND WHITE PEPPER

PUT THE CAULIFLOWER in a saucepan and cover with the cream and milk. Add the 1/4 cup butter and place over medium-low heat. Season generously with salt and pepper. Bring to a gentle simmer and cook until the florets are tender, about 15 minutes. Do not boil or the cream will overflow.

USING A SLOTTED spoon, transfer the cauliflower to a food processor. Add 1/4 cup of the hot cream mixture and pulse to combine. Add the remaining 2 tablespoons of butter and purée until smooth and creamy. Season generously with salt and pepper. Cover to keep warm.

CHAMPAGNE BEURRE BLANC

MAKES 1 CUP

	BEURRE BLANC (PAGE 220)
1/2	CUP DRY CHAMPAGNE
1/4	CUP CHAMPAGNE VINEGAR
1/2	HEAD CAULIFLOWER, STEMS TRIMMED
2	TABLESPOONS CANOLA OIL
	KOSHER SALT AND FRESHLY GROUND BLACK PEPPER

PREPARE THE BEURRE Blanc as directed on page 220, using the champagne and champagne vinegar.

PREHEAT THE OVEN to 400°F.

PLACE THE CAULIFLOWER in a baking dish, drizzle with the oil, and season generously with salt and pepper. Roast until the cauliflower is tender and slightly charred on the edges, 15 to 20 minutes. Chop the cauliflower into small pieces.

JUST BEFORE SERVING, fold the cauliflower into the Beurre Blanc.

CHAMPAGNE AÏOLI

MAKES 1 CUP

1	LARGE EGG YOLK
1	TABLESPOON CHAMPAGNE VINEGAR
1	CUP CANOLA OIL
	KOSHER SALT AND FRESHLY GROUND BLACK PEPPER

GARNISH

1/2	OUNCE CAVIAR, PREFERABLY OSETRA

PLACE THE YOLK and vinegar in a blender or food processor and process until combined. With the motor running, drizzle in the oil in a thin steady stream until emulsified and thick. Season with salt and pepper. Transfer the aïoli to a container, cover and refrigerate until ready to serve.

TO ASSEMBLE AND serve: Spoon 1/2 cup of the Cauliflower Purée onto each of 4 plates and spread it into a large circle with the back of the spoon. Lay a piece of Dover Sole on top, potato side up. Drizzle Champagne Beurre Blanc around the fish, being sure to evenly distribute the pieces of cauliflower. Put a dollop of Champagne Aïoli on top and garnish with a little caviar.

O 2

ONION, MALT

ROASTED SWEET ONION PURÉE

MAKES 2 CUPS

- 2   LARGE SWEET ONIONS, SUCH AS VIDALIA, MAUI,
     OR WALLA WALLA, UNPEELED AND QUARTERED
- 2   TABLESPOONS CANOLA OIL
     KOSHER SALT AND FRESHLY GROUND BLACK PEPPER
- 1/2 CUP (1 STICK) UNSALTED BUTTER

PREHEAT THE OVEN to 400°F.

PLACE THE ONIONS in a baking dish, drizzle with the oil, and season generously with salt and pepper. Cover the pan tightly with aluminum foil. Transfer to the oven and roast until the onions are completely tender and beginning to burst, about 30 minutes.

REMOVE THE FOIL and let the onions cool a bit. When cool enough to handle, peel and discard the skins. Place the onions in a blender or food processor and process until chunky. Add the butter and blend until smooth and thick. Season generously with salt and pepper. Cover to keep warm.

MALT VINEGAR BEURRE BLANC

MAKES 3/4 CUP

- BEURRE BLANC (PAGE 220)
- 1/2 CUP DRY WHITE WINE, SUCH AS SAUVIGNON BLANC
- 1/4 CUP MALT VINEGAR
- 2   TABLESPOONS UNSALTED BUTTER
- 1   LARGE SWEET ONION, SUCH AS VIDALIA, MAUI,
     OR WALLA WALLA, THINLY SLICED (ABOUT 2 CUPS)
     KOSHER SALT AND FRESHLY GROUND BLACK PEPPER
- 1/2 CUP CHICKEN STOCK (PAGE 222)

PREPARE THE BEURRE Blanc as directed on page 220, using the dry white wine and malt vinegar.

MELT THE BUTTER in a sauté pan over medium heat. Add the onions and stir to coat. Season lightly with salt and pepper. Cook, stirring constantly, until the onions are translucent, about 10 minutes. Add the stock and simmer for 10 more minutes until reduced by one-third.

JUST BEFORE SERVING, fold the onions into the Beurre Blanc.

CLASSIC TARTAR SAUCE

MAKES 1 CUP

- 1   LARGE EGG YOLK
- 2   TABLESPOONS FRESH LEMON JUICE
- 1   CUP CANOLA OIL

2   CORNICHONS, DRAINED AND CHOPPED

2   TABLESPOONS MINCED RED ONION

1   TABLESPOON FINELY GRATED LEMON ZEST

1   TABLESPOON DRIED ONION FLAKES

1   TABLESPOON CAPERS, DRAINED AND CHOPPED

1   TABLESPOON CHOPPED FRESH FLAT-LEAF PARSLEY

     KOSHER SALT AND FRESHLY GROUND BLACK PEPPER

PLACE THE YOLK and lemon juice in a blender or food processor and process until combined. With the motor running, drizzle in the oil in a thin steady stream until emulsified and thick, about 1 minute.

TRANSFER THE MAYONNAISE to a bowl and add the cornichons, red onion, lemon zest, dried onion, capers, and parsley. Season lightly with salt and pepper. Mix well. Cover and refrigerate until ready to serve.

GARNISH

4   CHIVE BLOSSOMS OR CHIVE POINTS

TO ASSEMBLE AND serve: Spoon 1/2 cup of the Roasted Onion Purée on each of 4 plates and spread into a large circle with the back of the spoon. Lay a piece of Dover Sole on top, potato side up. Drizzle the Malt Vinegar Beurre Blanc around the fish, being sure to evenly distribute the onions. Put a dollop of Tartar Sauce on top and garnish with a chive blossom.

0 3

SALSIFY, TRUFFLE

TRUFFLE SALSIFY

Salsify resembles a thin parsnip and has a starchy potato-like texture that is satiny when puréed. When peeling salsify, put them in a bowl of water acidulated with lemon juice to prevent discoloration.

MAKES ABOUT 2 CUPS

1   POUND SALSIFY, PEELED AND CUT INTO 3-INCH PIECES

2   CUPS HEAVY CREAM

     KOSHER SALT AND FRESHLY GROUND BLACK PEPPER

2   TABLESPOONS TRUFFLE BUTTER (SEE SOURCES, PAGE 242)

PLACE THE SALSIFY in a large saucepan and cover with the cream. Season lightly with salt and pepper. Simmer over medium-low heat until the salsify is fork tender, about 30 minutes.

USING A SLOTTED spoon or tongs, transfer the salsify to a food processor and reserve the cream. Add the truffle butter and 1/4 cup of the warm cream to the salsify. Purée until smooth and creamy. Generously season with salt and pepper. Cover to keep warm.

BEURRE ROUGE

MAKES 1 CUP

     BEURRE ROUGE (PAGE 220)

1   CUP DRY RED WINE, SUCH AS CABERNET SAUVIGNON

1/4 CUP RED WINE VINEGAR

4   STALKS SALSIFY, SLICED (ABOUT 1 CUP)

2   TABLESPOONS SUGAR

PREPARE THE BEURRE Rouge as directed on page 220, using 1/2 cup of the red wine and the red wine vinegar.

COMBINE THE SALSIFY, sugar, and remaining 1/2 cup red wine in a small saucepan over medium-low heat. Simmer until the salsify is tender and a deep burgundy red, about 15 minutes.

JUST BEFORE SERVING, fold in the salsify.

TRUFFLE AÏOLI

MAKES 1 CUP

1   LARGE EGG YOLK
1   TABLESPOON TRUFFLE VINEGAR (SEE SOURCES, PAGE 242)
1   CUP CANOLA OIL
2   TABLESPOONS WHITE TRUFFLE OIL
1   TABLESPOON CHOPPED TRUFFLE SHAVINGS
    KOSHER SALT AND FRESHLY GROUND BLACK PEPPER

GARNISH

4   PAPER-THIN SLICES FRESH TRUFFLE

PLACE THE YOLK and vinegar in a blender or food processor and process until combined. With the motor running, drizzle in the canola oil in a thin steady stream until emulsified and thick. Drizzle in the truffle oil and process to blend.

TRANSFER THE MAYONNAISE into a bowl and fold in the truffle shavings. Season lightly with salt and pepper. Mix well. Cover and refrigerate until ready to serve.

TO ASSEMBLE AND serve: Spoon 1/2 cup of the Truffle Salsify onto each of 4 plates and spread into a large circle with the back of the spoon. Lay a piece of Dover Sole on top, potato side up. Drizzle the Beurre Rouge around the fish, being sure to evenly distribute the salsify. Put a dollop of Truffle Aïoli on top and garnish with a shaving of truffle.

SEARED BLACK BASS, CRISPY PORK BELLY, AND CITRUS CONFIT

01
CORIANDER, MEYER LEMON

BLACK BELUGA LENTILS, CARAMELIZED PARSNIP AND MEYER LEMON CONFIT,
CORIANDER OIL

02
CURRY, BLOOD ORANGE

RED LENTILS, CARAMELIZED PUMPKIN AND BLOOD ORANGE CONFIT,
CURRY OIL

03
CARDAMOM, RED GRAPEFRUIT

FRENCH GREEN LENTILS, CARAMELIZED PARSLEY ROOT
AND RUBY RED GRAPEFRUIT CONFIT, CARDAMOM OIL

WHEN I SET OUT TO CREATE A NEW DISH, SEASONALITY PLAYS A VITAL ROLE. THIS DISH FLAUNTS A DEEPLY SATISFYING COMPOSITION OF WINTER INGREDIENTS AND IS IDEAL TO ENJOY WHEN THERE IS A CHILL IN THE AIR. THE HEARTY LENTILS OFFSET THE CRISPY SKIN OF THE FISH AND THE CRACKLING PORK BELLY. THERE IS PLENTY OF DENSITY GOING ON, SO IT IS REALLY IMPORTANT TO BALANCE THE WEIGHT SO THE DISH IS NOT TOO HEAVY. ADDING ACIDITY IS A FUNDAMENTAL WAY TO DO SO, AND SOME OF THE STRONGEST ACIDIC FLAVORS COME FROM CITRUS. IN THIS DISH, THE JEWEL-TONED FRUITS USED IN THE CONFITS NOT ONLY ADD A SPLASH OF COLOR, BUT ALSO PROVIDE SOME RELIEF FROM THE RICHNESS. MEYER LEMON, BLOOD ORANGE, AND RUBY GRAPEFRUIT HAVE A MODERATE ACIDIC LEVEL AND MORE SWEETNESS THAN THEIR EVERYDAY COUNTERPARTS. FRAGRANT SPICES ADD A POWERFUL PUNCH TO ROUND OUT THE EARTHY INTENSITY. CORIANDER HAS A DISTINCTIVELY CITRUSY AND MUSTY AROMA, CURRY HAS A FIERY AND SMOKY FLAVOR, AND CARDAMOM HAS A FLORAL GRAPEFRUIT-LIKE ESSENCE CONTAINING SOME WOODY UNDERTONES. THIS VIBRANT COMBINATION COMES ACROSS WITH MARVELOUS CLARITY AND DIMENSION.

WINE SUGGESTION

DOMAINE DUJAC CHAMBOLLE MUSIGNY, BURGUNDY, FRANCE 2002

A perfumey Pinot Noir from Burgundy is the answer for this complex dish. This soft and velvety wine has rich flavors of black cherry, cola, cumin, olive, and cardamom. The wine also has a sweetness and freshness that will carry the spices forward. Any Pinot Noir will work as long as it is not too heavy. Rich white wines such as Roussanne and Viognier can also be used.

SEARED BLACK BASS
MASTER RECIPE

Black bass is commonly caught off the coastal waters of Rhode Island. The most attractive feature of this sea bass is its unique exterior—a black-and-white checkerboard-like appearance with brilliant texture and taste. When properly cooked, the crispy, edible skin has a lot of character and is my absolute favorite part of the fish. The sweet, mild, white flesh has a distinct flavor and its low oil content makes it very lean. The natural oils in the skin seal in the fish's delicate moisture, particularly when it is seared in clarified butter.

FOUR   6-OUNCE BLACK BASS FILLETS, SKIN ON
        KOSHER SALT AND FRESHLY GROUND BLACK PEPPER
1/4   CUP CLARIFIED BUTTER (PAGE 221)

SEASON THE FISH well on both sides with salt and pepper. Place a large sauté pan over medium heat, add 2 tablespoons of the clarified butter, and swirl it around the pan to coat. When the butter is hot, carefully lay 2 fillets in the pan, skin side down. Gently press the fish with the back of a spatula so it does not curl up as it cooks. Cook until the skin is crisp and nicely browned, 3 to 5 minutes. Carefully flip the fillets over and cook the flesh side for just a few seconds to seal it. Transfer the fish to a platter and cover to keep warm.

REPEAT WITH THE 2 remaining fillets, adding more Clarified Butter as needed to keep the fish from sticking.

FOLLOW THE ASSEMBLY and serving directions for the recipe you are making.

CRISPY PORK BELLY
MASTER RECIPE

Pork belly, which comes from the underside of the hog, is basically uncured fresh bacon. The rosy meat is marbled with fat and when braised for hours (as it is here), the pork becomes so custardy soft that you can cut it with a spoon. The succulent fat crowned with a crackling skin is what makes it taste so damn delicious! Pork belly is typically an inexpensive cut, and a good butcher should carry it. Ask for unsalted, uncured belly, which is not the same as slab bacon or salt pork. Pork belly can also be found in Asian markets, as it is frequently used in that cuisine.

1   POUND PORK BELLY, EXCESS FAT TRIMMED AND SCORED
     KOSHER SALT AND FRESHLY GROUND BLACK PEPPER
3   TABLESPOONS CANOLA OIL
1   YELLOW ONION, COARSELY CHOPPED
6   CLOVES GARLIC, COARSELY CHOPPED
1/4 CUP COARSELY CHOPPED FRESH THYME
1/4 CUP COARSELY CHOPPED FRESH FLAT-LEAF PARSLEY SPRIGS
2   BAY LEAVES, PREFERABLY FRESH
1   TABLESPOON WHOLE BLACK PEPPERCORNS
1   CUP DRY WHITE WINE, SUCH AS SAUVIGNON BLANC
1   QUART CHICKEN STOCK (PAGE 222)

HEAVILY SEASON BOTH sides of the pork belly with salt and pepper. Place a Dutch oven or deep ovenproof skillet over medium-low heat and coat with 2 tablespoons of the oil. When the oil gets hazy, lay the pork belly in the pan and sear until the fat begins to render and crisp and the meat is brown, 10 minutes on each side.

PREHEAT THE OVEN to 350°F.

TRANSFER THE PORK belly to a side platter and carefully pour out all but 2 tablespoons of the rendered fat. Add the onion, garlic, thyme, parsley, bay leaves, and peppercorns. Sweat the vegetables in the pork fat, stirring often, until soft, about 15 minutes.

ADD THE WINE and continue to cook and stir until the liquid is reduced and looks syrupy, about 5 minutes. Turn the heat up to high, add the stock, and bring to a boil.

RETURN THE PORK belly to the pan; the liquid should just barely cover the meat. Cover tightly and transfer to the oven. Braise until the pork is very tender and a fork slides into the meat without any resistance, about 2 1/2 hours. Let the pork belly cool completely in the braising liquid. (The dish can be prepared to this point the night before and kept covered and refrigerated.)

REMOVE THE PORK from the liquid and pat dry with paper towels to eliminate any excess moisture and remove any solidified fat from the surface. Pass the pork cooking liquid through a fine-mesh strainer; you should have about 5 cups to use for cooking the lentils. Discard the solids.

USING A SHARP knife, cut the pork into 4 equal portions. Generously season the pieces of pork belly with salt and pepper.

HEAT A CAST-IRON skillet or deep ovenproof pan over medium heat and coat with the remaining tablespoon of oil. Once hot, place the pork belly in the pan, fat side down. Sear until the fat forms a very crispy crust, 5 to 10 minutes. Turn the pork over and cook the other side for another 5 minutes to brown the meat.

FOLLOW THE ASSEMBLY and serving directions for the variation you are making.

CITRUS CONFIT
MASTER RECIPE

This recipe can be made using any type of citrus—if preparing more than one variety at a time, use separate pans to avoid cross-over flavor. The leftover citrus-infused Simple Syrup is ideal to keep on hand to sweeten iced tea or mixed drinks. The softened citrus peels are handy to brighten up desserts and sauces or as a garnish. (Use the fruit for the variation you are making.)

2	MEYER OR REGULAR LEMONS, BLOOD ORANGES, OR RUBY RED GRAPEFRUIT, WELL-SCRUBBED
1	QUART SIMPLE SYRUP (PAGE 225)
5	FRESH THYME SPRIGS
1	BAY LEAF, PREFERABLY FRESH
1	TABLESPOON WHOLE BLACK PEPPERCORNS

USING A VEGETABLE peeler, remove the zest of the citrus, being careful to avoid the white pith. Cut the zest into long strips.

PLACE THE CITRUS zest in a small saucepan and cover with cold water. Place over high heat and bring to a boil. Boil for 30 seconds and then drain the water. Repeat this process 2 more times with fresh water to soften the citrus skin and remove any bitterness. Drain the blanched zest in a strainer.

COMBINE THE SIMPLE Syrup, thyme, bay leaf, and peppercorns in a saucepan and bring to a boil over high heat. Add the citrus zest and stir to submerge it in the liquid. Reduce the heat to low and gently simmer until the zest is tender and becomes translucent, about 20 minutes. Remove from heat and let cool. Pass through a fine-mesh strainer, reserving the syrup. Rinse the peel thoroughly with cold water. (The confit can be stored in the poaching liquid, covered and refrigerated, for up to 2 weeks.)

FOLLOW THE ASSEMBLY and serving directions for the recipe you are making.

O I

BLACK BELUGA LENTILS

2	PARSNIPS, PEELED AND HALVED
2	TABLESPOONS CORIANDER SEEDS
1	TABLESPOON WHOLE BLACK PEPPERCORNS
10	SPRIGS FRESH CILANTRO
1	LEMON VERBENA LEAF
1	STALK CELERY, HALVED
2	CLOVES GARLIC, SMASHED
6	CUPS (1 1/2 QUARTS) RESERVED PORK BELLY COOKING LIQUID
1	CUP DRIED BELUGA LENTILS
	KOSHER SALT AND FRESH GROUND BLACK PEPPER
2	TABLESPOONS FRESH MEYER LEMON JUICE
1/4	CUP (1/2 STICK) UNSALTED BUTTER, CUT INTO CHUNKS

COMBINE THE PARSNIPS, coriander, peppercorns, cilantro, verbena leaf, celery, and garlic in a double layer of cheesecloth, gather up the ends, and tie closed with kitchen string.

POUR THE PORK cooking liquid into a saucepan and place over low heat. Add the lentils and parsnip sachet and gently simmer, uncovered, until the lentils are soft, but not falling apart, about 20 minutes. Season with salt and pepper.

REMOVE AND DISCARD the sachet; there should still be about 1/2 cup of broth left in the pan. Stir in the lemon juice. Add the butter, stirring until melted.

CARAMELIZED PARSNIP AND MEYER LEMON CONFIT

1/2	CUP CANOLA OIL
1	TABLESPOON GROUND CORIANDER
1	PARSNIP, PEELED AND DICED (ABOUT 1 CUP)
	KOSHER SALT AND FRESHLY GROUND BLACK PEPPER
1	MEYER LEMON, CUT INTO SEGMENTS (SEE SEGMENTING CITRUS, PAGE 225)
1/4	CUP DICED MEYER LEMON CONFIT (FROM MASTER RECIPE)
	FRESH CILANTRO LEAVES, FOR GARNISH

COMBINE THE OIL and coriander in a small saucepan over low heat. Cook until fragrant, about 10 minutes; do not let boil. Remove from the heat and set aside to steep for 10 minutes to further infuse the flavor. Strain and discard the solids.

PLACE THE CORIANDER oil in a large sauté pan over medium heat. Add the parsnips, tossing to coat in the oil. Season with salt and pepper. Fry until the parsnips are tender and slightly charred on the edges, about 6 minutes. Add the lemon segments and Meyer Lemon Confit, tossing to combine. Heat through for a minute.

TO ASSEMBLE AND serve: Divide the Beluga Lentils among 4 plates, letting the broth puddle in the center. Lay a slice of Pork Belly on the lentils, crispy side up. Set a piece of Seared Black Bass across the top, skin side up. Spoon 2 generous tablespoons of the Parsnip and Lemon Confit around the plate, drizzling any remaining coriander oil on top. Garnish with cilantro leaves.

O 2

CURRY, BLOOD ORANGE

RED LENTILS

1/4	SMALL PUMPKIN, PEELED, SEEDED, AND CUT INTO CHUNKS
1	TABLESPOON WHOLE BLACK PEPPERCORNS
1	SPRIG FRESH ROSEMARY
1	FRESH CURRY LEAF
1	STALK CELERY, HALVED
2	CLOVES GARLIC, SMASHED
6	CUPS (1 1/2 QUARTS) RESERVED PORK BELLY COOKING LIQUID
1	CUP DRIED RED LENTILS
1	TABLESPOON YELLOW THAI CURRY
	KOSHER SALT AND FRESHLY GROUND BLACK PEPPER
1/4	CUP FRESH BLOOD ORANGE JUICE
1/4	CUP (1/2 STICK) UNSALTED BUTTER, CUT INTO CHUNKS

COMBINE THE PUMPKIN, peppercorns, rosemary, curry leaf, celery, and garlic in a double layer of cheesecloth, gather up the ends, and tie closed with kitchen string.

POUR THE PORK cooking liquid into a saucepan and place over low heat. Add the lentils, curry, and pumpkin sachet and gently simmer, uncovered, until the lentils are soft, but not falling apart, about 20 minutes. Season with salt and pepper.

REMOVE AND DISCARD the sachet; there should still be about 1/2 cup of broth left in the pan. Stir in the orange juice. Add the butter, stirring until melted.

CARAMELIZED PUMPKIN AND BLOOD ORANGE CONFIT

1/2	CUP CANOLA OIL
1	TABLESPOON THAI YELLOW CURRY
1/4	SMALL PUMPKIN, PEELED, SEEDED, AND CUT INTO CHUNKS (ABOUT 1 CUP)
	KOSHER SALT AND FRESHLY GROUND BLACK PEPPER
1	BLOOD ORANGE, CUT INTO SEGMENTS (SEE SEGMENTING CITRUS, PAGE 225)
1/4	CUP DICED BLOOD ORANGE CONFIT (FROM MASTER RECIPE)
	MINCED FRESH CHIVES, FOR GARNISH

COMBINE THE OIL and curry in a small saucepan over low heat. Cook until fragrant, about 10 minutes; do not let boil. Remove from the heat and set aside to steep for 10 minutes to further infuse the flavor. Strain and discard the solids.

PLACE THE CURRY oil in a large sauté pan over medium heat. Add the pumpkin, tossing to coat in the oil. Season with salt and pepper. Fry until the pumpkin is tender and slightly charred on the edges, about 6 minutes. Add the blood orange segments and Blood Orange Confit, tossing to combine. Heat through for a minute.

TO ASSEMBLE AND serve: Divide the Red Lentils among 4 plates, letting the broth puddle in the center. Lay a slice of Pork Belly on the lentils, crispy side up. Set a piece of the Seared Black Bass across the top, skin side up. Spoon 2 generous tablespoons of the Pumpkin and Blood Orange Confit around the plate, drizzling any remaining curry oil on top. Garnish with minced chives.

O 3

CARDAMOM, RED GRAPEFRUIT

FRENCH GREEN LENTILS

1	SMALL PARSLEY ROOT OR CELERY ROOT, PEELED AND CUT INTO CHUNKS
6	CARDAMOM PODS
1	TABLESPOON WHOLE BLACK PEPPERCORNS
6	SPRIGS FRESH FLAT-LEAF PARSLEY
1	BAY LEAF, PREFERABLY FRESH
1	STALK CELERY, HALVED
2	CLOVES GARLIC, SMASHED
5	CUPS (1 1/4 QUARTS) RESERVED PORK BELLY COOKING LIQUID
1	CUP DRIED FRENCH GREEN LENTILS
	KOSHER SALT AND FRESHLY GROUND BLACK PEPPER
2	TABLESPOONS FRESH RUBY RED GRAPEFRUIT JUICE
1/4	CUP (1/2 STICK) UNSALTED BUTTER, CUT INTO CHUNKS

COMBINE THE PARSLEY root, cardamom, peppercorns, parsley, bay leaf, celery, and garlic in a double layer of cheesecloth, gather up the ends, and tie closed with kitchen string.

POUR THE PORK cooking liquid into a saucepan and place over low heat. Add the lentils, curry, and parsley sachet and gently simmer, uncovered, until the lentils are soft, but not falling apart, about 20 minutes. Season with salt and pepper.

REMOVE AND DISCARD the sachet; there should still be about 1/2 cup of broth left in the pan. Stir in the orange juice. Add the butter, stirring until melted.

CARAMELIZED PARSLEY ROOT AND RUBY RED GRAPEFRUIT CONFIT

1/2	CUP CANOLA OIL
4	CARDAMOM PODS, COARSELY CRACKED
1	CUP DICED PARSLEY ROOT OR CELERY ROOT
	KOSHER SALT AND FRESHLY GROUND BLACK PEPPER
1/4	CUP DICED RUBY RED GRAPEFRUIT CONFIT (FROM MASTER RECIPE)
1	SMALL RUBY RED GRAPEFRUIT, CUT INTO SEGMENTS (SEE SEGMENTING CITRUS, PAGE 225)
	FRESH FLAT-LEAF PARSLEY LEAVES, FOR GARNISH

COMBINE THE OIL and cardamom in a small saucepan over low heat. Cook until fragrant, about 10 minutes; do not let boil. Remove from the heat and set aside to steep for 10 minutes to further infuse the flavor. Strain and discard the solids.

PLACE THE CARDAMOM oil in a large sauté pan over medium heat. Add the diced parsley root, tossing to coat in the oil. Season with salt and pepper. Fry until the parsley is tender and slightly charred on the edges, about 6 minutes. Add the grapefruit segments and the Ruby Red Grapefruit Confit, tossing to combine. Heat through for a minute.

TO ASSEMBLE AND serve: Divide the Green Lentils among 4 plates, letting broth puddle in the center. Lay a slice of Pork Belly on the lentils, crispy side up. Set a piece of Seared Black Bass across the top, skin side up. Spoon 2 generous tablespoons of the Parsley Root and Grapefruit Confit around the plate, drizzling any remaining cardamom oil on top. Garnish with a few fresh parsley leaves.

SAUTÉED ABALONE, FRESH FETTUCCINE, AND BROWN BUTTER SAUCE

01
BASIL, PINE NUT
GARLIC-BASIL BROWN BUTTER WITH PINE NUTS AND EGGPLANT, TOMATO CREAM

02
TARRAGON, ANCHOVY
CAPER-TARRAGON BROWN BUTTER WITH WHITE ANCHOVIES AND ZUCCHINI, GREEN GODDESS CREAM

03
PARSLEY, OLIVE
PEARL ONION–PARSLEY BROWN BUTTER WITH OLIVES AND PEPPERS, BLACK OLIVE CREAM

I AM A HUGE FAN OF ABALONE AND EAT IT PREPARED MANY DIFFERENT WAYS. IF PRESSED, I WOULD HAVE TO SAY EGG-BATTERED ABALONE WOULD BE MY REQUESTED LAST MEAL. I ALSO LOVE ABALONE THAT'S BEEN QUICKLY SEARED ON A GRILL, THEN GARNISHED WITH ONLY A SPRITZ OF LEMON JUICE. ABALONE IS COVETED FOR ITS SIZE, THICKNESS, AND DELICATE FLAVOR; HOWEVER, IT HAS A NATURAL CHEWY QUALITY SIMILAR TO CALAMARI, WHICH MAKES IT ESSENTIAL TO TENDERIZE WITH A MALLET. HERE, ITS MEATY NATURE CARRIES THE MEDITERRANEAN GARNISHES HOME, PAIRING PERFECTLY WITH THE SHARP-SALTY EDGE OF CAPERS, ANCHOVIES, AND OLIVES, DYNAMIC INGREDIENTS THAT MAKE THE DISH POP. THE PASTA IS THE THREAD THAT WEAVES TOGETHER ALL OF THE POTENT FLAVORS IN THIS TRIO. WHEN COOKING ABALONE, TIMING IS KEY; IT HAS TO BE SERVED HOT AND CANNOT SIT TOO LONG ONCE IT IS COOKED OR IT BECOMES RUBBERY. IN THE RESTAURANT, THIS WINDOW OF OPPORTUNITY IS ALWAYS A CHALLENGE DURING SERVICE, WHEN ORDERS ARE POURING IN. WHEN ATTEMPTING THIS DISH AT HOME, GET ALL THE COMPONENTS TOGETHER FIRST AND PREPARE THE ABALONE AT THE LAST MOMENT TO MAINTAIN ITS MELT-IN-YOUR-MOUTH TEXTURE.

ABALONE IS NOT EASILY FOUND IN THE MIDWEST OR EAST. SEE THE SOURCES (PAGE 242) FOR A PURVEYOR. CALAMARI MAY BE SUBSTITUTED.

FROM APRIL THROUGH NOVEMBER, AN EXCLUSIVE SUBCULTURE OF ADVENTUROUS DIVERS IN NORTHERN CALIFORNIA TAKES THE PLUNGE AND RISKS THEIR LIVES TO HARVEST ABALONE. THIS GOURMET GASTROPOD IS PRIZED BOTH FOR ITS LUSCIOUS FLAVOR AND OPALESCENT MOTHER-OF-PEARL SHELL. POPULAR OFF THE SONOMA AND MENDOCINO COASTS, "AB DIVING," AS IT IS CALLED LOCALLY, CAN BE A DANGEROUS ENDEAVOR. ABALONE TUCK THEMSELVES INTO THE DEEPEST CRACKS, CLINGING TO REEFS WHERE SEAWEED AND KELP ARE GROWING ON THE ROCKS AROUND THEM. THEY ARE WELL CAMOUFLAGED, SUCTIONED TIGHTLY IN DARK CREVICES AND HARD-TO-REACH PLACES. LAW FORBIDS SCUBA TANKS, SO YOU ARE RESTRICTED TO FREE-DIVE AND BASICALLY HOLD YOUR BREATH WHILE PRYING THE SNAIL-LIKE DELICACY FROM THE DEPTHS AND BRINGING THE TROPHY TO SHORE. SUFFICE IT TO SAY, DIVING FOR YOUR DINNER IS NOT AN EASY ACHIEVEMENT.

TO PRESERVE THE BEAUTIFUL IRIDESCENT ABALONE SHELLS, SOAK THEM IN BLEACH WATER FOR A COUPLE OF HOURS TO REMOVE ANY ALGAE, THEN RUN THEM THROUGH THE DISHWASHER A COUPLE OF TIMES TO CLEAN COMPLETELY.

WINE SUGGESTION

DOMAINE WEINBACH RIESLING 'SCHLOSSBERG' ST. CATHERINE, ALSACE, FRANCE 2002

Abalone needs a crisp and clean wine that will accentuate its sweet flavor, but it also needs a rich wine with acidity. This Riesling is dry and has a lot of intensity and power with a core mineral flavor. This exotic wine will cut through the flavored butter and add to the complexity of the abalone. A good alternative is a Chablis.

SAUTÉED ABALONE
MASTER RECIPE

SERVES 4

EIGHT   4- TO 5-OUNCE LIVE ABALONE, SHELLED AND CLEANED,
        OR LARGE CALAMARI TUBES, CLEANED
        KOSHER SALT AND FRESHLY GROUND BLACK PEPPER
1   CUP WONDRA FLOUR
4   LARGE EGGS
1   CUP CLARIFIED BUTTER (PAGE 221)

LINE A LARGE platter with a double thickness of paper towels and set aside.

LAY THE ABALONE side by side between 2 sheets of plastic wrap and place on a cutting board. Working from the center of the meat outward, gently pound the abalone with a meat mallet until they are about 1/4 inch thick. Season both sides with salt and pepper.

PLACE THE FLOUR in a shallow platter. In a shallow bowl, whisk together the eggs with 2 tablespoons of water to make an egg wash.

WORKING WITH 4 pieces at a time, dredge both sides of the abalone in the flour, then dip in the egg wash to coat completely, letting most of the excess drip off (you want enough egg to form a light crust).

PLACE 1/2 CUP of the Clarified Butter in a large sauté pan over medium heat. When the butter is nice and hot, add the abalone and fry until golden, less than 1 minute on each side. Do not overcook or the abalone will become tough and rubbery. Transfer the abalone to the prepared platter in a single layer and lightly season with salt. Cover to keep warm. Add the remaining Clarified Butter to the pan and repeat with the other 4 pieces of abalone.

FOLLOW THE ASSEMBLY and serving directions for the variation you are making.

BROWN BUTTER
MASTER RECIPE

MAKES 1/2 CUP

1/2   CUP (1 STICK) UNSALTED BUTTER
1   TABLESPOON FRESH LEMON JUICE
2   TABLESPOONS CHICKEN STOCK (PAGE 222)

PLACE THE BUTTER in a large sauté pan over medium heat and cook until it is foamy and just starts to brown on the edges. Swirl the pan occasionally to keep the color even. When a light brown color is achieved and the butter smells nutty, add the lemon juice; this will stop the butter from continuing to brown and potentially burn. The butter will bubble up. When the bubbles have died down, add the stock and generously season with salt and pepper. Brown butter sauce generally needs a fair amount of seasoning to prevent it from tasting oily.

RAISE THE HEAT slightly and bring the butter to a boil in order to emulsify and thicken it. Once thick, add ingredients for the variations you are making as directed in the recipe.

FETTUCCINE
MASTER RECIPE

PASTA DOUGH

MAKES 1 1/2 POUNDS FETTUCCINE

1 1/2	CUPS SEMOLINA FLOUR
1/2	CUP ALL-PURPOSE FLOUR, PLUS MORE FOR DUSTING
1	TEASPOON SALT
3	LARGE EGGS

IN AN ELECTRIC mixer fitted with a dough hook or paddle attachment, combine the semolina and all-purpose flours and salt. Add the eggs, 1 at a time, and continue to mix until the dough forms a mass.

SPRINKLE SOME ALL-PURPOSE flour on a clean, flat work surface. Place the dough in the center of the flour and knead and fold the dough until it is elastic and smooth. Gather the dough into a ball and wrap tightly in plastic. Set aside in a warm place to rest for about 30 minutes to allow the gluten to relax.

CUT THE DOUGH in half, wrap one half in plastic to prevent it from drying out while you work with the first piece. Flatten and shape the dough with your hands into a rectangle and roll it 2 or 3 times through the pasta machine, at the widest setting. If it sticks, dust with a little more flour. Pull and stretch the sheet of dough with the palm of your hand as it emerges from the rollers. Reduce the setting and crank the dough through 2 or 3 more times. Continue tightening and rolling until the sheet is approximately 12 inches long and about 1/4 inch thick (you should be able to see your hand through it). Set the sheet aside on a floured sheet pan and repeat the process with the remaining piece of dough.

WHEN BOTH SHEETS are done, cut them in half crosswise. Using the fettuccine attachment, run the sheets through the cutting slot. Separate the strands and put the noodles on a lightly floured baking sheet. Allow to dry for about 10 minutes before cooking.

WHEN READY TO cook, bring a large stockpot of salted water to boil over high heat. Add the fettuccine and boil for 3 minutes, stirring occasionally to prevent sticking. Quickly drain the pasta and toss it with the cream sauce for the variation you are making.

O I

BASIL, PINE NUT

GARLIC-BASIL BROWN BUTTER WITH PINE NUTS AND EGGPLANT

MAKES ABOUT 2 CUPS

6	CLOVES GARLIC, SLICED (ABOUT 1/4 CUP)
1/2	CUP WARM BROWN BUTTER (FROM MASTER RECIPE)
1	JAPANESE EGGPLANT, CUT INTO SMALL DICE (ABOUT 1 CUP)
	KOSHER SALT AND FRESHLY GROUND BLACK PEPPER
20	SWEET 100 TOMATOES, HALVED (ABOUT 1 CUP)
1/4	CUP FRESH BASIL LEAVES, CHOPPED
2	TABLESPOONS PINE NUTS, LIGHTLY TOASTED

PLACE THE GARLIC in a small saucepan and cover with cold water. Bring to a boil over high heat and immediately drain out the water. Repeat this process 2 more times with fresh water. This will soften the garlic and remove any bitterness.

PLACE THE BROWN Butter in a medium sauté pan over medium heat. Fold in the eggplant and garlic. Season with salt and pepper. Sauté for 1 to 2 minutes to tenderize the eggplant. Add the tomatoes, basil, and pine nuts, tossing a few seconds to combine.

TOMATO CREAM

MAKES 2 CUPS

4	FRESH BASIL LEAVES
2	SHALLOTS, CHOPPED
1/2	CUP DRY WHITE WINE, SUCH AS SAUVIGNON BLANC
1	TABLESPOON WHOLE BLACK PEPPERCORNS
	KOSHER SALT AND FRESHLY GROUND BLACK PEPPER
2	CUPS HEAVY CREAM
8	SUN-DRIED TOMATOES IN OIL, DRAINED AND CHOPPED

COMBINE THE BASIL, shallots, wine, and peppercorns in a small saucepan. Season with salt and pepper. Place over low heat and simmer until the liquid is reduced to about 2 tablespoons, about 5 minutes.

ADD THE CREAM and simmer until thick enough to coat the back of a spoon, about 10 minutes. Pass through a fine-mesh strainer into a clean saucepan and discard the solids.

PLACE THE PAN over medium heat and stir in the sun-dried tomatoes. Simmer until just tender and heated through, about 1 minute. Transfer the mixture to a blender or food processor and process until smooth. Taste and, if necessary, adjust the seasoning with salt and pepper. Cover and keep warm.

TO ASSEMBLE AND serve: Slip the Sautéed Abalone into the Garlic-Basil Brown Butter to heat through, turning to coat. Using a large fork, twirl servings of the coated fettuccine tightly into nests and place on each of 4 plates. Lean 2 Sautéed Abalone against the pasta and spoon the Garlic-Basil Brown Butter on top and around each plate.

O 2

TARRAGON, ANCHOVY

CAPER-TARRAGON BROWN BUTTER WITH WHITE ANCHOVIES AND ZUCCHINI

1/2	CUP WARM BROWN BUTTER (FROM MASTER RECIPE)
1	SMALL GREEN ZUCCHINI, DICED (ABOUT 1 CUP)
1	SMALL YELLOW ZUCCHINI, DICED (ABOUT 1 CUP)
	KOSHER SALT AND FRESHLY GROUND BLACK PEPPER
4	MARINATED WHITE ANCHOVIES, DRAINED AND CHOPPED
1	TABLESPOON CHOPPED FRESH TARRAGON
2	LEMONS, CUT INTO SEGMENTS (SEE SEGMENTING CITRUS, PAGE 225)
1	TABLESPOON CAPERS, DRAINED

PLACE THE BROWN Butter in a medium sauté pan over medium heat. Fold in the green and yellow zucchini. Season with salt and pepper. Sauté for 1 to 2 minutes to tenderize the squash. Add the anchovies, tarragon, lemon, and capers, tossing a few seconds to combine.

GREEN GODDESS CREAM

MAKES 2 CUPS

2	SHALLOTS, CHOPPED
	ZEST OF 1 LEMON, FINELY GRATED
1/2	CUP DRY WHITE WINE, SUCH AS SAUVIGNON BLANC
4	SPRIGS FRESH TARRAGON
4	SPRIGS FRESH FLAT-LEAF PARSLEY
1	TABLESPOON WHOLE BLACK PEPPERCORNS
	KOSHER SALT AND FRESHLY GROUND BLACK PEPPER
2	CUPS HEAVY CREAM
8	CHIVES, COARSELY CHOPPED
1/2	CUP WATERCRESS LEAVES, COARSELY CHOPPED
1/2	CUP FRESH PARSLEY LEAVES
1/4	CUP FRESH TARRAGON LEAVES

COMBINE THE SHALLOTS, zest, wine, tarragon and parsley sprigs, and peppercorns in a small saucepan. Season with salt and pepper. Place over low heat and simmer until the liquid is reduced to about 2 tablespoons, about 5 minutes.

ADD THE CREAM and simmer until thick enough to coat the back of a spoon, about 10 minutes. Pass through a fine-mesh strainer into a clean saucepan and discard the solids.

TRANSFER THE MIXTURE to a blender or food processor and add the chives, watercress, parsley leaves, and tarragon. Process until smooth. Taste and, if necessary, adjust the seasoning with salt and pepper. Cover to keep warm.

TO ASSEMBLE AND serve: Slip the Sautéed Abalone into the Caper-Tarragon Brown Butter to heat through, turning to coat. Using a large fork, twirl servings of the coated fettuccine tightly into nests and place on each of 4 plates. Lean 2 Sautéed Abalone against the pasta and spoon the Caper-Tarragon Brown Butter on top and around each plate.

03
PARSLEY, OLIVE

PEARL ONION—PARSLEY BROWN BUTTER WITH OLIVES AND PEPPERS

15	RED PEARL ONIONS, PEELED AND QUARTERED
1	CUP DRY RED WINE, SUCH AS MERLOT
1/2	CUP WARM BROWN BUTTER (FROM MASTER RECIPE)
1/4	CUP PICHOLINE OLIVES, PITTED AND SLICED
1/4	CUP NIÇOISE OLIVES, PITTED AND SLICED
1/4	CUP DICED RED BELL PEPPER
1/4	CUP DICED YELLOW BELL PEPPER
1	TABLESPOON CHOPPED FRESH FLAT-LEAF PARSLEY
	KOSHER SALT AND FRESHLY GROUND BLACK PEPPER

COMBINE THE PEARL onions and wine in a small saucepan over low heat. Bring to a simmer and cook until the onions are tender and deep purple, 10 minutes. Drain out any remaining wine.

PLACE THE BROWN Butter in a medium sauté pan over medium heat. Fold in the pearl onions, olives, peppers, and parsley.

SEASON WITH SALT and pepper, tossing a few seconds to soften.

BLACK OLIVE CREAM

MAKES 2 CUPS

3	SPRIGS FRESH FLAT-LEAF PARSLEY
3	SPRIGS FRESH THYME
2	SHALLOTS, CHOPPED
1/2	CUP DRY WHITE WINE, SUCH AS SAUVIGNON BLANC
1	TABLESPOON WHOLE BLACK PEPPERCORNS
	KOSHER SALT AND FRESHLY GROUND BLACK PEPPER
2	CUPS HEAVY CREAM
1	CUP NIÇOISE OLIVES, PITTED AND CHOPPED

COMBINE THE PARSLEY, thyme, shallots, wine, and peppercorns in a small saucepan. Season with salt and pepper. Place over low heat and simmer until the liquid is reduced to about 2 tablespoons, about 5 minutes.

ADD THE CREAM and simmer until thick enough to coat the back of a spoon, about 10 minutes. Pass through a fine-mesh strainer into a clean saucepan and discard the solids. Return to medium heat and mix in the olives. Simmer until just heated through, 1 minute.

TRANSFER THE MIXTURE to a blender or food processor and process until smooth. Taste and, if necessary, adjust the seasoning with salt and pepper. Cover to keep warm.

TO ASSEMBLE AND serve: Slip the Sautéed Abalone into the Onion-Parsley Brown Butter to heat through, turning to coat. Using a large fork, twirl servings of the coated fettuccine tightly into nests and place on each of 4 plates. Lean 2 Sautéed Abalone against the pasta and spoon the Onion-Parsley Brown Butter on top and around each plate.

TAPIOCA-CRUSTED RED SNAPPER

O1
SOY, GINGER
FRIED SUSHI RICE, SAUTÉED BOK CHOY, GINGER-SOY VINAIGRETTE

O2
SESAME, GARLIC
DRIED-FRUIT BASMATI, SAUTÉED SNOW PEAS, SESAME VINAIGRETTE

O3
LYCHEE, CHILE
FORBIDDEN RICE, FRIED JAPANESE EGGPLANT, SPICY LYCHEE VINAIGRETTE

MOST OFTEN WHEN I GO OUT TO DINNER, I CRAVE THE COMPLEXITY OF ASIAN FOOD. BY COMPLEXITY, I DON'T MEAN TRICKY COOKING TECHNIQUES, JUST THE FACT THAT IT TASTES SO RIGHT, FLAVOR-WISE. WHEN EXECUTED WELL, MOST ASIAN CUISINE TYPIFIES THE ZENITH OF SYMMETRY. UNFORTUNATELY, IF EVEN ONE OF THE ELEMENTS IS OUT OF WHACK, THE DISH CAN BE PLAIN TERRIBLE—THERE IS NOT MUCH ROOM FOR ERROR. A LOT OF WHAT I BELIEVE ABOUT BOLD AND BALANCED FLAVORS IS WHAT GOOD ASIAN COOKING IS ALL ABOUT. THE ASIAN MEDLEY OF SWEETNESS, ACIDITY, SPICINESS, AND FAT FIRES FULL THROTTLE TO HIT THE RIGHT NOTES IN THIS RECIPE. HOWEVER, IF ANY ONE OF THESE COMPONENTS ISN'T RIGHT, THIS ASIAN-INFLUENCED DISH WILL BE COMPLETELY WRONG. THEREFORE, WHEN MAKING THIS AT HOME, IT IS OF THE UTMOST IMPORTANCE TO FOLLOW THE EXACT MEASURES TO STRIKE THE CORRECT BALANCE OF FLAVOR.

THE THREE TYPES OF RICE HAVE THEIR OWN APPEAL, EACH EMPHASIZING A DIFFERENT TEXTURE AND FLAVOR. THE CHEWY SHORT-GRAIN SUSHI RICE IS COMPRESSED INTO A CAKE AND FRIED TO MAKE IT DENSE. BASMATI, A VERY LONG-GRAINED RICE WITH A SOFT TEXTURE, LENDS A PERFUMEY, NUTLIKE QUALITY TO ENHANCE THE FLAVORS OF THE DISH. INDIGO-COLORED FORBIDDEN RICE IS NOT ONLY EYE-CATCHING BUT ITS DISTINCTIVE FIRM SHAPE ADDS A TOOTHSOME BITE.

OTHER THAN THE ASSERTIVE FLAVORS, THE LESSON TO LEARN FROM THIS DISH IS THE ADAPTABILITY OF THE BATTER. THE BUTTERMILK AND TAPIOCA FLOUR COATING USED ON THE SNAPPER IS TRULY ALL-PURPOSE. WHENEVER YOU NEED TO BREAD SOMETHING, BE IT CHICKEN OR FISH, THIS BATTER IS A GREAT ONE TO PULL OUT. IT TAKES NO MORE EFFORT THAN DREDGING WITH REGULAR FLOUR, AND THE CRISP TAPIOCA FLOUR CRUST CAN HANDLE BEING BATHED WITH A SAUCE OR VINAIGRETTE WITHOUT GETTING SOGGY.

WINE SUGGESTION

DR. LOOSEN RIESLING 'WEHLENER SONNENUHR' KABINETT, MOSEL, GERMANY 2003

The unique perfume of Riesling will harmonize nicely with this dish. The sweet, sour, and spicy flavors will play very well with this semi-dry wine, and the fresh acidity will accentuate the earthy flavor of the red snapper.

TAPIOCA-CRUSTED RED SNAPPER
MASTER RECIPE

SERVES 4

FOUR	6-OUNCE RED SNAPPER FILLETS
	KOSHER SALT AND FRESHLY GROUND BLACK PEPPER
2	CUPS BUTTERMILK
1	CUP TAPIOCA FLOUR (CASSAVA FLOUR) (SEE SOURCES)
2	CUPS CORNSTARCH
1 1/2	CUPS CLARIFIED BUTTER (PAGE 221)
1/2	CUP (1 STICK) UNSALTED BUTTER

LINE A LARGE platter with a double thickness of paper towels and set aside.

LIBERALLY SEASON BOTH sides of the fish fillets with salt and pepper. Lay them in a single layer in a baking dish and pour the buttermilk over the top, turning to coat.

IN A LARGE shallow platter, combine the tapioca flour and cornstarch.

REMOVE ONE FILLET at a time from the buttermilk bath, letting the excess drip off. Dredge the fish in the flour mixture, coating both sides completely and evenly. The coating should be fairly thick.

PLACE A LARGE sauté pan or cast-iron skillet over medium heat. Pour in 3/4 cup of the Clarified Butter. Once the butter is hot, carefully place 2 fillets in the pan. Press the fish with the back of a spatula so it does not curl up as it cooks. When the edges of the fish begin to brown, add half of the unsalted butter and swirl it around as it melts. Continue cooking until the fish is golden and the crust is crispy on the bottom, about 3 minutes. Carefully turn the fillet over and continue to pan-fry until evenly browned, about 3 more minutes. Transfer the fish to the prepared platter. Season lightly with salt. Repeat the process with the remaining 2 snapper fillets.

FOLLOW THE ASSEMBLY and serving directions for the variation you are making.

O I

SOY, GINGER

FRIED SUSHI RICE

MAKES 8 CAKES

1	CUP SUSHI RICE OR OTHER SHORT-GRAIN WHITE RICE
1 1/4	CUPS WATER
1/4	CUP RICE VINEGAR
1	TABLESPOON SUGAR
1	TEASPOON KOSHER SALT
	WONDRA FLOUR, FOR DUSTING
	KOSHER SALT AND FRESHLY GROUND BLACK PEPPER
	CANOLA OIL, FOR FRYING

PLACE THE RICE in a colander under cold running water and rinse until the water runs clear. Drain well.

COMBINE THE RICE and water in a saucepan over medium-high heat and bring to a boil. When boiling, stir, cover, and reduce the heat to very low. Simmer until the water is absorbed and the rice is tender, 15 to 20 minutes. Remove from heat and let cool.

COMBINE THE VINEGAR, sugar, and salt in a small bowl, stirring to dissolve the sugar.

TRANSFER THE COOLED rice to a large bowl and drizzle with the vinegar mixture. Using a spatula, gently turn the rice to incorporate the liquid. Do not stir or mix because the grains can be smashed and become mushy. The rice should look shiny, be somewhat sticky, and have a nice balance of tart and sweet flavor.

COAT THE BOTTOM and sides of an 8-by-8-inch baking dish with nonstick spray. Dampen your fingers and spread the rice into the dish, pressing to an even, compact layer, about 1/4 inch thick. Cover with plastic wrap and refrigerate to cool and firm up for at least 15 minutes or up to overnight.

WHEN COOLED AND firm, carefully turn the rice square out onto a cutting board and cut into eight 1-inch-wide rectangular blocks.

LINE A PLATTER with paper towels and set aside.

SPREAD THE FLOUR on a platter and season with salt and pepper. Place 1/4 inch of canola oil in a large sauté pan over medium heat. Lightly dust both sides of the rice cakes in the seasoned flour, tapping off the excess. Working in batches, carefully lay the rice cakes in the hot oil. Fry until lightly golden, about 1 minute. Turn and fry the other side until golden, another minute. Transfer the rice cakes to the prepared platter. While they are still hot, season lightly with salt. Cover to keep warm.

SAUTÉED BOK CHOY

1	TABLESPOON CANOLA OIL
1	TABLESPOON SESAME OIL
1	SMALL SHALLOT, MINCED
1	CLOVE GARLIC, MINCED
1	TEASPOON MINCED FRESH GINGER
4	HEADS BABY BOK CHOY, TRIMMED AND QUARTERED
	KOSHER SALT AND FRESHLY GROUND BLACK PEPPER
	PINCH OF KOREAN RED PEPPER POWDER (KUCHO KARU), OR CAYENNE

PLACE THE CANOLA and sesame oils in a sauté pan over medium heat. Add the shallot, garlic, and ginger and sauté until fragrant, about 10 seconds. Add the bok choy and toss to coat. Add 2 tablespoons water so the bok choy wilts a bit. Season with salt, pepper, and red pepper powder. Cover to keep warm.

GINGER-SOY VINAIGRETTE

MAKES 1 2/3 CUPS

1	CUP WHITE SOY SAUCE (SHIRO SHOYU), SUCH AS MORITA (SEE SOURCES, PAGE 242)
1	TABLESPOON DARK SOY SAUCE
1/4	CUP RICE VINEGAR
1	TABLESPOON MINCED FRESH GINGER
1/2	CUP RICE BRAN OIL OR CANOLA OIL
1/2	TABLESPOON BLACK SESAME SEEDS
2	SCALLIONS, WHITE PART ONLY, SLICED

COMBINE THE WHITE and dark soy, vinegar, and ginger in a small saucepan and place over low heat to infuse the ginger flavor into the liquid, 1 to 2 minutes. Remove from the heat and whisk in the oil. Stir in the sesame seeds and scallions. Cover to keep warm.

TO ASSEMBLE AND serve: Place 2 Sushi Rice Cakes on each of 4 plates, just off center. Lay some of the Sautéed Bok Choy next to the cakes. Place a piece of the Tapioca-Crusted Red Snapper across the top. Spoon 3 to 4 tablespoons of the warm Ginger-Soy Vinaigrette over the fish and around each plate, being sure to evenly distribute the ginger, scallions, and sesame seeds in each serving.

O 2

SESAME, GARLIC

DRIED-FRUIT BASMATI

MAKES 4 CUPS

1 1/2	CUPS BASMATI RICE
2	KAFFIR LIME LEAVES
1	TABLESPOON UNSALTED BUTTER
1/2	TEASPOON KOSHER SALT
1 3/4	CUPS WATER
1/4	CUP DICED DRIED PINEAPPLE
1/4	CUP DICED DRIED PEAR
1/2	CUP PLUM WINE
1/2	RED BELL PEPPER, FINELY DICED
1/4	CUP FINELY DICED MANGO
2	TABLESPOONS SHELLED SOYBEANS (EDAMAME)
2	TABLESPOONS SLICED ALMONDS, TOASTED
2	TABLESPOONS FINELY CHOPPED FRESH CILANTRO
1/2	CUP SESAME VINAIGRETTE (RECIPE FOLLOWS)

COMBINE THE RICE, lime leaves, butter, salt, and water in a saucepan over medium-high heat and bring to a boil. When boiling, stir, cover, and reduce the heat to very low. Simmer until the rice is tender and all of the water is absorbed, 20 minutes. Remove from heat and let cool.

WHILE THE RICE is cooking, combine the dried pineapple, pear, and plum wine in a small saucepan. Bring to a boil over medium heat. Immediately remove from the heat and allow the fruit to steep in the wine to reconstitute and soften. After 10 minutes, drain out any wine that has not been absorbed by the fruit.

REMOVE AND DISCARD the lime leaves from the cooled rice and fluff the grains with a fork. Fold in the wine-soaked fruit, bell pepper, mango, soybeans, almonds, and cilantro. Add the Sesame Vinaigrette and stir to combine. Cover to keep warm.

SAUTÉED SNOW PEAS

1   TABLESPOON CANOLA OIL

1/2   POUND SNOW PEAS, STRINGS REMOVED

PINCH OF KOREAN RED PEPPER POWDER (KUCHO KARU), OR CAYENNE

PLACE A LARGE skillet over medium heat and film with the oil. Add the snow peas and sauté until crisp-tender, 1 to 2 minutes. Sprinkle with the red pepper powder and remove from the heat. Cover to keep warm.

SESAME VINAIGRETTE

MAKES 1 2/3 CUPS

2   CLOVES GARLIC, MINCED

1   RED JALAPEÑO, SEEDED AND MINCED

1   GREEN JALAPEÑO, SEEDED AND MINCED

JUICE OF 1 LIME

1   CUP SESAME OIL

1/2   CUP RICE VINEGAR

1/2   CUP FISH SAUCE (NAM PLA), SUCH AS THREE CRABS BRAND

COMBINE THE GARLIC, jalapeños, lime juice, oil, vinegar, and fish sauce in a small saucepan over low heat. Heat very slightly, until just warm and aromatic. Cover and keep warm.

TO ASSEMBLE AND serve: Mound about 1 cup of the Dried-Fruit Basmati on each of 4 plates, just off center. Lay some Sautéed Snow Peas next to the rice and place a piece of the Tapioca-Crusted Red Snapper across the top. Spoon 3 to 4 tablespoons of the warm Sesame Vinaigrette over the fish and around each plate, being sure to evenly distribute the garlic and chilies in each serving.

O 3

LYCHEE, CHILE

FORBIDDEN RICE

Forbidden rice grains look like black leather, though they're actually the deepest blue imaginable. Legend has it that Chinese emperors were once the sole consumers of forbidden rice, hence its name. Its firm texture and earthy and vaguely smoky taste holds up well to assertive flavors. Lotus Foods is a leading importer.

MAKES 4 CUPS

1 1/2	CUPS FORBIDDEN RICE
1 1/2	QUARTS WATER
1	TABLESPOON KOSHER SALT

PLACE THE RICE in a colander under cold running water and rinse until the water runs clear. Drain well.

COMBINE THE RICE and water in a saucepan over medium heat. Bring to a boil; reduce heat, and simmer for 40 minutes, uncovered, until the rice is tender but still firm, stirring occasionally. Remove from heat, stir in the salt, and let stand for 5 minutes to allow the grains to absorb the salt.

PASS THE RICE through a fine-mesh strainer and rinse under hot water to remove any excess starch. Return the rice to the saucepan and cover to keep warm.

FRIED JAPANESE EGGPLANT

	JUICE OF 1 LIME
1/2	CUP UNSWEETENED COCONUT MILK
1/2	CUP SWEET CHILE SAUCE, SUCH AS MAE PLOY
1/2	CUP CANOLA OIL
2	JAPANESE EGGPLANTS, TRIMMED, CUT LENGTHWISE IN 8 SLICES
	KOSHER SALT

LINE A PLATTER with paper towels and set aside.

COMBINE THE LIME juice, coconut milk, and chile sauce in a large sauté pan and bring to a simmer over medium-low heat. Reduce heat to low.

POUR THE OIL into a separate sauté pan and place over medium heat. Working in batches, fry the eggplant until lightly browned, about 1 minute on each side. Transfer to the prepared platter.

LAY THE EGGPLANT in the coconut milk mixture and simmer until the eggplant is well coated in the sauce but not so overcooked that it's falling apart, about 1 minute. Remove the eggplant from the sauce and cover to keep warm.

SPICY LYCHEE VINAIGRETTE

MAKES 2 CUPS

1/2	CUP LYCHEE SYRUP
6	TABLESPOONS SUGAR
2	CUPS FRESH ORANGE JUICE, STRAINED (FROM ABOUT 8 ORANGES)
1/2	CUP FRESHLY SQUEEZED LIME JUICE, STRAINED (FROM ABOUT 4 LIMES)
2	CUPS LOBSTER STOCK (PAGE 223)
	CANOLA OIL, FOR FRYING
2	LARGE SHALLOTS, CUT CROSSWISE INTO VERY THIN SLICES AND SEPARATED INTO RINGS

WONDRA FLOUR, FOR DUSTING

1 1/2 TABLESPOONS FISH SAUCE, SUCH AS THREE CRABS BRAND

4 LYCHEE NUTS, SLICED IN STRIPS

2 TANGERINES OR ORANGES, CUT INTO SEGMENTS
(SEE SEGMENTING CITRUS, PAGE 225)

1 THAI BIRD CHILE OR JALAPEÑO, SLICED

1/4 CUP OPAL BASIL LEAVES OR ITALIAN BASIL

1/4 CUP THAI BASIL LEAVES

COMBINE THE LYCHEE syrup and sugar in a 2-quart saucepan, stirring to combine. Place over medium heat and cook until the sugar melts into a light caramel, about 5 minutes. Add the orange and lime juices, followed by the Lobster Stock. Bring to a simmer and then lower the heat and cook at a bare simmer until reduced by half, about 40 minutes. It is very important to reduce the vinaigrette slowly, as the citrus juice has a tendency to become bitter when the acid is rapidly cooked down.

WHILE THE VINAIGRETTE is cooking, line a plate with paper towels and set aside. Heat 1 inch of oil in a wide pan to 300°F. Toss the shallot rings in the flour to lightly dust. Transfer the shallots to a mesh strainer and shake to remove any excess flour. Place the shallots in the hot oil and fry until light golden and crispy, about 1 minute. Using a slotted spoon, scoop the fried shallots out of the oil and drain on the prepared plate. While still hot, season them lightly with salt.

STIR THE FISH sauce into the vinaigrette. Just before serving, add the fried shallots, lychees, chile, tangerine sections, and basil leaves.

TO ASSEMBLE AND serve: Lay 2 slices of Fried Eggplant in the center of each of 4 plates. Mound 1 cup of Forbidden Rice on top of the eggplant and place a piece of the Tapioca-Crusted Red Snapper across the top. Spoon 3 to 4 tablespoons of the warm Lychee Vinaigrette over the fish and around each plate, being sure to evenly distribute the shallots, lychees, tangerine sections, chilies, and basil in each serving.

CHAPTER THREE

MEAT ENTRÉE TRIOS

As much as I love cooking fish, after having a seafood restaurant for twelve years, I was ready for a change. When I opened MICHAEL MINA, I was determined to explore new dimensions in the preparation of meats.

Juiciness and flavor are two important components when it comes to meat quality. Both factors are influenced by the cut of meat you choose and how it's cooked. I first experimented with slow-poaching lamb in warm olive oil and beef in clarified butter. The outcomes were amazing and opened an entirely new avenue of cooking. The meat gave up none of its mass and retained all its inherent flavor and moisture while cooking evenly throughout. Cooking meat slowly in this fashion also kept it from shrinking and toughening. By then searing the meat *after* it is poached, you achieve maximum tenderness while still producing a caramelization on the outside of the meat. It is now my favorite method to prepare different types of meat.

In this chapter, I examine both the more traditional methods of cooking meat—searing and roasting—as well as the poaching approach. The two meats that are seared and roasted are protected by a nice layer of fat, which not only adds succulence but also helps retain juiciness. The rich skin on the squab provides some armor for the breast meat, and the pancetta wrapping on the pork loin ensures that the lean meat will stay moist and tender. Although some of the recipes may seem complex, I think that you will find that once you have gathered your *mise en place* (the French term for the organization of all the ingredients necessary to complete a dish), the actual preparation time will be relatively short.

BUTTER-POACHED KOBE BEEF RIB EYE
WITH PINOT NOIR REDUCTION

O1
HORSERADISH, ONION

HORSERADISH MASHED POTATOES, ROASTED CIPOLLINI ONIONS,
HORSERADISH CREAM, BUTTERMILK ONION RINGS

O2
TARRAGON, ASPARAGUS

SALT-BAKED YUKON POTATOES, GRILLED ASPARAGUS, CLASSIC BÉARNAISE

O3
GARLIC, SPINACH

POTATO CAKES, SAUTÉED GARLIC SPINACH, FOIE GRAS EMULSION

THERE ARE PLENTY OF GREAT OLD STEAKHOUSES ACROSS THE COUNTRY—IZZY'S IN SAN FRANCISCO AND PETER LUGER'S IN NEW YORK COME TO MIND. LARGE PLATTERS OF THICK, JUICY STEAK SURROUNDED BY AN ABUNDANCE OF SIDE PLATES STIRS UP CONVERSATION AROUND THE LIVELY TABLES. THIS STEAKHOUSE-STYLE TRIO ECHOES THE GREAT AMERICAN SPIRIT WITH A MODERN ADAPTATION OF PROVEN FLAVORS AND TECHNIQUES. MY AIM IS TO OFFER FAMILIAR YET UNINTIMIDATING INGREDIENTS AND PRESENT THEM IN A REALLY DRAMATIC FASHION TO INSTIGATE THE "WOW" FACTOR. I AM NOT REINVENTING THE FLAVOR WHEEL HERE—IF YOU ARE IN THE MOOD FOR STEAK, IT IS SIMPLE TO GRASP THAT PINOT NOIR, HORSERADISH, BÉARNAISE, AND ASPARAGUS ARE PRETTY SAFE BETS. BUT BETWEEN THE WORLD-CLASS BEEF, THE METHOD OF COOKING, AND THE PRESENTATION, THIS MEAT-AND-POTATOES DISH IS ANYTHING BUT MUNDANE. POACHING THE KOBE BEEF NICE AND SLOW IN CLARIFIED BUTTER IS A NONAGGRESSIVE WAY TO GET THE MOST OUT OF IT. THE THEORY BEHIND THIS PREPARATION IS THAT BY FIRST COOKING THE BEEF IN THE BUTTER, THEN SEARING IT, THE MEAT WILL NOT TIGHTEN UP AND SHRINK FROM THE HIGH HEAT. BRIEFLY SEARING THE BEEF LEAVES THE INTERIOR MEDIUM-RARE AND THE OUTSIDE CARAMELIZED JUST ENOUGH FOR A LITTLE CHARRED FLAVOR. THE MELT-IN-YOUR-MOUTH TEXTURE IS MEANT TO BE CLOSER TO A FINE HUNK OF TUNA THAN BEEF.

TO ME, RIB EYE IS ONE OF THE MOST FLAVORFUL CUTS OF MEAT. I PREFER IT TO FILET BECAUSE THE MEATY FLAVOR IS MORE INTENSE AND IT HAS A FIRM CUT. THE COMBINED CHARACTERISTICS OF UNMATCHED FLAVOR, TENDERNESS, AND CONSISTENCY MAKE KOBE RIB EYE MY CUT OF CHOICE.

WINE SUGGESTION

LEWIS CABERNET SAUVIGNON RESERVE, NAPA VALLEY 2002

This ripe and powerful Cabernet Sauvignon is a perfect match for beef and especially for the rich preparations of the rib eye in this all-American dish, with three classic preparations. A big Syrah could very well be used as a substitute.

SERVES 4

BUTTER-POACHED KOBE BEEF RIB EYE
MASTER RECIPE

Tales of the Kobe beef cattle being massaged with sake and fed a special diet enriched with beer are culinary legend. It is reputed that all the love and care the cows receive help produce meat that's extraordinarily tender, finely marbled, and full flavored. If you have never tasted this buttery, nearly sweet beef before, you are in for a culinary revelation. However, Kobe beef that you see on menus in the States most likely isn't genuine Kobe. Just as the only true champagne is bottled in France's Champagne, the only beef that merits the official Kobe name is actually from that region of Japan. Thankfully, Kobe-style beef is now raised domestically. Here, as in Japan, the livestock come from the heirloom breed "Wagyu," which translates to "Japanese cattle." In the U.S., Kobe beef is a crossbreed of American cattle (usually Black Angus) and Wagyu, which are raised in accordance with exacting Kobe standards. I stand by the Idaho ranch Snake River Farms for their methodical, specialized regimen and hormone-free ethics (see Sources, page 242). They sell a full range of cuts and grades of high-quality beef that is properly aged and handled with care.

6	CUPS (1 1/2 QUARTS) CLARIFIED BUTTER (PAGE 221)
3	CLOVES GARLIC, SMASHED
2	BAY LEAVES, PREFERABLY FRESH
6	FRESH THYME SPRIGS
FOUR	6-OUNCE BONELESS RIB EYE STEAKS, PREFERABLY KOBE-STYLE
	KOSHER SALT AND FRESHLY GROUND BLACK PEPPER
	MALDON SEA SALT, FOR SERVING
1	CUP PINOT NOIR REDUCTION (PAGE 221)

BRING A LARGE saucepan of water to a simmer over medium-low heat. Combine the Clarified Butter, garlic, bay leaves, and thyme in a metal bowl or pan just large enough to sit over the simmering water without letting the bottom touch. Gently heat the butter to 135°F on a frying thermometer. Make sure the butter hovers somewhere between 135 and 140°F, as this will ensure that the meat is cooked to a perfect medium-rare.

SEASON THE BEEF heavily with salt and pepper, and completely submerge the steaks in the warm butter. The temperature of the fat will drop slightly. Using tongs to rotate the meat occasionally, poach for a minimum of 25 to 30 minutes or up to an hour or more. As long as the temperature of the butter stays below 140°F the meat won't overcook. Check the temperature often with the thermometer so that it remains a constant temperature.

WHEN READY TO serve, using tongs, remove the beef from the pan, allowing the excess butter to drip off. Season it well with salt and pepper. Place a large sauté pan over medium-high heat, and when hot, coat with 2 tablespoons of the Clarified Butter. Add the steaks and sear all sides until well browned. (At this point, the meat is already cooked through from the poaching; you just want a slight crust on the outside for texture.) Transfer the beef to a cutting board and let rest for at least 10 minutes to allow the juices to redistribute. Slice each steak against the grain into about 5 slices. Season lightly with Maldon sea salt.

FOLLOW THE ASSEMBLY and serving directions for the variation you are making.

O I

HORSERADISH, ONION

HORSERADISH MASHED POTATOES

MAKES ABOUT 3 CUPS

4 RUSSET POTATOES, PEELED AND QUARTERED
1 TABLESPOON KOSHER SALT, PLUS MORE FOR SEASONING
1 CUP HEAVY CREAM
2 TABLESPOONS UNSALTED BUTTER
2 TABLESPOONS GRATED FRESH OR PREPARED HORSERADISH
   FRESHLY GROUND BLACK PEPPER

PLACE THE POTATOES in a large saucepan and cover with cold water. Add about 1 tablespoon of salt to the water. Place over medium heat and bring to a boil. Reduce the heat and cook at a gentle simmer until there is no resistance when a fork is inserted into the potatoes, 20 to 25 minutes.

DRAIN THE POTATOES and immediately pass them through a food mill or potato ricer into a large mixing bowl. (If you do not have a ricer or food mill you can use a fork for chunky potatoes or a hand mixer or immersion blender for a smoother consistency.)

PLACE THE CREAM in a small saucepan over low heat to warm through. Add the cream to the potatoes along with the butter and horseradish. Stir with a wooden spoon to blend. Season with salt and pepper. You can add more or less cream to achieve the consistency that you like. Cover and keep warm over low heat.

ROASTED CIPOLLINI ONIONS

1/2 POUND CIPOLLINI ONIONS, PEELED (ABOUT 2 CUPS)
2   TABLESPOONS CANOLA OIL
2   SPRIGS FRESH THYME
1   BAY LEAF, PREFERABLY FRESH
     KOSHER SALT AND FRESHLY GROUND BLACK PEPPER

PREHEAT THE OVEN to 400°F.

PLACE THE ONIONS on a large piece of aluminum foil and drizzle with the oil. Toss the thyme and bay leaf on top and season generously with salt and pepper. Fold up the edges and pinch the foil tightly to seal. Place the package on a sheet pan and roast until the onions are very tender, about 30 minutes.

HORSERADISH CREAM

MAKES 2/3 CUP

2   SHALLOTS, SLICED
1/2 CUP DRY WHITE WINE, SUCH AS SAUVIGNON BLANC
1   CUP HEAVY CREAM
1   TABLESPOON GRATED FRESH OR PREPARED HORSERADISH
     KOSHER SALT AND FRESHLY GROUND BLACK PEPPER

COMBINE THE SHALLOTS and wine in a saucepan over medium-low heat. Bring to a simmer and cook until almost dry, about 5 minutes. Stir in the cream and horseradish. Continue to simmer and stir until the mixture is thick enough to coat the back of a spoon, 8 to 10 minutes. Do not allow the cream to boil. Pass the horseradish cream through a fine-mesh strainer to smooth out the sauce. Season with salt and pepper. Cover and keep warm.

BUTTERMILK ONION RINGS

1	MEDIUM RED ONION, CUT CROSSWISE INTO 1/8-INCH-THICK SLICES
1	CUP BUTTERMILK
	CANOLA OIL, FOR DEEP-FRYING
1	CUP WONDRA FLOUR
	KOSHER SALT AND FRESHLY GROUND BLACK PEPPER

SEPARATE THE ONION slices into rings, discarding the centers. Place in a shallow baking dish and pour the buttermilk on top, tossing to coat. Set aside to marinate for at least 20 minutes.

LINE A LARGE plate with paper towels and set aside.

FILL A LARGE heavy saucepan or deep fryer three-quarters full with oil, about 2 quarts. Heat to 360°F on a frying thermometer attached to the side of the pan.

SPREAD THE FLOUR out on a platter and generously season with salt and pepper. Dredge the onion rings in the seasoned flour, coating evenly. Shake off the excess. Carefully submerge the rings in the hot oil, stirring gently to ensure they don't stick together and will cook evenly. Fry until light golden, 30 seconds to 1 minute. Using a slotted spoon, transfer the onion rings to the prepared plate. Lightly season with salt. Serve hot.

TO ASSEMBLE AND serve: Evenly divide the Horseradish Mashed Potatoes among 4 plates, mounding just off center. Fan the Rib Eye slices over the potatoes and nestle the Roasted Onions next to them. Pour 1/4 cup of the Pinot Noir Reduction around the meat and drizzle some of the Horseradish Cream on top. Garnish with the hot Onion Rings.

O 2

TARRAGON, ASPARAGUS

SALT-BAKED YUKON POTATOES

At the restaurant, we serve this dish with small marble potatoes so guests enjoy a one-bite personal baked potato. For a more substantial serving, you can use creamer-sized potatoes. Baking the potatoes in salt not only adds flavor, but also aids in even cooking, as the salt helps to conduct the heat to the interior.

SERVES 4

2	CUPS ROCK SALT
4	YUKON GOLD POTATOES, CREAMER SIZE
1/4	POUND BACON STRIPS
2	TABLESPOONS UNSALTED BUTTER, AT ROOM TEMPERATURE
1	TEASPOON MINCED FRESH TARRAGON
	KOSHER SALT AND FRESHLY GROUND BLACK PEPPER
1/2	CUP CRÈME FRAÎCHE
2	TABLESPOONS MINCED FRESH CHIVES

PREHEAT THE OVEN to 450°F.

SPRINKLE A THIN layer of rock salt on the bottom of a small baking dish. Nestle the potatoes into the salt, making sure that they are spaced evenly. Completely cover the potatoes with the remaining rock salt. Transfer to the oven and bake until a knife can slide into the potatoes without resistance, about 1 hour.

WHILE THE POTATOES are baking, place a sauté pan over medium heat. Add the bacon and fry until crisp. Drain on a plate lined with paper towels. When cool, crumble the bacon and set aside.

IN A SMALL bowl, combine the butter and tarragon. Season lightly with salt and pepper. Set aside.

WHEN COOKED, REMOVE the potatoes from the salt crust, being sure to brush off all the excess. Cut the potatoes lengthwise and scoop out some of the insides with a spoon, leaving a thick shell; push the ends together to crown the top. Spoon about 1/2 tablespoon of the tarragon butter in each hollowed-out potato, top with crème fraîche, crumbled bacon, and chives.

GRILLED ASPARAGUS

1	BUNCH ASPARAGUS, BOTTOMS TRIMMED
	ZEST OF 1 LEMON, FINELY GRATED
2	TABLESPOONS EXTRA-VIRGIN OLIVE OIL
	KOSHER SALT AND FRESHLY GROUND BLACK PEPPER

PREHEAT AND OIL a grill or preheat a broiler.

IF THE ASPARAGUS is woody you may need to peel the tough outer stalk. Toss the asparagus with the lemon zest, oil, and salt and pepper. Place the asparagus on the grill or under the broiler, turning as needed until evenly browned. Take care that the tips do not burn. When the asparagus is tender, transfer to a plate and cover to keep warm.

CLASSIC BÉARNAISE

MAKES 1 1/4 CUPS

2	SHALLOTS, CHOPPED
2	STEMS FRESH TARRAGON
1/4	CUP CHAMPAGNE VINEGAR

1/4 CUP DRY WHITE WINE, SUCH AS SAUVIGNON BLANC

3 LARGE EGG YOLKS

1 CUP WARM CLARIFIED BUTTER (PAGE 221)

2 TABLESPOONS MINCED FRESH TARRAGON LEAVES

KOSHER SALT AND FRESHLY GROUND BLACK PEPPER

COMBINE THE SHALLOTS, tarragon stems, vinegar, and wine in a small saucepan over medium heat. Cook until all but about 2 tablespoons of the liquid has evaporated. Strain, discarding the solids. Set aside to cool slightly.

COMBINE THE SHALLOT reduction and egg yolks in a stainless steel bowl. Whisk together until foamy. Place the bowl over a saucepan containing barely simmering water (or use a double boiler). The water should not touch the bottom of the bowl, as this will cook the eggs too quickly. Cook, whisking constantly, until yellow ribbons start to form. Slowly drizzle in the Clarified Butter and continue to whisk until thick and creamy. Remove from the heat, stir in the minced tarragon, and season with salt and pepper. Serve immediately. It is important that the sauce not cool down or it will break.

TO ASSEMBLE AND serve: Puddle 2 tablespoons of the Béarnaise on each of 4 plates, just off center. Arrange an equal portion of the Grilled Asparagus on top. Fan the Rib Eye slices over the asparagus and nestle the Salt-Baked Potatoes next to them. Pour 1/4 cup of the Pinot Noir Reduction around the meat.

03

GARLIC, SPINACH

4 POTATO CAKES (SEE PAGE 176) 3-INCH SIZE

FOIE GRAS EMULSION (SEE PAGE 197)

SEARED FOIE GRAS (SEE PAGE 29)

PREPARE THE POTATO Cakes according to the directions in the recipe.

PREPARE THE FOIE Gras Emulsion according to the directions in the recipe.

PREPARE THE SEARED Foie Gras according to the directions in the recipe.

SAUTÉED GARLIC SPINACH

SERVES 4

2 TABLESPOONS UNSALTED BUTTER

2 CLOVES GARLIC, MINCED

1 POUND SPINACH, WELL-WASHED, STEMMED, AND DRIED (PREFERABLY SAVOY)

KOSHER SALT AND FRESHLY GROUND BLACK PEPPER

MELT THE BUTTER in a large sauté pan over medium-low heat. Add the garlic and sauté until tender and fragrant. Using a wooden spoon, fold in the spinach to coat it in the garlic butter. Season with salt and pepper. Sauté just until wilted. Transfer the spinach to a clean kitchen towel to drain off the excess liquid. Cover and keep warm.

TO ASSEMBLE AND serve: Set a Potato Cake in the center of each of 4 plates. Place a small pile of Sautéed Spinach on top. Fan the Rib Eye slices over the spinach and set a Seared Foie Gras medallion on top. Pour 1/4 cup of the Pinot Noir Reduction around the meat and drizzle the Foie Gras Emulsion on top.

OLIVE OIL-POACHED RACK OF LAMB

O 1
CUCUMBER, MINT
CUCUMBER RAITA, MINT GREMOLATA, HEIRLOOM TABBOULEH

O 2
RED PEPPER, ROSEMARY
HARISSA RATATOUILLE, ROSEMARY GREMOLATA,

ROSEMARY-SCENTED BABY POTATOES

O 3
CURRY, CILANTRO
MATSUTAKE GARAM MASALA, CILANTRO GREMOLATA, DATE BASMATI

MORE OFTEN THAN NOT, RACK OF LAMB IS ROASTED ON THE BONE, AS THIS METHOD RESULTS IN MOISTER MEAT, WITH THE BONE PROVIDING PROTECTION AND FLAVOR. HOWEVER, THE EXTERIOR AT THE BASE OF THE BONE IS THE TOUGHEST SPOT TO ROAST EVENLY WITHOUT THE EXTERIOR GETTING OVERDONE AND THE TIPS BURNED. I FIND THAT POACHING THE LAMB YIELDS CONSISTENT RESULTS; IT IS PERFECTLY COOKED WITH THE ENTIRE EYE EVENLY RED. FROM A RESTAURANT STANDPOINT, THIS COOKING METHOD IS ALSO A BONUS BECAUSE THE LAMB CAN HOLD IN THE OIL AND THEN BE QUICKLY SEARED AT THE LAST MINUTE. ASK THE BUTCHER TO REMOVE THE CHINE BONE (BACKBONE) FROM EACH RACK OF LAMB, TO CLEAN AND FRENCH THE RIBS, AND TRIM THE FAT CAP ON THE MEAT.

IN THIS RECIPE, GENTLY POACHING THE LAMB IN FRUITY OLIVE OIL ENHANCES THE MEDITERRANEAN THEME OF THE ENTIRE DISH. THE PROGRESSION OF TASTES BUILDS ONE UPON ANOTHER. CUCUMBER AND TABBOULEH IS A FRESH OPENER, FOLLOWED BY THE POWERFUL TEAM OF HARISSA AND ROSEMARY, ENDING WITH A STRONG FINISH OF CURRY AND DATES. THE PALETTE OF TRIOS WORKS SEPARATELY AS WELL.

WINE SUGGESTION

QUPÉ SYRAH *HILLSIDE*, SANTA MARIA VALLEY 2001

Qupé is one of the greatest California Syrah producers. The smoky and gamy flavors of Syrah and lamb are a pairing made in heaven. Other wines such as Chateauneuf du Pape and domestic Grenache also pair nicely.

OLIVE OIL–POACHED RACK OF LAMB
MASTER RECIPE

SERVES 4

6   CUPS OLIVE OIL
4   SPRIGS FRESH ROSEMARY
2   SHALLOTS, HALVED
2   BAY LEAVES, PREFERABLY FRESH
1   HEAD OF GARLIC, HALVED
2   RACKS OF LAMB (1 1/2 POUNDS EACH), TRIMMED AND FRENCHED
     KOSHER SALT AND FRESHLY GROUND BLACK PEPPER
     MALDON SEA SALT

BRING A LARGE saucepan of water to a simmer over medium-low heat. Combine the oil, rosemary, shallots, bay leaves, and garlic in a metal bowl or pan just large enough to sit over the simmering water without letting the bottom touch. Gently heat the oil to 135°F on a frying thermometer. Make sure the oil hovers somewhere between 135 and 140°F, as this will ensure that the meat is cooked to a perfect medium-rare.

SEASON THE LAMB heavily with salt and pepper, and completely submerge the meat in the warm oil. The temperature of the fat will drop slightly. Using tongs to rotate the meat occasionally, poach for a minimum of 25 to 30 minutes or up to an hour or more. As long as the temperature of the oil stays below 140°F the meat won't overcook. Check the temperature often with the thermometer so that it remains a constant temperature.

WHEN READY TO serve, using tongs, remove the lamb from the pan, allowing the excess oil to drip off. Season it well with salt and pepper. Place a large sauté pan over medium-high heat and, when hot, coat with 2 tablespoons of the oil. Add the lamb and sear both sides until well browned. (At this point, the meat is already cooked through from the poaching; you just want a slight crust on the outside for texture.) Transfer the lamb to a cutting board and let rest for at least 10 minutes to allow the juices to redistribute. Carve the lamb into chops. Season lightly with Maldon sea salt.

FOLLOW THE ASSEMBLY and serving directions for the variation you are making.

O I

CUCUMBER RAITA

Raita, a fresh yogurt sauce that typically accompanies curries and other Indian dishes, is designed to be a cooling counter-balance to spiciness. Draining the yogurt and patting the cucumber dry removes excess liquid that would otherwise make the raita runny.

2	CUPS PLAIN WHOLE-MILK YOGURT
6	FRESH DILL SPRIGS, CHOPPED
1	ENGLISH CUCUMBER, PEELED, SEEDED, HALVED, THINLY SLICED IN HALF MOONS, AND PATTED DRY
	JUICE OF 1/2 LEMON
1/4	TEASPOON PAPRIKA
	KOSHER SALT AND FRESHLY GROUND BLACK PEPPER

LINE A STRAINER with cheesecloth and set over a bowl. Place the yogurt in the strainer and cover with plastic wrap. Transfer the bowl and strainer to the refrigerator to drain overnight.

THE NEXT DAY, combine the drained yogurt, dill, cucumber, lemon, and paprika in a small bowl. Season generously with salt and pepper. Stir well to combine. Cover and refrigerate for at least 30 minutes to let the flavors marry. Stir again before serving.

MINT GREMOLATA

1	LEMON
1	CLOVE GARLIC
1/4	TEASPOON KOSHER SALT
1/4	CUP CHOPPED FRESH MINT
1/4	CUP EXTRA-VIRGIN OLIVE OIL
	FRESHLY GROUND BLACK PEPPER

USING A VEGETABLE peeler or sharp paring knife, carefully remove wide strips of lemon zest. Do not include the bitter white pith. Finely chop the zest into small pieces. (Although it may seem faster to simply use a zester or microplane, too much oil comes out of the peel, making the gremolata clumpy.) Cut the peeled lemon in half and squeeze out the juice.

PLACE THE GARLIC clove on a cutting board and sprinkle with the salt. With the side of a chef's knife, mash and smear the garlic into a coarse paste.

IN A SMALL bowl, mix the lemon zest, lemon juice, garlic paste, mint, and oil. Season with a pinch of pepper. Cover and set aside.

HEIRLOOM TABBOULEH

1	CUP BULGUR WHEAT (FINE-MEDIUM GRIND)
1	CUP HOT WATER
3	ASSORTED RIPE HEIRLOOM TOMATOES, SUCH AS BRANDYWINE, GREEN ZEBRA, AND SUNGOLD, PEELED, CORED, SEEDED, AND CHOPPED
2	SCALLIONS, WHITE AND GREEN PARTS, FINELY CHOPPED
1	CUP CHOPPED FRESH FLAT-LEAF PARSLEY
1/2	CUP CHOPPED FRESH MINT
1/2	TEASPOON GROUND CUMIN
1/4	TEASPOON ALLSPICE

KOSHER SALT AND FRESHLY GROUND BLACK PEPPER

JUICE OF 1 LEMON

1/4 CUP EXTRA-VIRGIN OLIVE OIL

PLACE THE BULGUR in a large heatproof bowl and pour in the hot water. Cover and let stand for about 20 minutes to rehydrate until all of the water is absorbed.

IN A MIXING bowl, combine the tomatoes, scallions, parsley, and mint. Toss the salad well to incorporate the ingredients. Add the cumin, allspice, salt and pepper. Add the bulgur, lemon juice, and olive oil. Fold together to incorporate. You can serve immediately, but the flavor will improve if the tabbouleh sits for a couple of hours at room temperature.

TO ASSEMBLE AND serve: Mound equal portions of the Heirloom Tabbouleh in the center of each of 4 plates. Stand 2 Rack of Lamb chops around it and drizzle with the Mint Gremolata. Serve the Cucumber Raita in small bowls on the side.

0 2

RED PEPPER, ROSEMARY

HARISSA RATATOUILLE

HARISSA SAUCE

MAKES 1 1/2 CUPS

2	ROASTED RED PEPPERS, PEELED, SEEDED, AND COARSELY CHOPPED
2	CLOVES GARLIC, MINCED
1	SMALL RED CHILE, COARSELY CHOPPED
1	TABLESPOON MINCED FRESH FLAT-LEAF PARSLEY
1/4	CUP EXTRA-VIRGIN OLIVE OIL
1	TEASPOON RED PEPPER FLAKES
1	TEASPOON GROUND CORIANDER
1	TEASPOON GROUND CARAWAY
1	TEASPOON GROUND CUMIN
1	TEASPOON KOSHER SALT

COMBINE THE PEPPERS, garlic, chile, parsley, oil, pepper flakes, coriander, caraway, cumin, and salt in a food processor. Pulse until the sauce is well blended and smooth, adding a little more oil or water to thin it out if necessary.

HARISSA WILL KEEP covered and refrigerated for up to 1 week.

RATATOUILLE

1/4	CUP PLUS 1 TABLESPOON OLIVE OIL
1	YELLOW BELL PEPPER, PEELED, SEEDED, AND DICED
1	RED BELL PEPPER, PEELED, SEEDED, AND DICED
1	SMALL GREEN ZUCCHINI, DICED
1	SMALL YELLOW ZUCCHINI, DICED
1	JAPANESE EGGPLANT, DICED
	KOSHER SALT AND FRESHLY GROUND BLACK PEPPER
1/2	RED ONION, DICED
1	CLOVE GARLIC, MINCED
1/4	CUP TOMATO PASTE

PINCH OF GROUND CORIANDER

PINCH OF GROUND FENNEL SEED

PLACE A LARGE sauté pan over medium-high heat and coat with 1/4 cup of the oil. Once the oil is hazy, add the peppers and cook for 1 minute. Add the zucchini and eggplant and sauté until the vegetables soften slightly but retain their crunch and vibrant color, 3 to 5 minutes. Season with salt and pepper and transfer to a large bowl.

RETURN THE PAN to medium-high heat and coat with the remaining tablespoon of oil. Add the onion and garlic and cook until translucent, about 2 minutes. Season with salt and pepper. Stir in the tomato paste, along with 1/4 cup of water, and continue to cook until thick and deep red. Remove from heat and add to the bowl of sautéed vegetables. Season with coriander, fennel, salt, and pepper, folding to incorporate. Cover to keep warm. Just before serving, fold 1/2 cup of the Harissa Sauce into the ratatouille.

ROSEMARY GREMOLATA

1	LEMON
1	CLOVE GARLIC
1/4	TEASPOON KOSHER SALT
2	TABLESPOONS CHOPPED FRESH ROSEMARY
1/4	CUP EXTRA-VIRGIN OLIVE OIL
	FRESHLY GROUND BLACK PEPPER

USING A VEGETABLE peeler or sharp paring knife, carefully remove wide strips of lemon zest. Do not include the bitter white pith. Finely chop the zest into small pieces. (Although it may seem faster to simply use a zester or microplane, too much oil comes out of the peel, making the gremolata clumpy.) Cut the peeled lemon in half and squeeze out the juice.

PLACE THE GARLIC clove on a cutting board and sprinkle with the salt. With the side of a chef's knife, mash and smear the garlic into a coarse paste.

IN A SMALL bowl, mix the lemon zest, lemon juice, garlic paste, rosemary, and oil. Season with a pinch of pepper. Cover and set aside.

ROSEMARY-SCENTED BABY POTATOES

1	POUND NEW POTATOES, SCRUBBED
	KOSHER SALT AND FRESHLY GROUND BLACK PEPPER
2	CUPS EXTRA-VIRGIN OLIVE OIL
4	SHALLOTS, THICKLY SLICED
2	SPRIGS FRESH ROSEMARY
1	TABLESPOON CHOPPED FRESH ROSEMARY NEEDLES, FOR GARNISH

PLACE THE POTATOES in a small saucepan and season with salt and pepper. Pour in enough oil to cover the potatoes completely. Add the shallots and rosemary sprigs. Place over medium heat and simmer until the potatoes are fork tender, about 20 minutes.

REMOVE FROM THE heat and strain. Remove and discard the rosemary. Transfer the potatoes and shallots to a serving bowl and season with salt and pepper, tossing to combine. Garnish with chopped rosemary.

TO ASSEMBLE AND serve: Mound equal portions of the Ratatouille onto each of 4 plates. Stand 2 Rack of Lamb chops around it and drizzle with the Rosemary Gremolata. Serve the Rosemary Potatoes in small bowls on the side.

O 3

MATSUTAKE GARAM MASALA

A special autumn delicacy, the Japanese mushroom matsutake ("pine mushroom") is prized for its magnificently spicy scent, similar to cinnamon. The strong, foresty-clean fragrance is a result of where it grows—under the base of old pine trees (and curiously never in the same place twice). This mushroom imitates the truffle, which lends its earthy perfume to any preparation it encounters. The matsutake's steaklike texture resembles the meaty oyster or porcini mushroom, which may be used as a substitute. Fresh matsutakes are not easily cultivated and are available only in limited amounts in the fall, so they tend to be pricey. Dried matsutakes can be purchased year-round.

2	CUPS DRIED MATSUTAKE MUSHROOMS (MAY SUBSTITUTE OYSTER OR PORCINI), WIPED OF GRIT AND SLICED
1/4	CUP CANOLA OIL
4	CLOVES GARLIC, COARSELY CHOPPED
1	YELLOW ONION, COARSELY CHOPPED
3-INCH	PIECE FRESH GINGER, PEELED AND CHOPPED
	KOSHER SALT AND FRESHLY GROUND BLACK PEPPER
2	TO 3 TABLESPOONS GARAM MASALA OR CURRY POWDER
4	ROMA TOMATOES, COARSELY CHOPPED
1	TEASPOON SUGAR
1	CUP DRY WHITE WINE, SUCH AS SAUVIGNON BLANC
2	CUPS CHICKEN STOCK (PAGE 222)
2	TABLESPOONS UNSALTED BUTTER

PLACE THE MUSHROOMS in a small heatproof bowl with 2 cups boiling water. Set aside to steep until they are very soft, about 20 minutes. Pass the mushrooms and liquid through a fine-mesh strainer or coffee filter, discarding the liquid. Rinse the mushrooms under running water to remove any residual sand. Set aside.

PLACE A SAUCEPAN over medium heat and coat with the oil. When the oil is hot, add the garlic, onion, and ginger and sauté until moisture has cooked off and the vegetables are caramelized, about 10 minutes. Season with salt and pepper. Stir in the garam masala and cook until fragrant, 2 minutes. Add the tomatoes and continue to cook and stir until they soften and the vegetable mixture has thickened, about 5 minutes. Sprinkle in the sugar.

ADD THE WINE and stir to deglaze the pan. Cook until the liquid is almost totally evaporated, about 3 minutes. Add the stock and simmer until reduced by half, about 10 minutes. Using a standard or immersion blender, blend the vegetable mixture until it is a fairly smooth and slightly thick sauce.

PLACE A CLEAN medium sauté pan over medium heat and add the butter. When melted, add the mushrooms. Raise the heat to medium-high and cook, stirring occasionally, until their moisture evaporates and the mushrooms begin to brown, about 6 minutes. Season with salt and pepper. When the mushrooms are caramelized, add 2 cups of the garam masala sauce, stirring to combine. Cover to keep warm.

CILANTRO GREMOLATA

1	LEMON
1	CLOVE GARLIC
1/4	TEASPOON KOSHER SALT
1/4	CUP CHOPPED FRESH CILANTRO
1	TABLESPOON EXTRA-VIRGIN OLIVE OIL
	FRESHLY GROUND BLACK PEPPER

USING A VEGETABLE peeler or sharp paring knife, carefully remove wide strips of lemon zest. Do not include the bitter white pith. Finely chop the zest into small pieces. (Although it may seem faster to simply use a zester or microplane, too much oil comes out of the peel, making the gremolata clumpy.) Cut the peeled lemon in half and squeeze out the juice.

PLACE THE GARLIC clove on a cutting board and sprinkle with the salt. With the side of a chef's knife, mash and smear the garlic into a coarse paste.

IN A SMALL bowl, mix the lemon zest, lemon juice, garlic paste, cilantro, and oil. Season with a pinch of pepper. Cover and set aside.

DATE BASMATI

1 1/2	CUPS BASMATI RICE
2	CUPS WATER
1	TABLESPOON UNSALTED BUTTER
1	TEASPOON KOSHER SALT
	PINCH OF SAFFRON THREADS
8	DATES, PITTED AND CHOPPED
2	TABLESPOONS CHOPPED FRESH CILANTRO

IN A SMALL saucepan, combine 3/4 cup of the rice, 1 cup water, 1/2 tablespoon butter, and 1/2 teaspoon salt. In another small saucepan, combine the remaining rice, water, butter, and salt, along with the saffron. Place both saucepans over medium-high heat and bring to a boil.

WHEN BOILING, GIVE a stir, cover, and reduce the heat to very low. Simmer until the water has been absorbed and the rice is tender, about 20 minutes. Remove from the heat and set aside, covered, for 5 minutes. Fluff the rice with a fork.

JUST BEFORE SERVING, combine the white and saffron rices, taking care to distribute the colors evenly. Fold in the dates and cilantro.

TO ASSEMBLE AND serve: Mound an equal portion of the Date Basmati onto each of 4 plates. Stand the 2 Rack of Lamb chops around it, and drizzle with the Cilantro Gremolata. Serve the Matsutake Garam Masala in small bowls on the side.

SEARED SQUAB BREAST, SQUAB LEG CONFIT, SQUAB STOCK, AND DEMI-GLACE

O 1
STAR ANISE, ORANGE

STAR ANISE AND FENNEL FARRO, NAVEL ORANGE MARMALADE, SAFFRON FOAM

O 2
CUMIN, APPLE

CUMIN AND BEET BARLEY, GREEN APPLE MARMALADE, RED PEPPER FOAM

O 3
CINNAMON, CHERRY

CINNAMON AND MOREL COUSCOUS, BING CHERRY MARMALADE, ARUGULA FOAM

I GET PARTICULARLY CREATIVE WHEN FEATURING GAME BIRDS ON THE MENU BECAUSE THEIR ASSERTIVE FLAVORS ARE ALWAYS ATTENTION GETTERS. SQUAB (ALSO CALLED PIGEON) IS A BIRD ABOUT 1 MONTH OLD WITH TENDER RED MEAT AND A LIGHT GAMY FLAVOR. ALTHOUGH TECHNICALLY POULTRY, SQUAB DEFINITELY DOES NOT TASTE JUST LIKE CHICKEN— IT IS ACTUALLY MUCH MORE LIKE BEEF OR LAMB. ITS PRONOUNCED FLAVOR IS BEST APPRECIATED WHEN COOKED ON THE RARE SIDE. SQUAB TASTES ALMOST LIKE A REALLY INTENSE DUCK, ENLIVENED BY FRUITY AND ACIDIC FLAVORS. SQUAB ACCENTED WITH MEDALLIONS OF FOIE GRAS IS A PRETTY LUSH PAIRING (IT IS ALSO PRETTY PHENOMENAL). THE TROIKA OF GRAINS IN THE VARIATIONS IS A WONDERFUL VEHICLE TO SUSTAIN THESE TRANSCENDENT FLAVORS, PROVIDING A NUTTY TEXTURE AND AN EARTHY BACKDROP TO ANCHOR THE DISH. LECITHIN, OFTEN THE NATURAL EMULSIFIER THAT KEEPS CHOCOLATE AND COCOA BUTTER FROM SEPARATING IN A CANDY BAR, IS THE MAGIC POWDER THAT STABILIZES THE FOAMS ON THE SQUAB, KEEPING THEM AERATED WITH TINY BUBBLES FOR SEVERAL MINUTES. IT IS POSSIBLE TO STILL FROTH THE LIQUID WITHOUT THE LECITHIN, BUT THE FOAM WILL NOT HOLD AS LONG. LECITHIN IS AVAILABLE IN POWDER, LIQUID, OR PELLETLIKE GRANULES, AND ALL ARE SUITABLE IN THIS APPLICATION.

WINE SUGGESTION

COPAIN PINOT NOIR 'HEIN,' ANDERSON VALLEY 2003

A ripe and voluptuous Pinot Noir marries very well with this squab preparation. Because the dish is somewhat sweet, the wine needs to be soft and have loads of fruit. A red Burgundy might work, but it may be too austere (unless we use a modern producer). Copain is one of the new stars producing excellent wines from California's Anderson Valley.

SEARED SQUAB BREAST
MASTER RECIPE

FOUR	1-POUND WHOLE SQUABS, INNARDS AND EXCESS FAT REMOVED
	KOSHER SALT AND FRESHLY GROUND BLACK PEPPER
2	TABLESPOONS CANOLA OIL
3	SPRIGS FRESH THYME
1	SHALLOT, SLICED
2	TABLESPOONS UNSALTED BUTTER
4	SEARED FOIE GRAS MEDALLIONS (PAGE 29)

USING A SHARP boning knife, remove the wings, legs, and breasts from the squab. Reserve the carcasses and wings for the Squab Stock and the legs for the Squab Leg Confit.

SEASON THE SQUAB breasts generously with salt and pepper. Heat the oil in a large sauté pan over medium-high heat. When hot, lay the squab, skin side down, in the hot pan and sear until crisp, 3 to 5 minutes. Add the thyme, shallot, and butter. Using tongs, turn the squab and cook for an additional 2 to 3 minutes, basting with the butter. Transfer the squab to a platter and set aside to rest 5 minutes.

FOLLOW THE ASSEMBLY and serving directions for the variation you are making.

SQUAB LEG CONFIT
MASTER RECIPE

Although the confit is delicious the day it is made, it gets even better after a day or two in the refrigerator. Don't throw away the leftover duck fat; it adds that extra something to fried potatoes and eggs.

2	BAY LEAVES, PREFERABLY FRESH
1	CARDAMOM POD
2	TABLESPOONS CORIANDER SEEDS
1	TABLESPOON WHOLE BLACK PEPPERCORNS
1	TEASPOON FRESH THYME LEAVES
1	CUP KOSHER SALT
1/3	CUP SUGAR
8	SQUAB LEGS, RESERVED FROM THE 4 WHOLE SQUAB
	ABOUT 2 CUPS WARM RENDERED DUCK FAT, TO COVER (SEE SOURCES)

COMBINE THE BAY leaves, cardamom, coriander seeds, peppercorns, and thyme in a dry skillet over low heat. Toast for just a minute to release the fragrant oils, shaking the pan so they do not scorch. Remove from the heat and place in a spice mill or clean coffee grinder. Grind to a coarse powder. Transfer to a bowl and stir in the salt and sugar to evenly combine.

SPREAD A QUARTER of the salt cure on the bottom of a small baking dish. Rub some of the remaining salt cure over the squab legs to completely cover. Arrange the legs in a single layer in the baking dish. Sprinkle the remaining salt cure on top to bury the legs. Cover with plastic wrap and refrigerate for 2 to 4 hours.

PREHEAT THE OVEN to 275°F.

REMOVE THE SQUAB legs from the cure, rinse well under cold water, and pat dry with paper towels. Arrange the legs in a single layer in a small baking pan. Pour the warm duck fat over them to cover. Cover the pan tightly with aluminum foil. Transfer to the oven and roast until the meat is very tender and falling off the bone, about 2 1/2 hours. Remove from the oven and let the squab cool completely in the fat.

ONCE COOL, REMOVE the legs from the pan. Pull the meat off the bones, discarding the skin and bones. You should have about 1 cup of shredded meat. Cover and refrigerate. Reserve the fat for another use, if desired (see headnote).

USE AS DIRECTED in the recipe you are making.

SQUAB STOCK
MASTER RECIPE

MAKES 2 QUARTS

1/4	CUP CANOLA OIL
4	SQUAB CARCASSES, RESERVED FROM 4 WHOLE SQUAB
8	SQUAB WINGS, RESERVED FROM 4 WHOLE SQUAB
4	CLOVES GARLIC, SMASHED
1	YELLOW ONION, CHOPPED
1	STALK CELERY, CHOPPED
1	CARROT, CHOPPED
4	SPRIGS FRESH THYME
4	SPRIGS FRESH FLAT-LEAF PARSLEY
1	BAY LEAF, PREFERABLY FRESH
1	TABLESPOON WHOLE BLACK PEPPERCORNS
1	CUP DRY WHITE WINE, SUCH AS SAUVIGNON BLANC
3	QUARTS CHICKEN STOCK (PAGE 222)

HEAT THE OIL in a stockpot over medium-high heat. Lay the squab carcasses and wings in the pot and sear, turning frequently, for 8 to 10 minutes, until well browned on all sides. Carefully pour off all but 2 tablespoons of the rendered fat. Add the garlic, onion, celery, carrot, thyme, parsley, bay leaf, and peppercorns. Cook, stirring often, until the vegetables have sweated their liquid and caramelized, about 15 minutes.

ADD THE WINE and stir to deglaze the pan, scraping up the brown bits from the bottom with a wooden spoon. Simmer until the wine has reduced, about 3 minutes. Add the Stock and simmer until all the flavors have come together and the stock has reduced and thickened, 30 to 40 minutes.

USING TONGS, REMOVE and discard the squab pieces. Pass the stock through a fine-mesh strainer into a clean container. You should have 2 quarts of fairly viscous squab stock.

USE AS DIRECTED in the recipe you are making.

SQUAB DEMI-GLACE

1	QUART SQUAB STOCK (FROM MASTER RECIPE)
2	TABLESPOONS COLD UNSALTED BUTTER, CUT INTO CHUNKS

PLACE THE SQUAB Stock in a medium saucepan over medium-low heat and simmer until the liquid is reduced to a little more than 1 cup, 20 to 30 minutes. The Demi-Glace should have deep color and be thick enough to coat the back of a spoon. Just before serving, whisk in the cold butter to finish the sauce. Keep warm.

FOLLOW THE ASSEMBLY and serving directions for the variation you are making.

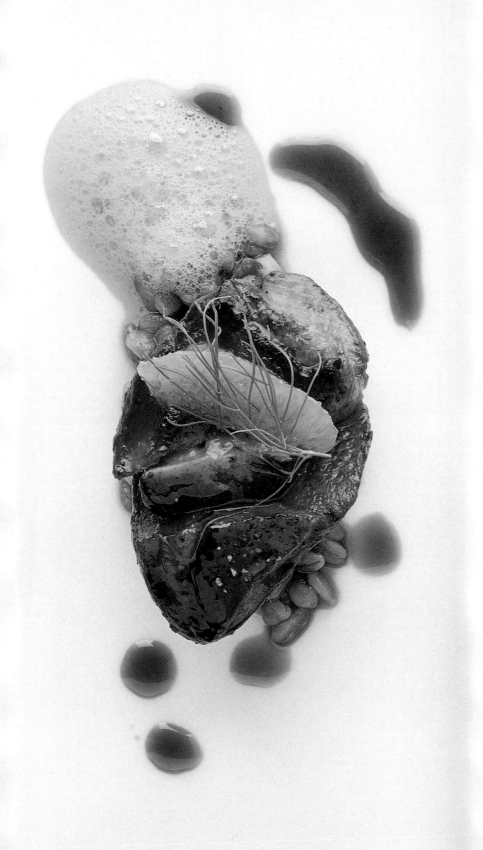

O I

STAR ANISE, ORANGE

STAR ANISE AND FENNEL FARRO

3	TABLESPOONS CANOLA OIL
1/2	YELLOW ONION, MINCED
1/2	FENNEL BULB, TRIMMED, CORED, AND MINCED, FRONDS RESERVED
4	WHOLE STAR ANISE
1	BAY LEAF, PREFERABLY FRESH
2	TEASPOONS GROUND FENNEL
1	CUP WHOLE-GRAIN FARRO
	KOSHER SALT AND FRESHLY GROUND BLACK PEPPER
2	CUPS SQUAB STOCK (FROM MASTER RECIPE)
1/2	CUP SQUAB CONFIT (FROM MASTER RECIPE), CHOPPED

HEAT A SAUCEPAN over medium-low heat and coat with the oil. When hot, add the onion and fennel. Sauté until the vegetables have sweated their liquid and are translucent, about 4 minutes. Add the star anise, bay leaf, and fennel, and sauté until fragrant, about 1 minute. Stir in the farro and toss to toast lightly. Season with salt and pepper.

WHEN THE FARRO smells nutty, after 3 to 5 minutes, pour in the stock, and give it a stir. Bring to a boil, lower the heat, cover, and simmer until the farro has popped open and is tender and fluffy, 25 to 30 minutes. Season well with salt and pepper.

REMOVE AND DISCARD the star anise and bay leaf. Fold in the Squab Confit to evenly distribute and heat through. Cover to keep warm.

JUST BEFORE SERVING, blanch the reserved fennel fronds and purée in a blender with 2 tablespoons of cold water until smooth and bright green. Mix the fennel liquid into the farro to evenly distribute.

Note: Farro. This nutritious ancient Italian grain has fed the Mediterranean and Near Eastern populations for thousands of years. A hulled grain, farro cooks up beautifully, retaining the firm chewy texture of wheat berries because it is low in gluten and thus is not overly starchy. The nutty flavor and sturdy texture can hold up to robust flavors such as meat, red wine, and onion. Farro is processed in a whole or cracked form, but I prefer whole because it holds up better; either can be found in specialty food stores or mail-order suppliers. Grains like millet, spelt, bulgur, and barley also make good candidates.

NAVEL ORANGE MARMALADE

	JUICE OF 6 NAVEL ORANGES (ABOUT 2 CUPS)
	ZEST OF 1 NAVEL ORANGE
1	SHALLOT, SLICED
1	WHOLE STAR ANISE
1	TABLESPOON WHOLE BLACK PEPPERCORNS
1/2	CUP SUGAR
1/2	TEASPOON POWDERED FRUIT PECTIN
1	NAVEL ORANGE, CUT INTO SEGMENTS (PAGE 225)
2	TABLESPOONS CHOPPED FENNEL FRONDS

COMBINE THE ORANGE juice, zest, shallot, star anise, and peppercorns in a small saucepan over low heat. Bring to a simmer and cook gently for 10 minutes to infuse the aromatics. Strain through a fine-mesh sieve into a clean saucepan, discarding the solids.

PLACE OVER HIGH heat and add the sugar, stirring to dissolve. Mix in the pectin and, stirring constantly, boil hard until the mixture thickens, about 1 minute. Remove from the heat and fold in the orange segments and fennel fronds.

SAFFRON FOAM

PINCH OF SAFFRON THREADS
1   TABLESPOON LECITHIN

COMBINE THE SAFFRON and 1/2 cup hot water in a small bowl. Steep for 1 minute to bleed out the color. Stir in the lecithin.

JUST BEFORE YOU are ready to plate the dish, buzz the saffron water with an immersion blender, placing the blades just below the surface and moving them up and down to foam the top (it should resemble steamed milk for cappuccino). Blend until thick and frothy. Rake off the foamy surface with a tablespoon.

TO ASSEMBLE AND serve: Preheat the broiler. Using a sharp knife, cut each Squab Breast into 3 slices. Cut the Seared Foie Gras medallions into 4 slices. Starting with a piece of squab, alternate the foie gras and squab pieces on a lined sheet pan. Spoon a few tablespoons of the Orange Marmalade over the pieces to lightly glaze. Place under the broiler and broil just until the sugar begins to caramelize, about 1 minute.

MOUND EQUAL PORTIONS of the Fennel Farro among each of 4 serving plates. Shingle an equal portion of the glazed meats on top of the grain, and garnish with the remaining marmalade. Drizzle the Squab Demi-Glace around the plates and place a couple of spoonfuls of the Saffron Foam on top.

0 2

CUMIN, APPLE

CUMIN AND BEET BARLEY

4   RED BABY BEETS, SCRUBBED
4   TABLESPOONS CANOLA OIL
    KOSHER SALT AND FRESHLY GROUND BLACK PEPPER
3   CUPS SQUAB STOCK (FROM MASTER RECIPE)
1/2 YELLOW ONION, MINCED
    GRATED ZEST OF 1 LEMON
1   TABLESPOON GROUND CUMIN
1   CUP BARLEY
1/2 CUP SQUAB CONFIT (FROM MASTER RECIPE), CHOPPED

PREHEAT THE OVEN to 375°F.

RUB THE BEETS with 2 tablespoons of the oil and season with salt and pepper. Wrap each beet individually in aluminum foil and place on a baking pan. Transfer to the oven and roast until a knife meets no resistance when a beet is pierced, 30 to 40 minutes. Carefully unwrap the beets, and when cool enough to handle, rub off the skins with paper towels. Coarsely chop the beets and put them in a blender or food processor with 1 cup of the Squab Stock. Process to a smooth purée. Set aside.

HEAT THE REMAINING 2 tablespoons oil in a saucepan over medium heat. Once the oil becomes hazy, add the onion and sauté until translucent, about 5 minutes. Add the lemon zest and cumin, stirring until fragrant. Season with salt and pepper.

ADD THE BARLEY and toss to toast lightly. Stir in the beet purée and remaining 2 cups of Squab Stock, and bring to a boil. Lower the heat, cover, and simmer until the barley is tender and looks crimson red, 25 to 30 minutes. Season well with salt and pepper.

REMOVE FROM THE heat and fold in the Squab Confit to distribute and heat through. Cover to keep warm.

GREEN APPLE MARMALADE

1	GRANNY SMITH APPLE, PEELED, CORED, AND CHOPPED
	JUICE AND ZEST OF 1 LEMON
1	SHALLOT, SLICED
1	CINNAMON STICK
1	TABLESPOON WHOLE BLACK PEPPERCORNS
2	CUPS APPLE JUICE, PREFERABLY FRESH
3/4	CUP SUGAR
1	TEASPOON POWDERED FRUIT PECTIN
1/2	RED APPLE
1/2	GREEN APPLE
2	TABLESPOONS CHOPPED FRESH CHERVIL

COMBINE THE APPLE, lemon juice and zest, shallot, cinnamon, peppercorns, and apple juice in a saucepan over low heat. Simmer gently for 10 minutes to infuse the aromatics. Pass through a fine-mesh strainer into a clean saucepan, discarding the solids.

PLACE OVER HIGH heat and add the sugar, stirring to dissolve. Mix in the pectin and, stirring constantly, boil hard until the mixture thickens, about 1 minute. Remove from the heat. Using a small melon baller, scoop out balls from the red and green apples, including the skin (typically called a parisienne ball). If you prefer, cut the apples into small dice. Fold in the apple balls and chervil.

RED PEPPER FOAM

1	ROASTED RED PEPPER, PEELED
1	TABLESPOON LECITHIN

PASS THE PEPPER through a juicer. Place the juice in a small saucepan over medium heat. Bring to a simmer and stir in the lecithin.

JUST BEFORE YOU are ready to plate the dish, buzz the pepper juice with an immersion blender, placing the blades just below the surface and moving them up and down to foam the top (it should resemble steamed milk for cappuccino). Blend until thick and frothy. Rake off the foamy surface with a tablespoon.

TO ASSEMBLE AND serve: Preheat the broiler. Using a sharp knife, cut each Squab Breast into 3 slices. Cut the Seared Foie Gras medallions into 4 slices. Starting with a piece of squab, alternate the foie gras and squab pieces on a foil-lined sheet pan. Spoon a few tablespoons of the Green Apple Marmalade over the pieces to lightly glaze. Place under the broiler and broil just until the sugar begins to caramelize, about 1 minute.

MOUND EQUAL PORTIONS of the Beet Barley among each of 4 serving plates. Shingle an equal portion of the glazed meats on top of the grain, and garnish with the remaining marmalade. Drizzle the Squab Demi-Glace around the plates and place a couple of spoonfuls of the Red Pepper Foam on top.

O3

CINNAMON, CHERRY

CINNAMON AND MOREL COUSCOUS

2	TABLESPOONS OLIVE OIL
1/2	YELLOW ONION, MINCED
6	MOREL MUSHROOMS, CHOPPED
1/4	TEASPOON GROUND CINNAMON
1	CUP COUSCOUS
	KOSHER SALT AND FRESHLY GROUND BLACK PEPPER
1	CUP SQUAB STOCK (FROM MASTER RECIPE)
1/2	CUP SQUAB CONFIT (FROM MASTER RECIPE), CHOPPED

PLACE A SAUCEPAN over medium-low heat and coat with the oil. When hot, add the onion and mushrooms. Sauté until the vegetables have sweated their liquid and the moisture has evaporated, about 4 minutes. Sprinkle in the cinnamon and sauté until fragrant, 1 minute. Add the couscous and toss to toast lightly. Season with salt and pepper.

ADD THE SQUAB Stock, give it a stir, and bring to a boil. Lower the heat, cover, and simmer until the couscous is tender, 10 to 15 minutes. Season well with salt and pepper.

FLUFF THE COUSCOUS with a fork and fold in the Squab Confit to distribute and heat through. Cover to keep warm.

BING CHERRY MARMALADE

1	CUP PITTED BING CHERRIES, FRESH (OR FROZEN AND THAWED), CHOPPED
1	CUP CHERRY JUICE
	JUICE AND ZEST OF 1 LIME
1	SHALLOT, SLICED
1	CINNAMON STICK
1	TABLESPOON WHOLE BLACK PEPPERCORNS
3/4	CUP SUGAR
1/2	TEASPOON POWDERED FRUIT PECTIN
4	FRESH BASIL LEAVES, CUT INTO SLIVERS
1/4	CUP SLICED BING CHERRIES

COMBINE THE CHOPPED cherries and cherry juice, lime juice and zest, shallot, cinnamon, and peppercorns in a medium saucepan over low heat. Simmer gently for 10 minutes to infuse the aromatics. Pass through a fine-mesh strainer into a clean saucepan, discarding the solids.

PLACE OVER HIGH heat and add the sugar, stirring to dissolve. Mix in the pectin and, stirring constantly, boil hard until the marmalade thickens, about 1 minute. Remove from the heat and fold in the basil and sliced cherries.

ARUGULA FOAM

2	TABLESPOONS KOSHER SALT
1	CUP ARUGULA LEAVES
1	TABLESPOON LECITHIN

PREPARE AN ICE bath. Bring a large saucepan of water to a rolling boil over high heat and add the salt. Add the arugula, stirring the leaves into the water to immerse. Blanch for 30 seconds. Pour into a strainer and immediately plunge into the ice bath to stop the cooking process and lock in the vibrant green color. Remove the strainer from the ice water. Squeeze the arugula dry with a paper towel, and coarsely chop.

PLACE THE ARUGULA in a blender or food processor and add 1/2 cup ice water. Process to a smooth purée, about 1 minute. Pour the arugula purée into a small saucepan over medium heat. Bring to a simmer and stir in the lecithin.

JUST BEFORE YOU are ready to plate the dish, buzz the arugula water with an immersion blender, placing the blades just below the surface and moving them up and down to foam the top (it should resemble steamed milk for cappuccino). Blend until thick and frothy. Rake off the foamy surface with a tablespoon.

TO ASSEMBLE AND serve: Preheat the broiler. Using a sharp knife, cut each Squab Breast into 3 slices. Cut the Seared Foie Gras medallions into 4 slices. Starting with a piece of squab, alternate the foie gras and squab pieces on a foil-lined sheet pan. Spoon a few tablespoons of the Cherry Marmalade over the pieces to lightly glaze. Place under the broiler and broil just until the sugar begins to caramelize, about 1 minute.

MOUND EQUAL PORTIONS of the Morel Couscous among each of 4 serving plates. Shingle an equal portion of the glazed meats on top of the grain, and garnish with the remaining marmalade. Drizzle the Squab Demi-Glace around the plates and place a couple of spoonfuls of the Arugula Foam on top.

CRISPY LOIN OF KUROBUTA PORK, PULLED PORK

O1
ORANGE, CARROT
ORANGE-GLAZED CARROTS, KUMQUAT RELISH, CARROT RISOTTO

O2
APPLE, SAGE
RED WINE-GLAZED CABBAGE, APPLE RELISH, APPLE AND PORK RAVIOLI WITH HAZELNUT BROWN BUTTER

O3
TOMATO, CORN
CREAMED CORN, BARBECUED PORK, TOMATO RELISH, CORN FRITTERS

THIS RUSTIC PROCESSION OF PORK WAS FIRST INTRODUCED AT THE LAUNCHING OF MICHAEL MINA IN SAN FRANCISCO, AND FOLKS STILL ASK ME ABOUT IT. IT IS MY VERSION OF HOME-STYLE PORK, BUT THE LEVEL OF FLAVOR GOES WELL BEYOND WHAT DINERS EXPECT FROM THESE SEEMINGLY ORDINARY INGREDIENTS. THE APPROACH IS BOTH CASUAL AND REFINED AS THE PRIMARY PROTEIN GETS ACCESSORIZED IN PARALLEL WAYS. PORK LOIN IS A FAIRLY LEAN AND MELLOW CUT, SO WRAPPING IT WITH FATTIER ITALIAN BACON (PANCETTA) NOT ONLY IMPARTS FLAVOR BUT HELPS TENDERIZE THE MEAT. MY PULLED PORK SHOULDER HAS A COMPLETELY DIFFERENT TAKE THAN THE LOIN, WITH ITS DELICIOUSLY FATTY MEAT THAT LITERALLY FALLS APART, AND IT CAN BE MADE A DAY OR TWO IN ADVANCE.

WINE SUGGESTION
CHÂTEAU DE BEAUCASTEL CHÂTEAUNEUF-DU-PAPE, RHÔNE, FRANCE 2001

Château de Beaucastel is a blend of 13 grape varieties (mostly Grenache). This is a big wine with exotic flavors of blackberry, tea, and white pepper. The spiciness of the wine matches well with the spice elements in the dish (especially the barbecued pork). Other alternatives could be a soft Syrah, rich Pinot Noir, or even a Zinfandel.

CRISPY LOIN OF KUROBUTA PORK
MASTER RECIPE

Often called the Kobe of pork, Kurobuta pork is a mighty fine piece of meat. The Berkshire breed, known industry-wide by its Japanese name, Kurobuta, is prized for its high fat content and unparalleled juiciness. Unlike traditional white pork that tends to be bland and dry, Kurobuta is visibly different. The meat is deep pink in color and well marbled, a unique characteristic for pork. Its superior flavor and meaty texture makes it taste almost like steak.

ONE	3-POUND BONELESS PORK LOIN, PREFERABLY KUROBUTA, EXCESS FAT TRIMMED
1/4	POUND PANCETTA, THINLY SLICED
1/4	CUP CANOLA OIL
	KOSHER SALT AND FRESHLY GROUND BLACK PEPPER

CUT THE LOIN in half lengthwise and then again crosswise, so you wind up with 4 pieces of equal size. Unravel the spiraled slices of pancetta into long, thin strips. Coil the pancetta around the pork loin to cover completely. Season all sides generously with salt and pepper.

PREHEAT THE OVEN to 375°F.

PLACE A LARGE ovenproof sauté pan over medium heat and coat with the oil. When the oil gets hazy, lay the pork in the pan, and sear, turning with tongs, until the pancetta is crispy on all sides, about 8 minutes.

CAREFULLY POUR OFF the fat and transfer the pan to the oven. Roast the pork for about 10 minutes, turning halfway through cooking to ensure even browning, until a meat thermometer inserted into the center registers 140°F.

REMOVE FROM THE oven and transfer the pork to a cutting board. Let rest for 10 minutes to allow the juices to settle. The internal temperature will also continue to rise from the carry-over heat. Cut the pork loin into 1/4-inch-thick slices. It should be rosy pink in the center.

FOLLOW THE ASSEMBLY and serving directions for the variation you are making.

PULLED PORK
MASTER RECIPE

1/4	CUP DARK BROWN SUGAR, LIGHTLY PACKED
2	TABLESPOONS KOSHER SALT
2	TABLESPOONS PAPRIKA
1	TABLESPOON FRESHLY GROUND BLACK PEPPER
1/2	TABLESPOON GROUND CORIANDER
1/2	TEASPOON DRY MUSTARD
1/2	TEASPOON ONION POWDER
ONE	3-POUND BONELESS PORK BUTT
1 1/2	CUPS APPLE JUICE
1/2	CUP WATER

COMBINE THE BROWN sugar, salt, paprika, pepper, coriander, mustard, and onion powder together in a small bowl. Rub the spice blend all over the pork and marinate, covered and refrigerated, for as long as you can, as little as 1 hour or up to overnight.

PREHEAT THE OVEN to 300°F.

LAY THE PORK on a rack in a roasting pan. Add the apple juice and water. Cover the pan tightly with aluminum foil and transfer to the oven. Roast for 5 hours. Remove the foil and continue to cook the pork until the outside is brown and the meat is very tender and falling apart, about 30 minutes.

REMOVE THE PORK from the oven and transfer to a large platter. Let the meat rest for about 10 minutes. While still warm, shred the pork into small pieces using 2 forks or your hands; you should have about 4 cups of shredded meat. Put the pulled pork in a bowl and set aside. This may be done a day or two in advance and stored, covered and refrigerated.

FOLLOW THE ASSEMBLY and serving directions for the variation you are making.

O I

ORANGE, CARROT

ORANGE-GLAZED CARROTS

1/2	CUP CARROT JUICE, STRAINED
1/2	CUP ORANGE JUICE, STRAINED
1/2	POUND BABY CARROTS, TOPS TRIMMED, QUARTERED LENGTHWISE
2	TABLESPOONS UNSALTED BUTTER
	KOSHER SALT AND FRESHLY GROUND BLACK PEPPER

COMBINE THE CARROT and orange juices in a small saucepan over medium heat. Simmer until slightly thickened, about 10 minutes. Lay the carrots in the juice, tossing to coat. Continue to simmer until the carrots are just tender, about 2 minutes. Stir in the butter and lightly season with salt and pepper. The sauce should be thick enough to glaze the carrots. Cover to keep warm.

KUMQUAT RELISH

MAKES 1 CUP

16	KUMQUATS, THINLY SLICED (ABOUT 1 CUP)
	JUICE OF 1 ORANGE (ABOUT 1/2 CUP)
1	JALAPEÑO, STEMMED AND THINLY SLICED
1/4	CUP SUGAR

PLACE THE KUMQUATS in a small saucepan and cover with cold water. Place over high heat and bring to a boil. Drain the water and then repeat this process two more times using fresh water. This will soften the kumquats and remove their bitterness.

ADD THE ORANGE juice, jalapeño, and sugar to the blanched kumquats and place the saucepan over medium heat. Bring to a simmer and cook until they are coated in a golden syrup, 3 to 5 minutes. Remove from the heat and set aside to come to room temperature.

CARROT RISOTTO

3	CUPS CHICKEN STOCK (PAGE 222)
1	TABLESPOON CANOLA OIL
1	TABLESPOON UNSALTED BUTTER
1/2	YELLOW ONION, CUT INTO SMALL DICE
1	CUP CARNAROLI OR ARBORIO RICE
	KOSHER SALT AND FRESHLY GROUND BLACK PEPPER
1/2	CUP DRY WHITE WINE, SUCH AS SAUVIGNON BLANC
1	CUP PULLED PORK (FROM MASTER RECIPE)
1	CUP CARROT JUICE
1/2	CUP FINELY GRATED PARMIGIANO-REGGIANO

PLACE THE CHICKEN Stock in a small saucepan over medium-low heat; keep warm at a low simmer. Do not let it boil.

PLACE A LARGE sauté pan over medium heat and add the oil and butter. When the butter has melted, add the onion and sauté until translucent, about 3 minutes. Add the rice, and stir until the grains are opaque and slightly toasted, 1 to 2 minutes. Season with salt and pepper.

ADD THE WINE and stir to deglaze the pan. Cook until the liquid has almost totally evaporated, about 1 minute. Pour in 1 cup of the warm stock, stirring with a wooden spoon, until the rice has absorbed all the liquid. Add another cup and keep stirring while adding the stock 1 cup at a time, allowing the rice to drink it in before adding more. Taste the risotto; it should be al dente—definitely not mushy but not raw either.

AFTER 15 MINUTES, fold in the Pulled Pork. Add the carrot juice as your last dose of liquid. Cook, stirring, for an additional 3 to 5 minutes to incorporate the pork and heat through. Remove from the heat and stir in the cheese. Taste and, if necessary, adjust the seasoning.

TO ASSEMBLE AND serve: Divide the Orange-Glazed Carrots among each of 4 plates. Distribute the Pork Loin slices equally on top of the carrots, and garnish with the Kumquat Relish. Serve the Carrot Risotto on the side.

02

APPLE, SAGE

RED WINE–GLAZED CABBAGE

1	CUP DRY RED WINE, SUCH AS CABERNET SAUVIGNON
1/4	CUP RED WINE VINEGAR
1/2	CUP APPLE JUICE
2	TABLESPOONS SUGAR
1	SMALL HEAD RED CABBAGE, CORED AND SHREDDED (ABOUT 2 QUARTS)
	KOSHER SALT AND FRESHLY GROUND BLACK PEPPER
3	TABLESPOONS UNSALTED BUTTER

COMBINE THE WINE, vinegar, apple juice, and sugar in a large saucepan over medium heat. When the liquid is hot and the sugar dissolved, add the cabbage. Season generously with salt and pepper. Simmer, stirring occasionally until the cabbage is tender, 15 to 20 minutes. Just before serving, stir in the butter and let it melt into the cabbage.

APPLE RELISH

MAKES 1 CUP

1	GALA APPLE
1	GRANNY SMITH APPLE
1/2	CUP APPLE JUICE
3	TABLESPOONS HONEY
1	TABLESPOON CIDER VINEGAR
2	FRESH SAGE LEAVES, CUT INTO SLIVERS
	PINCH OF FRESHLY GRATED NUTMEG
	KOSHER SALT AND FRESHLY GROUND BLACK PEPPER

USING A SMALL melon baller, scoop out balls from each apple, including the skin (typically called a parisienne ball). If you prefer, you can cut the apples into a small dice.

COMBINE THE APPLE juice, honey, and vinegar in a small saucepan over medium heat. Add the apple balls and sage. Season with the nutmeg, salt, and pepper. Bring to a simmer and cook until the liquid gets syrupy and the apples soften slightly but still hold their shape, 1 to 2 minutes. Cover to keep warm.

APPLE AND PORK RAVIOLI WITH HAZELNUT BROWN BUTTER

MAKES 2 DOZEN RAVIOLI

2	TABLESPOONS UNSALTED BUTTER
1/4	YELLOW ONION, PEELED AND DICED
3	FRESH SAGE LEAVES, CHOPPED
1	LARGE GRANNY SMITH APPLE, PEELED, CORED, AND DICED
	KOSHER SALT AND FRESHLY GROUND BLACK PEPPER
1/4	CUP APPLE BRANDY, SUCH AS CALVADOS
2	CUPS PULLED PORK (FROM MASTER RECIPE), CHOPPED
1/4	CUP APPLESAUCE
2	TABLESPOONS MASCARPONE, AT ROOM TEMPERATURE
4	STORE-BOUGHT SHEETS FRESH PASTA DOUGH, OR 1 RECIPE PASTA DOUGH (SEE PAGE 71), 12 TO 14 INCHES LONG BY 4 INCHES WIDE
1	LARGE EGG
	ALL-PURPOSE FLOUR, FOR DUSTING

HAZELNUT BROWN BUTTER

1	RECIPE WARM BROWN BUTTER (SEE PAGE 70)
4	FRESH SAGE LEAVES, CHOPPED
1/4	CUP HAZELNUTS, TOASTED AND CHOPPED

TO MAKE THE ravioli: Melt the butter in a small sauté pan over medium-low heat. When it gets foamy, add the onion and sauté until translucent, about 1 minute. Add the sage and apple and cook until the apple is softened but not mushy, 2 minutes. Season with salt and pepper. Add the brandy and stir to deglaze the pan. Continue to cook until the liquid has evaporated, about 1 minute. Transfer the apple mixture to a bowl and let cool to room temperature.

FOLD THE PULLED Pork, applesauce, and mascarpone into the apple mixture to combine. Season generously with salt and pepper.

WHISK TOGETHER THE egg and 1 tablespoon water in a small bowl. Set aside.

DUST THE COUNTER and a sheet of pasta dough with flour. Using a 3-inch ring mold, cut out 12 circles. Working with 1 piece at a time, place a generous spoonful of the filling in the center of a pasta circle. Using a pastry brush, lightly coat the edge of the pasta around the filling. Top with another pasta circle to cover the filling. Using your fingertips, gently press out any air pockets around each mound of filling and seal the edges well. Dust the ravioli and a baking sheet with flour to prevent the pasta from sticking and lay out to dry slightly while assembling the remaining ravioli. You should get 6 filled ravioli per sheet of pasta.

WHEN READY TO serve, place the ravioli in plenty of boiling salted water and cook for 3 to 5 minutes (the ravioli will float to the surface when done). Using a strainer or slotted spoon, transfer the ravioli to a dry towel and dab dry.

TO MAKE THE Hazelnut Brown Butter: Place the Brown Butter in a small saucepan. Stir in the sage and hazelnuts, add the ravioli, and toss to coat. Serve immediately.

TO ASSEMBLE AND serve: Divide the Wine-Glazed Cabbage among each of 4 plates. Distribute the Pork Loin slices equally on top and garnish with a spoonful of the Apple Relish. Serve the Apple and Pork Ravioli with Hazelnut Brown Butter on the side.

O 3

CREAMED CORN

1	TEASPOON CANOLA OIL
3	SLICES OF BACON, CHOPPED
1	SHALLOT, MINCED
1/4	CUP DRY WHITE WINE, SUCH AS SAUVIGNON BLANC
2	EARS SWEET YELLOW CORN, KERNELS CUT FROM THE COB (ABOUT 2 CUPS)
3/4	CUP HEAVY CREAM
	KOSHER SALT AND FRESHLY GROUND BLACK PEPPER

PLACE A LARGE sauté pan over medium-low heat and add the oil. When hot, add the bacon and fry until the fat is rendered but the bacon is not yet crisp, about 1 minute. Stir in the shallot and cook for a minute to coat in the fat. Add the wine and stir to deglaze the pan, scraping up the bits from the bottom with a wooden spoon. Add the corn and the cream and season lightly with salt and pepper. Bring to a simmer and cook until the corn loses its starchiness and the sauce is thick, about 5 minutes. Cover and keep warm over low heat.

BARBECUED PORK

BARBECUE SAUCE

2	CUPS HICKORY OR APPLE-WOOD CHIPS, SOAKED FOR 10 MINUTES IN WATER AND DRAINED
5	ROMA TOMATOES, HALVED
3	RED BELL PEPPERS, HALVED, CORED, AND COARSELY CHOPPED
1	YELLOW ONION, COARSELY CHOPPED
1	JALAPEÑO, HALVED
2	TABLESPOONS CANOLA OIL
1/4	POUND APPLE-WOOD SMOKED SLAB BACON, CHOPPED
1/4	CUP DARK BROWN SUGAR, LIGHTLY PACKED
1	CUP KETCHUP
2	TEASPOONS DRY MUSTARD
1	TEASPOON FRESHLY GROUND BLACK PEPPER
1/2	CUP APPLE CIDER VINEGAR
1	QUART VEAL STOCK (SEE PAGE 222)
1	CUP ORANGE JUICE, STRAINED
4	CUPS PULLED PORK (FROM MASTER RECIPE)

TO MAKE THE barbecue sauce: First, smoke the vegetables.

TO SMOKE THE vegetables outdoors: Prepare a charcoal fire or preheat a gas grill to low heat. If using a gas grill, place all the wood chips in the smoker box; if using a charcoal grill, toss the wood chips on the coals. Place the tomatoes, peppers, onions, and jalapeño in a disposable pie pan on the grill and cover with the lid. Smoke until the vegetables have softened and smell smoky, 10 to 15 minutes.

TO SMOKE THE vegetables indoors: Open the windows. Place the wood chips in a disposable pie pan or roasting pan. Place the tomatoes, peppers, onions, and jalapeño in a steamer basket or perforated pan and set over the chips. Cover tightly with aluminum foil and place over low heat. Smoke until the vegetables have softened and smell smoky, 10 to 15 minutes. Remove from the smoker.

HEAT THE OIL in a large saucepan over medium-high heat. When hot, add the bacon and fry for 2 minutes to render the fat. Add the smoked vegetables and sauté until they begin to soften and caramelize, about 10 minutes. Sprinkle in the brown sugar, stirring to dissolve. Stir in the ketchup, mustard, and pepper. Add the vinegar, stirring for a minute to evaporate. Pour in the Veal Stock and orange juice. Reduce the heat to medium and simmer until the sauce is reduced by half and has thickened, 30 to 40 minutes.

POUR THE BARBECUE sauce into a food mill attached to a large saucepan. Run the sauce through the mill. Discard the solids. Taste and, if necessary, adjust the seasoning. Place the barbecue sauce over medium heat and fold in the pulled pork. Cook, stirring, to heat through, 3 to 5 minutes.

TOMATO RELISH

MAKES 1 CUP

1	TEASPOON CANOLA OIL
3	SLICES BACON, CHOPPED
1	TABLESPOON DARK BROWN SUGAR
1	TABLESPOON APPLE CIDER VINEGAR
1/2	JALAPEÑO, MINCED
1/2	CUP DICED TOMATOES, PEELED AND SEEDED
1/2	CUP DICED RED BELL PEPPER
1/4	CUP DICED RED ONION
1	TABLESPOON MINCED FRESH CHIVES
	KOSHER SALT AND FRESHLY GROUND BLACK PEPPER

PLACE THE OIL in a small saucepan over medium heat. When hot, add the bacon and fry until crisp, about 5 minutes. Stir in the brown sugar and vinegar to blend well.

ADD THE JALAPEÑO, tomatoes, bell pepper, onion, and chives. Season with salt and pepper and sauté for 1 minute to warm through and soften slightly. Remove from the heat and set aside to cool to room temperature.

CORN FRITTERS

MAKES 2 DOZEN FRITTERS

1 1/2	CUPS ALL-PURPOSE FLOUR
1	TABLESPOON PLUS 1 TEASPOON BAKING POWDER
1	TABLESPOON SUGAR
1/2	TABLESPOON KOSHER SALT, PLUS ADDITIONAL FOR SEASONING
1	TEASPOON CAYENNE
1/2	TEASPOON GROUND BLACK PEPPER
2	EARS SWEET YELLOW CORN, KERNELS CUT FROM THE COB (ABOUT 2 CUPS)
2	TABLESPOONS MINCED FRESH CHIVES
	APPROXIMATELY 1 CUP ICE WATER
	CANOLA OIL, FOR DEEP-FRYING

COMBINE THE FLOUR, baking powder, sugar, salt, cayenne, black pepper, corn, and chives in a medium mixing bowl. Whisk in ice water until the mixture has the consistency of cake batter. Cover and refrigerate while heating the oil.

HEAT 3 INCHES of canola oil in a heavy-bottomed saucepan or deep fryer to 360°F on a frying thermometer attached to the side of the pan. Line a plate with a double thickness of paper towels and set aside.

REMOVE THE BATTER from the refrigerator and carefully spoon heaping tablespoonfuls into the hot oil, adding no more than 6 at a time. Fry until the fritters are golden brown on all sides, turning often, 3 to 4 minutes. Using a slotted spoon, transfer the fritters to the prepared plate. While still hot, season with salt. Continue frying in batches of 6 until all of the batter is used.

TO ASSEMBLE AND serve: Divide the Creamed Corn among each of 4 plates. Distribute the Pork Loin slices equally on top and garnish with the Tomato Relish. Serve the Barbecued Pork on the side topped by a few Corn Fritters.

CHAPTER FOUR

DESSERT TRIOS

Pastry is a craft that's a huge passion of mine and a profession I lived and loved for 3 years early in my career. After graduating from the Culinary Institute of America, at the urging of my instructors and friends who understood my enthusiasms, I began my culinary career in the pastry kitchen. I have been forever grateful for this nudge as I now believe that the pastry arts are an essential part of a well-rounded chef's education. Many cooks delay the experience until after they have worked their way up the kitchen ladder, and it can be extremely difficult to go from being a sous chef to a beginner in the pastry kitchen.

Creating fine pastry is a little bit art, a pinch of magic, and a lot of chemistry. It is primarily structured around science; unlike savory cooking, there is no a-little-of-this-and-a-little-of-that. Measuring and weighing ingredients teaches precision and patience, and the process of working doughs with your hands also cultivates a gentle touch. There are many skills that are absorbed when dealing with desserts and pastries, and many of them translate to the savory kitchen as well.

Creating and preparing desserts teaches much about the theory of the culinary arts. In many ways, it also simplifies cooking, as you learn that one solid technique or recipe may have many different interpretations. For instance, pastry cream, crème anglaise, and an ice-cream base are essentially the same—they are made the same way with similar ingredients but the ratio used, the finishing process, and the flavors incorporated will yield a variety of results.

For a chef, desserts are an extremely important part of the meal—because they are the last dish to be savored by the diner, they are often the most memorable. The presentation must be spectacular and the flavors lasting. Since many desserts can easily be made ahead of time, they are also the course that the home cook can use to elicit a "Wow!" However, you do not have to be a pastry chef to master the recipes in this chapter, you just have to have a sweet tooth and a passion for warm, deep flavors that are timeless.

SUMMER BERRY COBBLER,
BERRY SUNDAE WITH MASCARPONE ICE CREAM

O I
RASPBERRY, VANILLA
RASPBERRY COBBLER WITH VANILLA STREUSEL, RASPBERRY SUNDAE

O 2
BLUEBERRY, LAVENDER
BLUEBERRY COBBLER WITH LAVENDER SCONE, BLUEBERRY SUNDAE

O 3
BLACKBERRY, CANDIED GINGER
BLACKBERRY COBBLER WITH CANDIED GINGER SHORTBREAD,
BLACKBERRY SUNDAE

THE SWEET SIMPLICITY OF THIS DESSERT REMINDS ME OF MY MOM BAKING BERRY PIES ADORNED WITH CREAM CHEESE IN THE SUMMERTIME. WHEN I WAS LITTLE, SHE WOULD LET ME PAINT THE BOTTOM OF THE PIE SHELL WITH SILKY CREAM CHEESE BEFORE PUTTING THE FRUIT ON TOP. THESE INDIVIDUAL COBBLERS CAPTURE THE SAME OLD-FASHIONED TASTE BY COUPLING LUSH BERRIES WITH ITALIAN MASCARPONE CREAM CHEESE. HERE, THE WARM COBBLERS ARE CROWNED BY MERINGUE BULKED UP WITH MASCARPONE. THE WHITE CLOUDS MELT INTO THE COBBLER AND GRANT A SUBTLE SWEETNESS WITHOUT PUSHING THE DISH OVERBOARD. THE COBBLERS ARE COVERED WITH THREE DIFFERENT CRUNCHY TOPPINGS THAT ARE A SNAP TO PUT TOGETHER. THE FLAVORS OF VANILLA, LAVENDER, AND GINGER TAKE THE PLUMP BERRIES IN UNEXPECTED DIRECTIONS. THE IDEA BEHIND THE HOT AND COLD VARIATIONS IS TO FIRST TAKE A BITE OF THE WARM COBBLER AND THEN FOLLOW WITH THE SUNDAE TO COOL YOUR PALATE. I PREFER TO TASTE EACH TYPE OF BERRY INDIVIDUALLY; WHEN MIXED, THE FLAVORS TEND TO ALL WASH TOGETHER AND BECOME NONDESCRIPT. THE MASCARPONE ICE CREAM SUNDAE NEEDS LITTLE EMBELLISHMENT; THE VELVETY SMOOTH TEXTURE IS REMINISCENT OF A BIG SLICE OF CHEESECAKE. AS A MODI-FICATION, CONSIDER USING THE SCONE AND SHORTBREAD TOPPING RECIPES TO MAKE BREAKFAST SCONES AND SHORTBREAD COOKIES; THEY WORK PERFECTLY.

WINE SUGGESTION
ROBERT WEIL RIESLING 'GRAFENBERG' AUSLESE, RHEINGAU, GERMANY 2002
In my opinion it is very hard to find a perfect wine pairing for any sweet dish. Many wines work, but since the sweetness and acidity change with every element, it is difficult to settle on just one wine. So I am suggesting one wine, but there could be many others that could work.

M

SUMMER BERRY COBBLER
MASTER RECIPE

2   PINTS FRESH BERRIES (RASPBERRIES FOR VARIATION 1;
    BLUEBERRIES FOR VARIATION 2; OR BLACKBERRIES FOR VARIATION 3)
1/4 CUP SUGAR
    PINCH OF SALT
1   TABLESPOON CORNSTARCH
    JUICE AND FINELY GRATED ZEST OF 1/2 LEMON
    STREUSEL, SCONE, OR SHORTBREAD TOPPING
    (FROM VARIATION RECIPES)

PREHEAT THE OVEN to 400°F.

COMBINE THE BERRIES, sugar, salt, cornstarch, lemon juice, and zest in a mixing bowl and fold gently. Divide the berry mixture among four 8-ounce ramekins or brûlée dishes.

PREPARE THE TOPPING for the variation you are making. Cover the berry mixture with the topping and set the cobblers on a baking pan. Place in the oven and bake until the topping is golden brown and the fruit juices are bubbling, 20 to 25 minutes.

MASCARPONE MERINGUE
MASTER RECIPE

1   CUP SUPERFINE SUGAR
1/3 CUP WATER
2   LARGE EGG WHITES, AT ROOM TEMPERATURE
1/2 CUP MASCARPONE, AT ROOM TEMPERATURE

COMBINE THE SUGAR and water in a small saucepan over medium heat, swirling the pan to dissolve the sugar completely. Attach a candy thermometer to the side of the pan to ensure a constant temperature. Bring the mixture to a boil, and boil until the mixture reaches 240°F (softball stage). Do not stir.

PLACE THE EGG whites in the bowl of a standing electric mixer fitted with a wire whip attachment, or use a hand-held electric beater. Whip the egg whites on medium speed until foamy and soft peaks begin to form. With the mixer running, pour the hot sugar syrup in a thin stream over the egg whites. Increase the speed to high, and whip until stiff and glossy, about 5 minutes. Continue until the meringue is opaque and has cooled to room temperature.

PLACE THE MASCARPONE in a mixing bowl and, using a rubber spatula, fold in one-third of the meringue to lighten, then gently fold in the rest. Do not overmix or the mascarpone will become grainy.

LINE A BAKING pan with parchment paper and lightly coat with nonstick spray. Spoon the mascarpone mixture into a pastry bag fitted with a large plain tip. Pipe out 3-inch disks of meringue onto the parchment (you will get at least 1 dozen, enough to make all 3 variations). Transfer to the freezer and chill at least 1 hour or up to overnight to harden.

FOLLOW THE ASSEMBLY and serving directions for the variation you are making.

MASCARPONE ICE CREAM
MASTER RECIPE

MAKES 1 QUART

2	CUPS MILK
1	CUP HEAVY CREAM
1/4	CUP SUGAR
8	LARGE EGG YOLKS
1	CUP LIGHT BROWN SUGAR, LOOSELY PACKED
1 1/2	CUPS MASCARPONE, AT ROOM TEMPERATURE
1	TEASPOON FRESH LEMON JUICE
	PINCH OF SALT

COMBINE THE MILK and cream in a large saucepan over medium heat and cook until bubbles just begin to form around the edges. Remove from heat and set aside.

PREPARE AN ICE bath.

IN A LARGE bowl, whisk together the sugar and egg yolks, until slightly thick and yellow. Very gradually ladle half of the hot milk mixture into the yolk and sugar mixture, whisking constantly. (Do not add too quickly or the eggs will scramble.) Return the tempered eggs back to the saucepan and whisk constantly over medium-low heat until the custard is thick enough to coat the back of a spoon and leaves a path when you run your finger across it, about 5 minutes.

REMOVE FROM THE heat and whisk in the brown sugar until dissolved. Pass the custard through a fine-mesh strainer into a clean container. Whisk in the mascarpone until thoroughly combined and free of lumps. Transfer the bowl to the ice bath and stir occasionally until well chilled. Once chilled, stir in the lemon juice and salt.

PLACE CUSTARD IN an ice-cream maker and process according to the manufacturer's directions. When the ice cream is done it will be the consistency of soft serve. To fully harden, place it in a plastic container with a cover and freeze for at least 2 hours.

FOLLOW THE ASSEMBLY and serving directions for the variation you are making.

O I

VANILLA STREUSEL TOPPING FOR RASPBERRY COBBLER

1	CUP ALL-PURPOSE FLOUR, SIFTED
1/2	CUP QUICK-COOKING OATS, NOT INSTANT
1/4	CUP SUGAR
1/4	CUP LIGHT BROWN SUGAR, LOOSELY PACKED
1	TEASPOON PURE VANILLA EXTRACT
1/4	TEASPOON SALT
1/4	CUP (1/2 STICK) COLD UNSALTED BUTTER, CUT INTO SMALL CHUNKS

COMBINE THE FLOUR, oats, white and brown sugars, vanilla, and salt in a medium bowl. Add the butter and, using your fingers, work it in until the mixture resembles coarse crumbs. Do not overmix.

SPRINKLE THE STREUSEL Topping on top of the Raspberry Cobbler and bake as directed in the master recipe.

RASPBERRY SUNDAE

RASPBERRY COULIS

3	PINTS FRESH RASPBERRIES
1	CUP SIMPLE SYRUP (SEE PAGE 225)
1	VANILLA BEAN, SPLIT AND SCRAPED
	JUICE OF 1/2 LEMON
4	TO 8 LARGE SCOOPS MASCARPONE ICE CREAM
	(FROM MASTER RECIPE)
	FRESH MINT LEAVES, FOR GARNISH

COMBINE 2 PINTS of the raspberries, the Simple Syrup, vanilla bean, and lemon juice in a saucepan over medium heat. Bring to a boil and cook, stirring gently, until the berries soften and release their natural juices, about 10 minutes.

REMOVE FROM THE heat and cool slightly. Place in a blender or food processor and process to a smooth purée. Pass the purée through a fine-mesh strainer, discarding the solids. You should have about 3/4 cup of coulis. Cover and refrigerate until chilled, at least 15 minutes.

TO ASSEMBLE AND serve: For the cobbler variation, place a disk of Mascarpone Meringue on top of the warm cobbler and allow it to melt. For the sundae variation, place a spoonful or two of the Raspberry Coulis into 4 wine glasses or small dessert bowls. Add an equal portion of the Mascarpone Ice Cream to each and drizzle some of the remaining coulis on top. Garnish with a few of the remaining raspberries and a leaf or two of mint.

O 2

BLUEBERRY, LAVENDER

LAVENDER SCONE TOPPING FOR BLUEBERRY COBBLER

1	CUP ALL-PURPOSE FLOUR
1	TABLESPOON SUGAR
1 1/2	TEASPOONS BAKING POWDER
1/4	TEASPOON KOSHER SALT
2	TABLESPOONS FINELY CHOPPED FRESH LAVENDER
	OR 1 TABLESPOON DRIED LAVENDER
2	TABLESPOONS COLD UNSALTED BUTTER, CUT INTO PIECES
1/2	CUP BUTTERMILK

SIFT THE FLOUR, sugar, baking powder, and salt into a mixing bowl. Add the lavender, stirring to combine. Using a fork or a pastry blender, cut in the butter. The mixture should look like coarse crumbs. Pour in the buttermilk and fold together with a rubber spatula, mixing just until the dough comes together.

DROP DOLLOPS OF the scone topping on top of each Blueberry Cobbler and bake as directed in the master recipe.

BLUEBERRY SUNDAE

BLUEBERRY COULIS

3	PINTS FRESH BLUEBERRIES
1	CUP SIMPLE SYRUP (PAGE 225)
1	TABLESPOON FRESH LAVENDER
	OR 1/2 TABLESPOON DRIED LAVENDER
	JUICE OF 1/2 LEMON
4	TO 8 LARGE SCOOPS MASCARPONE ICE CREAM
	(FROM MASTER RECIPE)
	FRESH MINT LEAVES, FOR GARNISH

COMBINE 2 PINTS of the blueberries, the Simple Syrup, lavender, and lemon juice in a saucepan over medium heat. Bring to a boil and cook, stirring gently, until the berries soften and release their natural juices, about 10 minutes.

REMOVE FROM THE heat and cool slightly. Place in a blender or food processor and process to a smooth purée. Pass the purée through a fine-mesh strainer, discarding the solids. You should have about 3/4 cup of coulis. Cover and refrigerate until chilled.

TO ASSEMBLE AND serve: For the cobbler variation, place a disk of Mascarpone Meringue on top of the warm cobbler and allow it to melt. For the sundae variation, place a spoonful or two of the Blueberry Coulis into 4 wine glasses or small dessert bowls. Add an equal portion of the Mascarpone Ice Cream to each and drizzle some of the remaining coulis on top. Garnish with a few of the remaining blueberries and a leaf or two of mint.

O 3

BLACKBERRY, CANDIED GINGER

CANDIED GINGER SHORTBREAD TOPPING FOR BLACKBERRY COBBLER

1	CUP ALL-PURPOSE FLOUR
1/4	CUP SUGAR
1/4	TEASPOON SALT
1/4	TEASPOON GROUND CINNAMON
4	PIECES CANDIED GINGER, FINELY CHOPPED
1/2	CUP (1 STICK) COLD UNSALTED BUTTER, CUT INTO CHUNKS

SIFT THE FLOUR, sugar, salt, and cinnamon into a mixing bowl. Add the candied ginger, stirring to combine. Using a fork or a pastry blender, cut in the butter, mixing just until the dough comes together.

DROP DOLLOPS OF the shortbread topping on top of each Blackberry Cobbler and bake as directed in the master recipe.

BLACKBERRY SUNDAE

BLACKBERRY COULIS

3	PINTS FRESH BLACKBERRIES
1	CUP SIMPLE SYRUP (PAGE 225)
2	PIECES CANDIED GINGER, HALVED
	JUICE OF 1/2 LEMON
4	TO 8 LARGE SCOOPS MASCARPONE ICE CREAM
	(FROM MASTER RECIPE)
	FRESH MINT LEAVES, FOR GARNISH

COMBINE 2 PINTS of the blackberries, the Simple Syrup, candied ginger, and lemon juice in a saucepan over medium heat. Bring to a boil and cook, stirring gently, until the berries soften and release their natural juices, about 10 minutes.

REMOVE FROM THE heat and cool slightly. Place in a blender or food processor and process to a smooth purée. Strain the blackberry purée through a fine-mesh sieve, discarding the solids. You should have about 3/4 cup of coulis. Cover and refrigerate until chilled.

TO ASSEMBLE AND serve: For the cobbler variation, place a disk of Mascarpone Meringue on top of the warm cobbler and allow it to melt. For the sundae variation, place a spoonful or two of the Blackberry Coulis into 4 wine glasses or small dessert bowls. Add an equal portion of the Mascarpone Ice Cream to each and drizzle some of the remaining coulis on top. Garnish with a few of the remaining blackberries and a leaf or two of mint.

STONE FRUIT PAIN PERDU
WITH CRÈME FRAÎCHE SHERBET

O 1
CHERRY, FIREWEED HONEY
CHERRY CRÈME FRAÎCHE SHERBET, CHERRY CARAMEL SAUCE,
ROASTED CHERRIES

O 2
PEACH, ORANGE BLOSSOM HONEY
PEACH CRÈME FRAÎCHE SHERBET, PEACH CARAMEL SAUCE, ROASTED PEACHES

O 3
PLUM, CLOVER HONEY
PLUM CRÈME FRAÎCHE SHERBET, PLUM CARAMEL SAUCE, ROASTED PLUMS

WHEN I INDULGE IN DESSERT, I INSTINCTUALLY GRAVITATE TOWARD FRUIT-BASED DESSERTS BECAUSE THEY POSSESS NATURAL ACIDITY, SWEETNESS, AND BODY. I ANTICIPATE THE ARRIVAL OF SUMMER FRUITS: THEY HAVE SO MANY APPLICATIONS AND COME IN A KALEIDOSCOPE OF FLAVORS AND COLORS. THE FAMILY OF STONE FRUITS INCLUDES PEACHES, NECTARINES, PLUMS, APRICOTS, AND CHERRIES, AND IS SO NAMED DUE TO THE HARD PITS. STONE FRUITS ARE EITHER PERFECTLY RIPE AND JUICY OR MEALY AND FLAVORLESS. WHEN CAUGHT AT THE PEAK OF RIPENESS, A GOOD PLUM, LIKE A GOOD PEACH, OFFERS SOME OF THE MOST DELECTABLE BITES OF SUMMER. THE NICE THING IS THAT DIFFERENT VARIETIES OF STONE FRUIT POP UP THROUGHOUT THE SUMMER; CERTAIN VARIETALS ARE BETTER IN JUNE, FOR INSTANCE, THAN IN JULY. VISIT FARMERS' MARKETS TO SHOP IN-SEASON FROM LOCAL GROWERS AND ALWAYS TASTE BEFORE YOU BUY.

THE ORIGIN OF THIS DESSERT WAS AS A BUTTERY BRIOCHE BREAD PUDDING. BUT AS MUCH AS I LOVE BRIOCHE BREAD PUDDING, THE MUSHINESS—AND I USE THAT WORD IN THE ABSOLUTE BEST SENSE—DID NOT OFFER ENOUGH OF A CONTRAST TO THE SOFT FRUIT. I WANTED SOMETHING YOU COULD SINK YOUR TEETH INTO, AND BRIOCHE FRENCH TOAST WAS THE ANSWER. THE EGG BATTER AND BROWNING ON THE GRIDDLE GIVES THE BREAD A FIRM EXTERIOR SO IT DOESN'T GET TOO SOFT. THIS IS HAUTE COMFORT FOOD. FRENCH TOAST IS A FAVORITE AT BISTROS AND BRASSERIES, AND THE FRENCH ACTUALLY CALL IT *PAIN PERDU*, WHICH MEANS "LOST BREAD." THE STORY IS THAT WAS A THRIFTY WAY OF REVIVING BREAD A DAY OR TWO PAST ITS PRIME. STORE-BOUGHT BRIOCHE MAKES A FINE SUBSTITUTE FOR THE RECIPE ON PAGE 144.

M

THE REFRESHING SHERBET ADDS LIGHTNESS. ICE CREAM WOULD BE OVER THE TOP BE-
CAUSE THERE IS SO MUCH CREAM ENRICHING THE *PAIN PERDU*. THE CULMINATION WOULD
BE TOO HEAVY AND YOU'D START TO OVERPOWER THE FRUIT FACTOR.

WINE SUGGESTION

KRACHER WELSCHRIESLING TBA, ILLMITZ, AUSTRIA 2001

SERVES 4

BRIOCHE
MASTER RECIPE

MAKES 1 LOAF

1	OUNCE FRESH CAKE YEAST, OR ONE (1/4-OUNCE) ENVELOPE ACTIVE DRY YEAST
3	TABLESPOONS WARM WATER
7	LARGE EGGS
5	CUPS ALL-PURPOSE FLOUR, PLUS MORE AS NEEDED
1/3	CUP SUGAR
1	TEASPOON KOSHER SALT
1	CUP (2 STICKS) UNSALTED BUTTER, AT ROOM TEMPERATURE, PLUS MORE FOR GREASING

PROOF THE YEAST by combining it with the warm water in a medium bowl. Let stand for 5 minutes until foam appears (this indicates the yeast is active). Add 6 of the eggs to the dissolved yeast, whisking to combine.

SIFT THE FLOUR, sugar, and salt into the bowl of a standing electric mixer fitted with a paddle attachment, or use a handheld electric beater. Begin mixing on low speed. Add the egg mixture in 3 additions, stopping the machine periodically to scrape the dough off the paddle and the sides of the bowl. Mix for a good 5 minutes to blend well (the dough will be thick and a bit lumpy). Add the butter, a couple of tablespoons at a time, mixing well between each addition. When all the butter is incorporated, increase the speed to medium and beat until the dough is smooth and slightly sticky, about 5 minutes.

SCRAPE THE DOUGH from the bowl and shape into a round. Place in a large greased bowl and cover with plastic wrap or a damp towel. Set aside in a warm spot to rise until doubled in size, about 2 hours. Test the dough by pressing 2 fingers into it; if the indents remain, the dough has risen adequately.

TURN THE DOUGH out onto a lightly floured counter and gently fold it over several times to deflate. Do not over-work or the dough will be dense and difficult to shape.

BUTTER A 9x5-INCH loaf pan. Pat the dough into a rectangle about 1/2 inch thick. Roll it into a cylinder and place in the prepared pan, seam side down. Make sure the dough touches all sides of the pan. Loosely drape plastic wrap over the dough and set aside on the counter to rise until the top of the dough is level with the rim of the pan, about 1 hour.

PREHEAT THE OVEN to 350°F. Beat the remaining egg in a small bowl.

REMOVE THE PLASTIC wrap from the loaf pan. Using a pastry brush, coat the top of the loaf with the beaten egg. Transfer to the oven and bake until well browned on top, 30 to 40 minutes, rotating the pan halfway through. Re-move from the oven and immediately turn the brioche out on a wire rack to cool. When cool, cut into 1-inch slices. Trim off the crusts and cut each slice in half to give you 2 rectangles.

USE AS DIRECTED in the Pain Perdu master recipe.

PAIN PERDU
MASTER RECIPE

6	LARGE EGG YOLKS
2	TABLESPOONS SUGAR
	PINCH OF KOSHER SALT
1/2	VANILLA BEAN, SCRAPED
2	1/2 CUPS HEAVY CREAM
4	BRIOCHE SLICES (8 PIECES), HALVED
	(FROM MASTER RECIPE OR STORE-BOUGHT)
2	TABLESPOONS CLARIFIED BUTTER (PAGE 221)

IN A LARGE bowl, whisk together the egg yolks, sugar, salt, and vanilla. Gradually whisk in the cream. Pour the mixture into a shallow baking dish. Working in batches, if necessary, place the brioche pieces in the dish, turning to coat. Soak for about 5 minutes total.

PLACE THE CLARIFIED Butter in a large sauté pan or preferably on a griddle over medium heat. Remove the brioche from the egg mixture, allowing the excess to drip off. Lay the bread in the pan and cook until evenly golden, 1 to 2 minutes on each side. If you have time, put the French toast on a baking sheet and warm in a low oven (200°-250°F) for a few minutes to dry out slightly.

FOLLOW THE ASSEMBLY and serving directions for the variation you are making.

STONE FRUIT CARAMEL SAUCE
MASTER RECIPE

1	CUP CHOPPED STONE FRUIT (CHERRIES FOR VARIATION 1;
	PEACHES FOR VARIATION 2; PLUMS FOR VARIATION 3)
1/2	CUP (1 STICK) UNSALTED BUTTER
1	CUP SUGAR
1	TEASPOON FRESH LEMON JUICE
1/2	CUP HEAVY CREAM
	PINCH OF KOSHER SALT

PLACE THE FRUIT you are using in a blender or food processor with 2 tablespoons of water. Process into a smooth purée. Set aside.

MELT THE BUTTER in a saucepan over medium heat. When the foam subsides, stir in the sugar and lemon juice. Cook until the sugar melts and begins to caramelize into a copper-colored syrup, 5 to 7 minutes. Carefully stir in the fruit purée and boil for 1 minute to bring it together.

REMOVE FROM THE heat and slowly add the cream, a little at a time (it will bubble a bit so stand back as you pour). Stir to combine and set aside to cool.

FOLLOW THE ASSEMBLY and serving directions for the variation you are making.

O 1

CHERRY, FIREWEED HONEY

CHERRY CRÈME FRAÎCHE SHERBET

MAKES ABOUT 1 QUART

1   CUP PITTED CHERRIES, PREFERABLY BING OR RAINIER,
    FRESH OR FROZEN AND THAWED, PLUS 1/2 CUP SLICED CHERRIES
    FOR GARNISH
2   CUPS SIMPLE SYRUP (PAGE 225)
1   CUP CRÈME FRAÎCHE
2   TABLESPOONS FRESH LEMON JUICE
1/8 TEASPOON PURE VANILLA EXTRACT
    PINCH OF KOSHER SALT

COMBINE THE PITTED cherries and Simple Syrup in a blender or food processor and process until very smooth. Pass the cherry purée through a fine-mesh strainer into a bowl. Discard the solids. Whisk in the crème fraîche, lemon juice, vanilla, and salt. Refrigerate until cold. Place the mixture in an ice cream maker and process according to manufacturer's directions. Transfer to a covered plastic container and freeze until firm, at least 2 hours.

CHERRY CARAMEL SAUCE

PREPARE THE STONE Fruit Caramel Sauce as directed in the master recipe, using the chopped cherries.

ROASTED CHERRIES

2   CUPS PITTED CHERRIES, PREFERABLY BING OR RAINIER,
    FRESH OR FROZEN AND THAWED
2   TABLESPOONS FIREWEED HONEY
1/2 VANILLA BEAN, SCRAPED

PREHEAT THE OVEN to 350°F.

TOSS THE CHERRIES with the honey and vanilla in a bowl, then spread out in a baking dish. Transfer to the oven and bake until the fruit is slightly softened, 8 to 10 minutes.

TO ASSEMBLE AND serve: Arrange 2 pieces of the Pain Perdu on each of 4 plates. Top with an equal portion of the Roasted Cherries and Cherry Caramel Sauce, allowing the sauce to drip down the sides. Serve the Cherry Sherbet on the side, garnished with sliced cherries.

O 2

PEACH CRÈME FRAÎCHE SHERBET

MAKES ABOUT 1 QUART

2	PEACHES, PREFERABLY WHITE, PITTED AND COARSELY CHOPPED, PLUS 1 PEACH DICED, FOR GARNISH
2	CUPS SIMPLE SYRUP (PAGE 225)
1	CUP CRÈME FRAÎCHE
2	TABLESPOONS FRESH LEMON JUICE
1/8	TEASPOON PURE VANILLA EXTRACT
	PINCH OF KOSHER SALT

COMBINE THE CHOPPED peaches and Simple Syrup in a blender or food processor and process until very smooth. Pass the peach purée through a fine-mesh strainer into a bowl. Discard the solids. Whisk in the crème fraîche, lemon juice, vanilla, and salt. Refrigerate until cold.

TRANSFER THE MIXTURE to an ice cream maker and process according to manufacturer's directions. Transfer to a covered plastic container and freeze until firm, at least 2 hours.

PEACH CARAMEL SAUCE

PREPARE THE STONE Fruit Caramel Sauce as directed in the master recipe, using the chopped peaches.

ROASTED PEACHES

3	PEACHES, PREFERABLY WHITE, PITTED AND QUARTERED
2	TABLESPOONS ORANGE-BLOSSOM HONEY
1/2	VANILLA BEAN, SCRAPED

PREHEAT THE OVEN to 350°F.

TOSS THE PEACHES with the honey and vanilla in a bowl, then spread out in a baking dish. Transfer to the oven and bake until the fruit is slightly softened, 10 to 15 minutes.

TO ASSEMBLE AND serve: Arrange 2 pieces of the Pain Perdu on each of 4 plates. Top with an equal portion of the Roasted Peaches and Peach Caramel Sauce, allowing the sauce to drip down the sides. Serve the Peach Sherbet on the side, garnished with diced peaches.

03

PLUM, CLOVER HONEY

PLUM CRÈME FRAÎCHE SHERBET

MAKES ABOUT 1 QUART

6 BLACK OR RED PLUMS, PITTED AND COARSELY CHOPPED,
PLUS 1/2 CUP DICED PLUMS, FOR GARNISH

2 CUPS SIMPLE SYRUP (PAGE 225)

1 CUP CRÈME FRAÎCHE

2 TABLESPOONS FRESH LEMON JUICE

1/8 TEASPOON PURE VANILLA EXTRACT

PINCH OF KOSHER SALT

COMBINE THE CHOPPED plums and Simple Syrup in a blender and process until very smooth. Pass the plum purée through a fine-mesh strainer into a bowl. Discard the solids. Whisk in the crème fraîche, lemon juice, vanilla, and salt. Refrigerate until cold.

PLACE THE MIXTURE in an ice cream maker and process according to manufacturer's directions. Transfer to a covered plastic container and freeze until firm, at least 2 hours.

PLUM CARAMEL SAUCE

PREPARE THE STONE Fruit Caramel Sauce as directed in the master recipe, using the chopped plums.

ROASTED PLUMS

4 BLACK OR RED PLUMS, HALVED AND PITTED

2 TABLESPOONS CLOVER HONEY

1/2 VANILLA BEAN, SCRAPED

TOSS THE PLUMS with the honey and vanilla in a bowl, then spread out in a baking dish. Transfer to the oven and bake until the fruit is slightly softened, 10 to 15 minutes.

TO ASSEMBLE AND serve: Arrange 2 pieces of the Pain Perdu on each of 4 plates. Top with an equal portion of the Roasted Plums and Plum Caramel Sauce, allowing the sauce to drip down the sides. Serve the Plum Sherbet on the side, garnished with diced plums.

WARM CHOCOLATE PUDDING CAKE
WITH MILK SHAKE

O1
DARK CHOCOLATE, PEANUT BUTTER

DARK CHOCOLATE–PEANUT BUTTER GANACHE, PEANUT BUTTER MILK SHAKE,
CHOPPED PEANUTS

O2
WHITE CHOCOLATE, PRALINE

WHITE CHOCOLATE–PRALINE GANACHE, PRALINE MILK SHAKE,
CRUMBLED PRALINES

O3
MILK CHOCOLATE, MALT

MILK CHOCOLATE–MALT GANACHE, MALTED MILK SHAKE,
CHOCOLATE SHAVINGS

TIMELESS DESSERTS SUCH AS WARM CHOCOLATE CAKE OCCUPY A CERTAIN SOFT SPOT ON THE PALATES OF NOSTALGIC DINERS. LAVA CAKE, MOLTEN CHOCOLATE CAKE, PUDDING CAKE; CALL IT WHAT YOU WANT BUT A BIG REASON IT'S A STAPLE ON RESTAURANT MENUS IS THAT PEOPLE LOVE IT SO MUCH. FOR THE KITCHEN, THE ADDED BENEFIT IS THAT THE BATTER CAN BE MADE AHEAD OF TIME AND THE PETITE CAKES TAKE ONLY 15 MINUTES TO BAKE—WHICH CAN ALSO BE A TIMESAVER WHEN ENTERTAINING AT HOME. THIS RICH, BITTERSWEET DESSERT IS DEFINITELY FOR THE CHOCOLATE LOVER, AND EVERYBODY KNOWS AT LEAST ONE. THE INDIVIDUAL CAKES ARE FILLED WITH THREE DIFFERENT GANACHE CENTERS, FLAVORED WITH PEANUT BUTTER, PRALINE, AND MY FAVORITE, MALT. ONCE YOUR SPOON CUTS THROUGH THE TENDER, CAKEY EXTERIOR, A SMOOTH PUDDING-LIKE CENTER REVEALS ITSELF AND OOZES ONTO THE PLATE. WHILE THESE RICH CHOCO-LATE CAKES ARE FAIRLY SMALL, THEY PACK A PUNCH; A FEW BITES ARE ALL YOU NEED TO SATISFY. DESSERT SHOULD TOP OFF A MEAL, NOT TAKE AWAY FROM IT. I HAVE PAIRED EACH WARM CAKE WITH A CORRESPONDING COLD MILK SHAKE TO MATCH. IT IS A FUN WAY TO BRING OUT THE KID IN ALL OF US, OFFERING SOMETHING TO WASH DOWN THE GOOEY CAKE, WHILE STILL LAYERING THE FLAVORS. USE ONLY THE BEST QUALITY CHOCOLATE— IT MAKES ALL THE DIFFERENCE BETWEEN WAXY, VAGUELY CHOCOLATY FLAVOR AND DARK AND INTENSE RICHNESS. VALRHÔNA AND SCHARFFEN BERGER ARE TWO PREMIUM CHOCO-LATE MAKERS THAT I LIKE; THEIR RELATIVELY HIGH PERCENTAGE OF CACAO CONTENT (FROM 60 TO 70 PERCENT) GIVES FULL BODY AND AROMA TO THE CHOCOLATE, AND THE SWEETNESS AND THE BITTERNESS COME THROUGH AT DIFFERENT TIMES. ANY LEFTOVER

GANACHE CAN BE USED TO MAKE CHOCOLATE TRUFFLES. TO DO SO, SCOOP UP 1 TEASPOON OF THE GANACHE AND QUICKLY ROLL INTO A BALL. DUST WITH COCOA POWDER TO COAT. STORE, REFRIGERATED IN AN AIRTIGHT CONTAINER, FOR UP TO ONE WEEK.

WINE SUGGESTION

DOWS VINTAGE PORT 1983

SERVES 4

WARM CHOCOLATE PUDDING CAKE
MASTER RECIPE

6	OUNCES HIGH-QUALITY SEMISWEET OR BITTERSWEET CHOCOLATE, SUCH AS VALRHÔNA OR SCHARFFEN BERGER, FINELY CHOPPED
1/2	CUP (1 STICK) UNSALTED BUTTER
1/2	CUP PLUS 1 TEASPOON SUGAR
2	LARGE EGGS
1	LARGE EGG YOLK
1/4	CUP CAKE FLOUR, SIFTED
	PINCH OF KOSHER SALT
1/4	CUP COLD GANACHE (FOR THE VARIATION YOU ARE MAKING, RECIPES FOLLOW), PLUS MORE FOR SERVING
	CONFECTIONERS' SUGAR, FOR DUSTING

PREHEAT THE OVEN to 350°F. Coat the interiors of four 4-ounce ramekins with nonstick spray. Set aside on a baking pan.

PLACE THE CHOCOLATE in a heatproof bowl. In a small saucepan, combine the butter, 1/2 cup of the sugar, and 1/4 cup water over medium heat. Bring to a boil, stirring to dissolve the sugar and melt the butter. Remove from the heat and pour the mixture over the chocolate, stirring to blend.

PLACE THE EGGS, yolk, and the remaining teaspoon of sugar in the bowl of a standing electric mixer fitted with a wire whip attachment, or use a handheld electric beater. Beat on medium-high speed until the eggs are thick and yellow.

ADD THE MELTED chocolate and continue to whip until thoroughly blended. Add the flour and salt, beating to incorporate. Transfer the bowl to the refrigerator and chill until firm, at least 30 minutes or ideally up to overnight.

FILL THE PREPARED ramekins halfway with the batter. Place a tablespoon of Ganache in the center (make sure it is chilled so it is firm and does not ooze into the batter). Pour in enough cake batter to cover the Ganache. The ramekins should be about three-quarters full.

TRANSFER THE CAKES to the oven and bake until the sides are set and the tops are puffed but still soft, 15 to 18 minutes. Remove from the oven and let cool in the ramekins for 2 minutes before inverting onto 4 dessert plates.

FOLLOW THE ASSEMBLY and serving directions for the recipe you are making.

VANILLA ICE CREAM
MASTER RECIPE

MAKES 1 QUART

2	CUPS HEAVY CREAM
1	CUP MILK
1/2	CUP SUGAR
	PINCH OF KOSHER SALT
1	VANILLA BEAN, SPLIT LENGTHWISE
9	LARGE EGG YOLKS
1 1/2	TEASPOONS PURE VANILLA EXTRACT

PREPARE AN ICE bath.

COMBINE THE CREAM, milk, sugar, and salt in a large saucepan over medium heat. Scrape the seeds of the vanilla bean into the milk mixture; add the scraped bean pod for extra flavor. Bring to a simmer and cook gently until the sugar is dissolved, about 5 minutes. The temperature should reach 175°F (just scalding).

IN A LARGE mixing bowl, whisk the egg yolks until slightly thick and yellow. Using a ladle, very gradually add half the hot vanilla cream into the yolk mixture, whisking constantly (do not add too quickly or the eggs will scramble). Return the tempered eggs to the saucepan and whisk constantly over medium-low heat until the custard is thick enough to coat the back of a spoon and leaves a path when you run your finger across it, about 5 minutes.

PASS THE CUSTARD through a fine-mesh sieve into a clean bowl and transfer to the ice bath, stirring occasionally. When cool, stir in the vanilla extract.

PLACE THE CUSTARD in an ice-cream maker and process according to the manufacturer's directions. The ice cream will be the consistency of soft serve when it is done. To fully harden the ice cream, place in a covered plastic container and freeze for at least 2 hours.

FOLLOW THE DIRECTIONS for the Milk Shake you are making.

CHANTILLY CREAM
MASTER RECIPE

MAKES ABOUT 1 CUP

1/2	CUP HEAVY CREAM, COLD
1	TABLESPOON CONFECTIONERS' SUGAR

CHILL A MIXING bowl and wire whisk in the freezer for 10 minutes.

PLACE THE CREAM in the chilled bowl and whisk until it begins to foam and thicken. Add the sugar and continue to beat until the cream barely mounds. Do not overwhip.

THE CHANTILLY CREAM is used as a topping for the Milk Shakes.

O I

DARK CHOCOLATE, PEANUT BUTTER

DARK CHOCOLATE—PEANUT BUTTER GANACHE

8	OUNCES GOOD-QUALITY DARK CHOCOLATE, SUCH AS VALRHÔNA OR SCHARFFEN BERGER, FINELY CHOPPED
1	CUP HEAVY CREAM
1	CUP SMOOTH PEANUT BUTTER

PLACE THE CHOCOLATE in a mixing bowl. Combine the cream and peanut butter in a small saucepan over medium heat and cook until bubbles just begin to form around the edges.

REMOVE FROM HEAT and immediately pour the hot cream mixture over the chocolate in a steady stream. Let it sit for a few seconds to begin to melt. As soon as the chocolate begins to melt, using a whisk or rubber spatula, stir in a circular motion until the chocolate is completely smooth.

YOU SHOULD HAVE about 2 cups of Ganache. Reserve half for the Chocolate Cake and the remaining cup for the Milk Shake.

PEANUT BUTTER MILK SHAKE

1	CUP RESERVED DARK CHOCOLATE—PEANUT BUTTER GANACHE
1	CUP MILK, SCALDED
6	TO 8 LARGE SCOOPS VANILLA ICE CREAM (FROM MASTER RECIPE OR STORE-BOUGHT)
1/4	CUP SMOOTH PEANUT BUTTER
1/4	TO 1/2 CUP CHANTILLY CREAM (FROM MASTER RECIPE), FOR SERVING
2	TABLESPOONS PEANUTS, TOASTED AND CHOPPED, FOR GARNISH

PLACE THE GANACHE in a heatproof bowl. Pour the scalded milk over the Ganache, stirring until it looks like chocolate milk. Let cool.

PLACE THE ICE cream, chocolate milk mixture, and peanut butter in a blender and blend until thick and smooth.

DIVIDE EQUALLY AMONG 4 chilled glasses. Top with a heaping spoonful of Chantilly Cream and garnish with chopped peanuts.

TO ASSEMBLE AND serve: Heat about 1/4 cup of the Dark Chocolate—Peanut Butter Ganache in a microwave so it is pourable. Drizzle a tablespoon of the Ganache around each Chocolate Cake and dust with confectioners' sugar. Serve the Peanut Butter Milk Shake on the side.

O 2

WHITE CHOCOLATE, PRALINE

WHITE CHOCOLATE—PRALINE GANACHE

Similar to peanut butter in texture, praline paste is made with roasted hazelnut or almond butter and sugar. This smooth, creamy, caramel-colored paste is often used to make candy and other desserts. I have been known to have a spoonful or two right out of the can! I do not recommend trying to make it at home since nut butters ground with noncommercial equipment tend to be somewhat gritty. If your neighborhood baking supply shop or gourmet retailer does not carry praline paste, it can be ordered from the King Arthur Flour Baker's Catalog (see Sources, page 242). Nutella also makes a fine substitute.

8	OUNCES WHITE CHOCOLATE, FINELY CHOPPED
1	CUP HEAVY CREAM
1	CUP PRALINE PASTE OR NUTELLA

PLACE THE CHOCOLATE in a mixing bowl. Combine the cream and praline paste in a small saucepan over medium heat and cook until bubbles just begin to form around the edges.

REMOVE FROM HEAT and immediately pour the hot cream mixture over the chocolate in a steady stream. Let it sit for a few seconds to begin to melt. As soon as the chocolate begins to melt, using a whisk or rubber spatula, stir in a circular motion until the chocolate is completely smooth.

YOU SHOULD HAVE about 2 cups of Ganache. Reserve half for the Chocolate Cake and the remaining cup for the Milk Shake.

PRALINE MILK SHAKE

1	CUP RESERVED WHITE CHOCOLATE—PRALINE GANACHE
1	CUP MILK, SCALDED
1/4	CUP PRALINE PASTE OR NUTELLA
6	TO 8 LARGE SCOOPS VANILLA ICE CREAM
	(FROM MASTER RECIPE OR STORE-BOUGHT)
1/4	TO 1/2 CUP CHANTILLY CREAM (FROM MASTER RECIPE), FOR SERVING
1	PRALINE, CRUMBLED, FOR GARNISH

PLACE THE GANACHE in a heatproof bowl. Pour the scalded milk over the Ganache, stirring until it looks like chocolate milk. Let cool.

PLACE THE ICE cream, chocolate milk mixture, and praline paste in a blender and blend until thick and smooth.

DIVIDE EQUALLY AMONG 4 chilled glasses. Top with a heaping spoonful of Chantilly Cream and garnish with crumbled praline.

TO ASSEMBLE AND serve: Heat about 1/4 cup of the White Chocolate—Praline Ganache in a microwave so it is pourable. Drizzle a tablespoon of the Ganache around each Chocolate Cake and dust with confectioners' sugar. Serve the Praline Milk Shake on the side.

03

MILK CHOCOLATE, MALT

MILK CHOCOLATE–MALT GANACHE

8   OUNCES GOOD-QUALITY MILK CHOCOLATE,
    SUCH AS VALRHÔNA OR SCHARFFEN BERGER, FINELY CHOPPED
1   CUP HEAVY CREAM
1   CUP MALTED MILK POWDER OR LIQUID MALT

PLACE THE CHOCOLATE in a mixing bowl. Combine the cream and malt in a small saucepan over medium heat and cook until bubbles just begin to form around the edges.

REMOVE FROM HEAT and immediately pour the hot cream mixture over the chocolate in a steady stream. Let it sit for a few seconds to begin to melt. As soon as the chocolate begins to melt, using a whisk or rubber spatula, stir in a circular motion until the chocolate is completely smooth.

YOU SHOULD HAVE about 2 cups of Ganache. Reserve half for the Chocolate Cake and the remaining cup for the Milk Shake.

MALTED MILK SHAKE

1   CUP RESERVED MILK CHOCOLATE–MALT GANACHE
1   CUP MILK, SCALDED
6   TO 8 LARGE SCOOPS VANILLA ICE CREAM
      (FROM MASTER RECIPE OR STORE-BOUGHT)
1/4   CUP MALTED MILK POWDER OR LIQUID MALT
1/4   TO 1/2 CUP CHANTILLY CREAM (FROM MASTER RECIPE), FOR SERVING
2   TABLESPOONS SHAVED MILK CHOCOLATE, FOR GARNISH

PLACE THE GANACHE in a heatproof bowl. Pour the scalded milk over the Ganache, stirring until it looks like chocolate milk. Let cool.

PLACE THE ICE cream, chocolate milk mixture, and malt in a blender and blend until thick and smooth.

DIVIDE EQUALLY AMONG 4 chilled glasses. Top with a heaping spoonful of Chantilly Cream and garnish with shaved chocolate.

TO ASSEMBLE AND serve: Heat about 1/4 cup of the Milk Chocolate–Malt Ganache in a microwave so it is pourable. Drizzle a tablespoon of the Ganache around each cake and dust with confectioners' sugar. Serve the Malted Milk Shake on the side.

APPLE *FINANCIER*, SPICED HOLIDAY DRINKS

O 1

NUTMEG, COGNAC

NUTMEG CARAMEL, WARM EGGNOG

O 2

CINNAMON, RUM

CINNAMON BROWN BUTTER, HOT BUTTERED RUM

O 3

CLOVE, CALVADOS

CLOVE ANGLAISE, HOT APPLE CIDER

I ORIGINATED THIS DESSERT A FEW CHRISTMAS EVES AGO AND JUST FELL IN LOVE WITH IT. THE WARM DRINKS SAY HOLIDAY AND I HAVE MADE THEM AN ANNUAL TRADITION FOR DECEMBER AND JANUARY. THE RICH FRENCH TEA CAKE APTLY CALLED *FINANCIER* (PRO-NOUNCED FEE-NAHN-SYEH) IS A SPONGE BATTER MADE FROM GROUND ALMONDS BLENDED WITH BROWN BUTTER AND EGG WHITES. WHEN BAKED THEY ARE SOFT AND SPRINGY WITH A SLIGHTLY DOMED TOP AND CRUSTY FINISH. TRADITIONALLY BAKED IN RECTANGULAR PANS, THE CAKE PROBABLY GETS ITS NAME FROM THE FACT THAT THE SHAPE RESEMBLES A BAR OF GOLD. AT THE RESTAURANT, WE USE RING-SHAPED SAVARIN MOLDS AND FILL THE CENTER HOLE WITH WARM SAUTÉED APPLES. YOU CAN SUCCESSFULLY USE SMALL MUFFIN TINS OR RAMEKINS, OR REALLY ANY SMALL PANS WILL DO. WITHOUT THE FRUIT, THIS BATTER CAN BE MADE IN TINY MOLDS, LIKE COOKIES. THEY ARE TERRIFIC TO SERVE AFTER DINNER WITH WARM DRINKS. MANY TIMES *FINANCIER* COMES WITH ICE CREAM, WHICH IS GREAT, BUT SERVING IT WITH APPLES AND WINTER SPICES GIVES THE DAINTY CAKE SOME MUSCLE. THE BATTER WILL KEEP, COVERED AND REFRIGERATED, FOR TWO DAYS.

WINE SUGGESTION

ZIND-HUMBRECHT PINOT GRIS 'HEIMBOURG' VT, ALSACE 2001

SERVES 4 TO 8

APPLE *FINANCIER*
MASTER RECIPE

CAKE BATTER

1/2   CUP (1 STICK) UNSALTED BUTTER, CUT INTO CHUNKS,
      PLUS MORE FOR GREASING THE MOLDS
3/4   CUP CONFECTIONERS' SUGAR
1/2   CUP ALMOND FLOUR/MEAL OR GROUND BLANCHED ALMONDS
1/4   CUP CAKE FLOUR, PLUS MORE FOR DUSTING THE MOLDS
      PINCH OF KOSHER SALT
  4   LARGE EGG WHITES (ABOUT 1/2 CUP)
1/2   TEASPOON PURE VANILLA EXTRACT
      SAUTÉED SPICED APPLES (RECIPE FOLLOWS)

PLACE THE BUTTER in a saucepan over medium-low heat and slowly melt. Cook gently until the milk solids turn golden brown and the butter is amber-colored and smells nutty, about 5 minutes. Remove from the heat and set aside to cool slightly.

SIFT THE CONFECTIONERS' sugar, almond flour, flour, and salt into the bowl of a standing electric mixer fitted with a wire whip attachment, or use a handheld electric beater. Add the egg whites and mix on low speed for a minute or two to just combine. Add the vanilla and slowly drizzle in the cooled brown butter, blending until smooth. Scrape the batter into a bowl, cover, and refrigerate until firm, at least 30 minutes or up to overnight.

PREHEAT THE OVEN to 375°F. Butter and flour four or eight 4-ounce ramekins and place them on a sheet pan.

TRANSFER THE BATTER to a pastry bag fitted with a large plain tip (or no tip at all) and pipe into the prepared ramekins, filling to just below the rim. Bake until the cakes are lightly golden and springy to the touch, 10 to 15 minutes. Remove from the oven and cool in the ramekins for 2 minutes before inverting onto dessert plates.

SAUTÉED SPICED APPLES

  2   TABLESPOONS UNSALTED BUTTER
  2   CRISP, FIRM APPLES, SUCH AS SIERRA BEAUTY OR PINK LADY,
      PEELED, CORED, AND DICED
  2   TABLESPOONS SUGAR
      PINCH OF KOSHER SALT
1/4   CUP APPLE BRANDY, SUCH AS CALVADOS

MELT THE BUTTER in a large sauté pan over medium heat. When the foam subsides, add the apples, tossing to coat. Sprinkle in the sugar and sauté until the apples soften slightly and the sugar begins to caramelize. Add a pinch of salt to balance out the sweetness.

ADD THE BRANDY and continue to cook until the liquid has reduced and is syrupy, about 2 minutes. Remove from the heat.

FOLLOW THE ASSEMBLY and serving directions for the variation you are making.

M

APPLE PASTRY CREAM
MASTER RECIPE

MAKES ABOUT 2 CUPS

2	CRISP, FIRM APPLES, SUCH AS SIERRA BEAUTY OR PINK LADY, HALVED AND CORED
1	CINNAMON STICK
2	TABLESPOONS LIGHT BROWN SUGAR, LOOSELY PACKED
1/2	CUP APPLE JUICE, PREFERABLY FRESH
1/2	TABLESPOON FRESH LEMON JUICE
1	CUP MILK
1/2	VANILLA BEAN
4	LARGE EGG YOLKS
1/2	CUP SUGAR
2	TABLESPOONS ALL-PURPOSE FLOUR
1	CUP CHANTILLY CREAM (SEE PAGE 155)

PREHEAT THE OVEN to 400°F.

PLACE THE APPLES, skin side up, in a small baking dish. Add the cinnamon stick, brown sugar, apple juice, and lemon juice and cover the dish tightly with aluminum foil. Transfer to the oven and bake until the apples are very soft, about 30 minutes.

REMOVE FROM THE oven and transfer the baked apples to a food processor or blender, along with a couple tablespoons of the liquid from the baking dish. Purée until completely smooth. Pass the applesauce through a fine-mesh strainer. Discard the solids. You should have 1 cup applesauce. Cover and refrigerate until cool.

PLACE THE MILK in a small saucepan over medium-low heat. Scrape the seeds from the vanilla bean into the milk and add the scraped bean pod for extra flavor. Bring the milk to a brief simmer to infuse the flavor. Do not boil or it can overflow.

IN A LARGE bowl, whisk together the yolks, sugar, and flour, until slightly thickened and lemon-colored. Using a ladle, very gradually add half the hot vanilla milk into the yolk mixture, whisking constantly (do not add too quickly or the eggs will scramble). Return the tempered eggs to the pan and whisk constantly over medium-low heat until the pastry cream is thick enough to coat the back of a spoon and leaves a path when you run your finger across it, about 5 minutes.

PASS THE PASTRY cream through a fine-mesh strainer into a large bowl. Put a piece of plastic wrap directly on the surface of the pastry cream to prevent a skin from forming. Refrigerate until well chilled.

JUST BEFORE SERVING, fold the chilled applesauce and Chantilly Cream into the pastry cream until evenly blended. Reserve the Apple Pastry Cream, chilled, for the hot drinks.

O I

NUTMEG CARAMEL

MAKES ABOUT 1 CUP

1/2	CUP (1 STICK) UNSALTED BUTTER
1	CUP SUGAR
1	TEASPOON FRESH LEMON JUICE
1/2	TEASPOON FRESHLY GRATED NUTMEG
1/2	CUP HEAVY CREAM

MELT THE BUTTER in a 2-quart saucepan over medium heat. When the foam subsides, stir in the sugar, lemon juice, and nutmeg. Cook until the sugar melts and begins to caramelize into a copper-colored syrup, 5 to 7 minutes. Remove from the heat and slowly stir in the cream, a little at a time. It will bubble a bit so stand back as you pour. Stir to combine and keep warm over low heat.

EGGNOG

MAKES ABOUT 1 QUART

1	CUP HEAVY CREAM
1	CUP MILK
1/2	CUP SUGAR
	PINCH OF KOSHER SALT
1	VANILLA BEAN, SPLIT LENGTHWISE
6	LARGE EGG YOLKS
3/4	TO 1 CUP COGNAC
1/2	TEASPOON FRESHLY GRATED NUTMEG, PLUS MORE FOR GARNISH
1/4	TEASPOON GROUND CINNAMON
1	CUP APPLE PASTRY CREAM (FROM MASTER RECIPE), FOR SERVING

COMBINE THE CREAM, milk, sugar, and salt in a large saucepan over medium heat. Scrape the seeds from the vanilla bean into the milk mixture. Add the bean pod for extra flavor. Bring to a simmer and cook gently until the sugar is dissolved, about 5 minutes.

USING A LADLE, very gradually add half the hot vanilla cream into the yolk mixture, whisking constantly (do not add too quickly or the eggs will scramble). Return the tempered eggs to the pan and whisk constantly over medium-low heat until the custard is thick enough to coat the back of a spoon and leaves a path when you run your finger across it, about 5 minutes.

PASS THE EGGNOG through a fine-mesh strainer into a large bowl. Stir in the cognac, nutmeg, and cinnamon. If the eggnog seems too thick, thin it out with a little half-and-half or milk.

TO ASSEMBLE AND serve: Pool a couple of tablespoons of the Nutmeg Caramel on each of 4 dessert plates. Place an inverted *Financier* in the center and top with the Spiced Apples. Ladle an equal portion of the warm Eggnog into each of 4 mugs. Top each with about 1/4 cup of the Apple Pastry Cream and a sprinkle of ground nutmeg if desired. Serve the Eggnog on the side.

O 2

CINNAMON, RUM

CINNAMON BROWN BUTTER

MAKES ABOUT 1 CUP

1	CUP (2 STICKS) UNSALTED BUTTER
1	CINNAMON STICK
1	TABLESPOON FRESH LEMON JUICE
1/2	CUP SIMPLE SYRUP (PAGE 225)
1/4	CUP HEAVY CREAM
	PINCH OF KOSHER SALT

COMBINE THE BUTTER and cinnamon stick in a small saucepan over medium-low heat and cook until foamy and beginning to brown on the edges. Swirl the pan occasionally to keep the color even. When the butter is light brown and smells nutty, add the lemon juice to stop it from continuing to brown. The butter will bubble up. When the bubbling has died down, whisk in the Simple Syrup. Bring to a boil until the sauce is thick and emulsified, about 1 minute. Take care to stir around the sides of the pan to keep the butter from burning in spots.

REMOVE FROM THE heat and stir in the cream and a pinch of salt. Cover to keep warm.

HOT BUTTERED RUM

MAKES ABOUT 1 QUART

1	QUART WATER
1	TEASPOON GROUND CINNAMON, PLUS MORE FOR GARNISH
1/4	TEASPOON FRESHLY GRATED NUTMEG
	PINCH OF GROUND CLOVES
2	CUPS LIGHT BROWN SUGAR, LOOSELY PACKED
	PINCH OF KOSHER SALT
2	TABLESPOONS UNSALTED BUTTER
1/2	TO 3/4 CUP DARK RUM, SUCH AS MEYERS
1	CUP APPLE PASTRY CREAM (FROM MASTER RECIPE), FOR SERVING

COMBINE THE WATER, cinnamon, nutmeg, and cloves in a small saucepan over low heat. Gently warm for 15 minutes to infuse the spicy flavor; do not allow the water to boil and evaporate. Whisk in the brown sugar until melted.

MELT THE BUTTER in a small sauté pan over medium-low heat until nutty brown. Pour the brown butter into the water mixture, stirring to combine. Add the rum.

TO SERVE: POOL a couple of tablespoons of the Cinnamon Brown Butter on each of 4 dessert plates. Place an inverted *Financier* in the center and top with the Spiced Apples. Ladle an equal portion of the Hot Buttered Rum into each of 4 mugs. Top with about 1/4 cup of the Apple Pastry Cream and a sprinkle of ground cinnamon if desired. Serve the Hot Buttered Rum on the side.

O 3

CLOVE, CALVADOS

CLOVE ANGLAISE

MAKES ABOUT 1 CUP

1	CUP HEAVY CREAM
2	LARGE EGG YOLKS
1/4	CUP SUGAR
1/4	TEASPOON GROUND CLOVES
1	TEASPOON PURE VANILLA EXTRACT

PLACE THE CREAM in a small saucepan over medium-low heat. Cook until bubbles form around the edge of the pan, about 4 minutes. Remove from heat and set aside.

IN A SMALL mixing bowl, whisk together the egg yolks, sugar, cloves, and vanilla until slightly thickened and lemon-colored. Using a ladle, very gradually add half the hot vanilla cream into the yolk mixture, whisking constantly (do not add too quickly or the eggs will scramble). Return the tempered eggs to the pan and whisk constantly over medium-low heat until the custard is thick enough to coat the back of a spoon and leaves a path when you run your finger across it, about 5 minutes. Remove from heat and cover to keep warm.

HOT APPLE CIDER

MAKES ABOUT 1 QUART

1	QUART FRESH APPLE CIDER
12	DRIED APPLE RINGS
1	ORANGE, THINLY SLICED
2	TABLESPOONS LIGHT BROWN SUGAR
1	TEASPOON WHOLE CLOVES, PLUS GROUND CLOVES FOR GARNISH
1	TEASPOON ALLSPICE
1	TEASPOON CORIANDER SEEDS, TOASTED
	PINCH OF FRESHLY GRATED NUTMEG
1	TO 1 1/2 CUPS APPLE BRANDY, SUCH AS CALVADOS
1	CUP APPLE PASTRY CREAM (FROM MASTER RECIPE), FOR SERVING

COMBINE THE CIDER, dried apple, orange, sugar, cloves, allspice, coriander, and nutmeg in a 2-quart saucepan over medium-low heat. Bring to a simmer and cook for 10 minutes. Strain through a fine-mesh sieve into a pitcher. Discard the solids. Stir in the brandy.

TO SERVE: POOL a couple of tablespoons of the Clove Anglaise on each of 4 dessert plates. Place an inverted *Financier* in the center and top with the Spiced Apples. Ladle equal portions of the Hot Apple Cider into each of 4 mugs. Top each with about 1/4 cup of the Apple Pastry Cream and a sprinkle of ground clove, if desired. Serve the Hot Apple Cider on the side.

02

MICHAEL MINA CLASSICS

When I say "classics" in the kitchen, I am referring not to mom's macaroni and cheese or corned beef hash, but to those dishes that have become my signatures—the dishes that I make over and over again no matter the time, the place, or the year. They might be thought of as the culinary equivalent of an artist conceiving an original design or a writer expressing a unique, identifiable voice. To proclaim these dishes "classic" was never my intention; it's the diners who have deemed a particular dish a classic.

Although the waitstaff and managers supply the feedback necessary, I generally measure a classic dish by how many I have to make each night. And when a dish is still requested after it has been taken off the menu, I am sure that I have a classic in the making. Clearly, it is much more challenging for a chef to keep reinventing the wheel, but I believe that I now have enough classic dishes to give the kitchen staff a romp while allowing diners a selection of their favorite dishes.

Through the years, I've noticed that most of our popular dishes are those that guests can relate to and remember, even after they leave the restaurant. Many of the signature dishes are closely identified as redefined modern American classics, items people are familiar with and can describe easily. My Root Beer Float (see page 210) is a perfect example—a soda-shop favorite reconfigured with a contemporary twist. Once a dish becomes a classic, I have to practice restraint and resist the temptation to continue to tweak it, as diners notice even the tiniest change. Some of my signature dishes take on a life of their own and are known to people who have never even dined in my restaurants.

The core of a classic dish always remains, but I often add seasonal garnishes to keep it interesting to the staff and exciting for diners. And to take it to even greater heights, I invented interesting serving pieces for each dish. The caviar carts, the carving board for the Whole Fried Chicken (see page 198), and the individual copper pots used for the Lobster Potpie (see page 189) are prime examples. Many diners now count these tableside serving pieces as one of my trademarks.

As we develop new restaurant concepts, individual dishes become instant hits and consequently are identified as "classics" on a particular menu. The Sea Bass Tagine at SeaBlue and the Cioppino at Nobhill each define the style of the restaurant's cuisine. Here, I have chosen a small selection of my signature dishes—some because they are my personal favorites and some because they ring the bell for so many of our restaurants' guests. I hope that at least one of them will become a classic in your kitchen.

TARTARE OF AHI TUNA

AHI TUNA TARTARE BECAME AN INSTANT CLASSIC AT AQUA AND IS A PRIME EXAMPLE OF THE BALANCE OF BOLD FLAVORS THAT I CONSTANTLY STRIVE FOR. THE DISH IS CONSTRUCTED AROUND FOUR PILLARS OF TASTE THAT CONSTITUTE THE FOUNDATION OF MY CUISINE: SWEETNESS, SPICINESS, ACIDITY, AND FAT. SUSHI-GRADE AHI IS COMBINED WITH PIECES OF SWEET PEAR MACERATED IN TART LEMON JUICE. SCOTCH BONNET CHILIES BRING IN THE HEAT, AND SESAME OIL AND PINE NUTS ADD THE FAT THAT TIES IT TOGETHER. THE EGG YOLK EMULSIFIES AND ADDS A CREAMINESS TO THE DISH. WHILE THE PREPARATION IS RELATIVELY SIMPLE, THE RESULTING COMBINATION OF FLAVORS AND TEXTURES IS DAZZLING.

AS WITH ALL COLD PREPARATIONS, TAKE THE TIME TO CHILL YOUR SERVING PLATES TO ENSURE THE DISH IS ENJOYED AT THE PROPER TEMPERATURE. IT TAKES SOME PRACTICE TO SEPARATE SMALL QUAIL EGGS, SO BUY A FEW EXTRA UNTIL YOU GET THE HANG OF IT. IF YOU CANNOT FIND QUAIL EGGS, OMIT THEM—THE DISH WILL STILL BE TERRIFIC!

WINE SUGGESTION

SELBACH OSTER RIESLING 'SCHLOSSBERG' KABINETT, MOSEL, GERMANY 2002

Raw fish usually works only with white wines that are high in acid. For this dish, a semi-dry Riesling will uphold the spicy flavors and balance it out. The wine must also be fresh and unoaked. Alternatives are unoaked Chenin Blanc or rose Champagne.

MAKES 4 APPETIZER PORTIONS

1	TABLESPOON FRESH LEMON JUICE
1/2	CUP COLD WATER
1/2	FIRM BOSC OR BARTLETT PEAR, PEELED AND FINELY DICED
1/2	SMALL ORANGE SCOTCH BONNET CHILE, HALVED LENGTHWISE
1/2	SMALL GREEN JALAPEÑO, HALVED LENGTHWISE
1/2	SMALL RED JALAPEÑO, HALVED LENGTHWISE
1/4	CUP SESAME OIL
1	POUND SUSHI-QUALITY AHI TUNA, SUCH AS BLUEFIN OR YELLOWFIN, CUT INTO 1/4-INCH DICE
2	TABLESPOONS PINE NUTS, LIGHTLY TOASTED
2	CLOVES GARLIC, MINCED
1	TEASPOON KOSHER SALT
	DUSTING OF GROUND WHITE PEPPER
	DUSTING OF CHILI POWDER, PREFERABLY ANCHO
1/4	CUP FRESH MINT LEAVES, CHIFFONADE
4	QUAIL EGGS*
8	SLICES WHITE BREAD, LIGHTLY TOASTED AND CRUSTS REMOVED

MIX THE LEMON juice with the water in a small bowl. Add the pear and soak in the acidulated water for 15 minutes. This not only prevents the fruit from browning but also imparts a subtle acidic note.

SCRAPE THE SEEDS and membranes from the chilies into a small saucepan. Pour in the sesame oil and place over very low heat to infuse the spiciness, about 2 minutes; do not let the oil boil or it can become bitter. Pass the oil through a fine-mesh strainer, discarding the solids. Set aside to cool.

IN THE MEANTIME, get all the remaining ingredients together for the tuna tartare. All ingredients will be divided by 4 for preparation of each individual serving plate.

MINCE THE SEEDED chilies very fine and mix the three colors together. Drain the pears from the lemon water.

SET A 2 1/2-INCH ring mold (about 1 1/2 inches high) in the center of a chilled plate and spoon a quarter of the tuna, about 4 ounces, into it to fill. Press down gently with the back of a spoon to hold the tuna together. Make a small indentation in the center of the tuna with your finger; this will ultimately hold the egg yolk. Carefully remove the ring so the tartare keeps its round shape; repeat with the remaining servings.

WORKING CLOCKWISE AROUND the tuna, on each plate pile 1 1/2 teaspoons of the pine nuts at 3 o'clock, about 1/8 teaspoon of garlic at 5 o'clock, 1/8 teaspoon of the chilies at 7 o'clock, and 1 tablespoon of diced pears at 9 o'clock. Sprinkle each serving of tuna with 1/4 teaspoon of salt and a light dusting of white pepper, then sprinkle each with a little chili powder and a few strands of mint. Drizzle 1 1/2 teaspoons of the chile-infused sesame oil on top of the tuna and around each plate. Very carefully crack a quail egg, gently separating the yolk from the white. Discard the white. Slip the yolk into the little indent in the center of the tuna so it has a resting place. Cut the toast in half diagonally to form triangles and place on a side plate.

TO SERVE: AFTER presentation of the dish, using a fork and spoon, mix all the elements vigorously tableside. When everything is well combined, reform the tuna tartare into an appealing shape—e.g., a square or triangle.

*RAW EGG WARNING:

The American Egg Board states: "There have been warnings against consuming raw or lightly cooked eggs on the grounds that the egg may be contaminated with Salmonella, a bacteria responsible for a type of foodborne illness. Healthy people need to remember that there is a very small risk and treat eggs and other raw animal foods accordingly. Use only properly refrigerated, clean, sound-shelled, fresh, grade AA or A eggs. Avoid mixing yolks and whites with the shell."

CAVIAR PARFAIT

MY WIFE, DIANE, ABSOLUTELY LOVES CAVIAR. WHILE ON OUR HONEYMOON IN HAWAII, WE HAD A VERY TRAUMATIC AFTERNOON WHERE WE WERE CHASED BY A WILD BOAR ON A REMOTE PART OF THE ISLAND. THE FOLLOWING MORNING, I WANTED TO MAKE IT UP TO MY NEW BRIDE BY SERVING HER BREAKFAST IN BED. MY FRIEND CHEF JEAN-MARIE JOSSELIN HAS A RESTAURANT IN KAUAI CALLED A PACIFIC CAFE, AND I PROCURED ALL OF THE INGREDIENTS FROM HIM TO INVENT A "LOVE LETTER" DISH THAT BRINGS CAVIAR FRONT AND CENTER. I ORIGINALLY CRAFTED THE PARFAIT BY HAND WITHOUT A RING MOLD AND LAYERED IT ALMOST LIKE A CAKE. THIS ROMANTIC CLASSIC HAS BEEN ON MY MENU EVER SINCE AND IS AN ELEGANT WAY TO KICK OFF A SPECIAL MEAL. THE PARFAITS CAN BE MADE A DAY IN ADVANCE; THE ONLY THING THAT NEEDS TO BE COOKED AT THE LAST MINUTE ARE THE POTATOES. IT IS IMPORTANT TO KEEP THE ORDER AND RATIO OF THE LAYERS IN MIND; TOO MUCH SALMON OR CRÈME FRAÎCHE THROWS THE COMPONENTS OFF BALANCE.

WINE SUGGESTION

EGLY-OURIET BLANC DE NOIRS CHAMPAGNE NV

A rich sparkling wine is the only answer to this simple but rich combination of caviar and its accompaniments. The salty caviar needs a refreshing finish. An alternative is a dry Riesling or chilled pure vodka.

MAKES 4 APPETIZER PORTIONS

EGG SALAD (RECIPE FOLLOWS)

WHIPPED CRÈME FRAÎCHE (RECIPE FOLLOWS)

POTATO CAKES (RECIPE FOLLOWS)

6   OUNCES SMOKED SALMON, FINELY CHOPPED (ABOUT 1 CUP)

4   OUNCES CAVIAR, PREFERABLY OSETRA

FRESH DILL LEAVES, FOR GARNISH

EGG SALAD

4   LARGE HARD-BOILED EGGS, PEELED

1 1/2   TEASPOONS FINELY CHOPPED FLAT-LEAF PARSLEY

1   TABLESPOON MINCED RED ONION

KOSHER SALT AND FRESHLY GROUND BLACK PEPPER

PUSH THE HARD-BOILED eggs through a strainer into a small bowl (be sure that the mesh is large enough to allow the egg to pass through the holes). Add the parsley and red onion and toss gently to incorporate. Season lightly with salt and pepper. This may be made a day in advance and stored, covered and refrigerated.

WHIPPED CRÈME FRAÎCHE

3/4   CUP CRÈME FRAÎCHE

2   TEASPOONS FINELY CHOPPED FRESH CHIVES

1   TEASPOON FINELY GRATED LEMON ZEST (FROM 1 LEMON)

GENEROUS PINCH OF KOSHER SALT AND FRESHLY GROUND

BLACK PEPPER

COMBINE THE CRÈME fraîche, chives, and lemon zest in a mixing bowl. Using an electric mixer, beat until very stiff, about 3 minutes. Season with salt and pepper. May be made a day in advance and stored, covered and refrigerated.

POTATO CAKES

2   RUSSET POTATOES (ABOUT 1 1/4 POUNDS)

1/2   LARGE EGG WHITE

2   TABLESPOONS CHOPPED FRESH CHIVES

GENEROUS PINCH OF KOSHER SALT, PLUS ADDITIONAL TO TASTE

CANOLA OIL, FOR FRYING

PREHEAT THE OVEN to 375°F.

WRAP THE POTATOES in aluminum foil and place them in a small baking pan. Transfer to the oven and bake until tender but not totally cooked through, approximately 40 minutes. To test, slice the potatoes in half; the "eye" in the center of the flesh should be opaque and about the size of a quarter. Par-baking the potatoes prevents them from oxidizing.

REFRIGERATE THE POTATOES until completely cool (if they are hot when you grate them, they can become gummy from the starch). This may be done the night before.

PEEL THE POTATOES. Using a box grater, coarsely grate them into a mixing bowl. Fold in the egg white and chives to bind the mixture together; season with a generous pinch of salt.

COAT THE INSIDE of a 3-inch ring mold with nonstick cooking spray. Pack the potatoes into the mold to form a 1/2-inch-high cake. Transfer to a plate, and continue making potato cakes until you have 4. The potato cakes can be formed ahead and refrigerated, for up to a day in advance, but it is best to fry them just before serving.

JUST BEFORE SERVING, shallow fry the potato cakes. Line a plate with a double thickness of paper towels and set aside. Heat 1 inch of oil in a large skillet or electric fryer to 350°F on a frying thermometer. Remove the potato cakes from their mold and add them to the oil. Fry until golden brown and crispy, 4 to 5 minutes, turning several times. Using a slotted spatula, remove the cakes to the prepared plate. While they are still hot, season with a light sprinkling of salt.

COAT THE INTERIORS of four 3-inch ring molds with nonstick spray. Set the molds on a plate or pan. Scoop 4 tablespoons of the Egg Salad into each mold, pressing gently with the bottom of a glass to create an even, compact layer. Repeat the process with the smoked salmon, creating a layer on top of the egg salad. Spoon 2 tablespoons of the Crème Fraîche over the salmon and even it out with the back of a spoon. Finish with about 1 ounce of caviar to cover the top completely, distributing it evenly with your fingers without smashing. Each component should create a distinctive layer; it is crucial that the layers are packed tight so the parfait does not fall apart when you remove the ring. Ideally, the assembly of the parfait should be done in advance and chilled for at least 1 hour to set up or it may "melt" when unmolded. If desired, the dish can be prepared up to this point the day before; simply cover the molds tightly with plastic and refrigerate.

TO ASSEMBLE AND serve: Place a warm Potato Cake in the center of each of 4 plates. Working gently, press the bottom of the parfait to release the seal. Working close to the plate, carefully shake the parfait out through the bottom of the mold and onto the Potato Cake. Garnish the plates with dill and any leftover egg salad.

BLACK MUSSEL SOUFFLÉ
WITH CHARDONNAY-SAFFRON CREAM

THIS DISH HAS BEEN REGARDED AS A CLASSIC FROM THE BEGINNING. FOR SEVERAL YEARS I WORKED AS A PASTRY CHEF AND HAVE ALWAYS LOVED SOUFFLÉS, BOTH SAVORY AND SWEET. THE IDEA BEHIND THIS CONCOCTION CAME FROM ONE OF MY FAVORITE MEALS: SITTING DOWN TO A BIG BOWL OF STEAMED MUSSELS AND DIPPING CRUSTY BREAD IN THE INTENSE, SAVORY BROTH. THE PÂTE À CHOUX DOUGH'S STRUCTURE IS MORE STABLE THAN A STANDARD SOUFFLÉ (MADE PREDOMINANTLY OF EGG WHITES), SO THE SOUFFLÉ IS LESS APT TO DEFLATE. THE WINE AND SAFFRON SAUCE POURED INTO THE SOUFFLÉ IS A SOPHISTICATED WAY TO MARRY ALL THESE TIMELESS FLAVORS.

WINE SUGGESTION

LOUIS MICHEL CHABLIS 'MONTÉE DE TONNERRE' 1ER CRU, BURGUNDY, FRANCE 2000

This dish needs a wine that will stand up to the pungency of saffron. I suggest a creamy Chardonnay with crisp acidity or a dry Riesling with a soft texture. I often surprise guests by suggesting an Austrian Riesling.

MAKES 6 APPETIZER PORTIONS (1 1/3 CUPS SAUCE)

1 1/2	CUPS MILK
1/4	CUP (1/2 STICK) UNSALTED BUTTER, PLUS ADDITIONAL FOR GREASING THE MOLDS
1 1/2	CUPS ALL-PURPOSE FLOUR, PLUS ADDITIONAL FOR DUSTING MOLDS
12	LARGE EGGS (YOU WILL BE USING 6 YOLKS AND 12 WHITES)
3	CUPS CHARDONNAY
8	SHALLOTS, 4 FINELY CHOPPED, 4 COARSELY CHOPPED
5	CLOVES GARLIC, FINELY CHOPPED
2	TABLESPOONS CANOLA OIL
2	POUNDS MUSSELS, SCRUBBED AND DEBEARDED
10	FLAT-LEAF PARSLEY STEMS
2	TABLESPOONS CHOPPED FRESH PARSLEY LEAVES
1 1/4	TEASPOONS KOSHER SALT
1/2	TEASPOON FRESHLY GROUND BLACK PEPPER
1 1/2	CUPS HEAVY CREAM
	PINCH OF SAFFRON THREADS
	PINCH OF CORNSTARCH

TO MAKE THE Pâte à Choux, combine the milk and butter in a heavy-bottomed saucepan over medium heat and bring to a boil. When the butter is completely melted, dump the flour in all at once. Reduce the heat to low and stir vigorously until the dough pulls away from the sides of the saucepan and forms a mass, about 3 to 5 minutes. The dough should not stick to your hands when pressed. You want whatever extra milk the flour doesn't soak up to evaporate. The drier the dough, the more eggs it will hold later. This is what helps make a stable and light soufflé.

SCRAPE THE PÂTE à Choux into the bowl of a standing electric mixer fitted with a paddle attachment. Mix the dough on medium-low speed to cool it off almost completely before beginning to incorporate the eggs (no steam should be rising from the dough).

WITH THE MACHINE running, add the 6 egg yolks, 1 at a time, periodically stopping to scrape down the sides of the bowl. The dough should be sticky and bright yellow. The dough may be prepared a day in advance, covered and refrigerated, or kept frozen for up to 1 month.

COMBINE 1 CUP of the wine, the finely chopped shallots, and garlic in a small saucepan and place over medium heat. Cook until the liquid has totally evaporated, about 15 minutes. Scrape the softened shallots and garlic into the dough.

PLACE THE OIL in a large saucepan over medium-high heat. Add the coarsely chopped shallots and sauté until softened, about 1 minute. Add the mussels, the remaining 2 cups of wine, and parsley stems. Give everything a thorough toss and then cover the pan. Steam until the mussels open, about 6 to 8 minutes.

STRAIN THE MUSSEL broth through a colander into another saucepan. You should have 2 cups of liquid. Set aside while shelling the mussels.

PULL THE MUSSELS out of their shells, discarding any unopened ones. Either by hand or in a food processor, finely chop the mussels. Add the mussels, chopped parsley, salt, and pepper to the dough. Mix the dough with the paddle until all the ingredients are combined.

PLACE THE MUSSEL broth over medium heat and simmer until reduced to 1/2 cup, about 15 to 20 minutes. Pour in the cream, lower the heat, and gently simmer until the sauce is thick enough to coat the back of a spoon, about 8 to 10 minutes. Stir in the saffron. The sauce will become bright yellow. Remove from the heat and cover to keep warm.

IN A SEPARATE clean bowl, beat the 12 egg whites and cornstarch until they hold medium stiff peaks. Fold one-third of the whites into the dough to lighten it. Then gently fold in the remaining whites.

PREHEAT THE OVEN to 375°F. Prepare six 8-ounce soufflé dishes by greasing with softened butter and dusting with flour, shaking off any excess. This coating will keep the soufflés from sticking to the sides and allow them to rise evenly.

USING AN ICE cream scoop, spoon the batter into the prepared dishes, filling to just below the rim. Shake them gently so the batter settles. Place the dishes on a baking pan. Transfer to the middle rack of the oven and bake for about 25 to 30 minutes. The soufflés are done when they puff over the rim by about an inch, the outside crust is golden, and the center is still a bit loose and creamy. Do not overbake.

TO SERVE: PLACE the soufflé dishes on individual plates and present the sauce on the side in a gravy boat or creamer with a spout. Ask each guest to crack open the crust of the Mussel Soufflé with a spoon and pour in the Saffron Cream.

PRAWNS STUFFED WITH DUNGENESS CRAB, ORANGE-JALAPEÑO HOLLANDAISE, HOT-AND-SOUR SAUCE WITH CUCUMBER NOODLES

WITHOUT A DOUBT, THE BOOMING FLAVORS OF THIS DISH ARE BOLD. THE COMPLEX COMBINATION HAS IT ALL—IT IS SPICY, SWEET, AND SOUR, WITH THE CREAMINESS OF THE HOLLANDAISE BINDING IT TOGETHER. THE UNDERCURRENT OF CHILIES BRINGS ON A LINGERING HEAT THAT TANTALIZES AND PERKS UP THE TASTE BUDS. THIS APPETIZER IS SERVED AT MICHAEL MINA AND IS COMMONLY ENJOYED AS A BAR SNACK AND AS A SUBSTANTIAL FIRST COURSE. I LOVE THE TEXTURE OF COOKED CUCUMBERS BECAUSE THEY ARE TENDER YET STILL REMAIN CRISP. WHEN YOU THINK ABOUT IT, A CUCUMBER IS BASICALLY A PICKLE; HERE THEY ARE PICKLED IN THE VINEGAR SAUCE. I THINK THAT CREAMY HOLLANDAISE ON SWEET CRAB IS A DECADENT PAIRING; IT IS MY ODE TO JAPANESE DYNAMITE CRAB. THE ZESTY HOT-AND-SOUR SAUCE IS EXTREMELY VERSATILE; TRY IT AS A DRESSING ON ASIAN GREENS OR AS A DIPPING SAUCE FOR STEAMED LOBSTER OR SHRIMP.

THERE ARE A NUMBER OF COMPONENTS TO THIS DISH. I SUGGEST PREPARING THE CAYENNE MAYONNAISE AND HOT-AND-SOUR SAUCE IN ADVANCE AND REFRIGERATING. WHEN YOU ARE READY TO MAKE THE ENTIRE DISH, PREPARE THE HOLLANDAISE SAUCE AND KEEP WARM WHILE YOU MAKE THE PRAWNS, AND BOIL THE CUCUMBER NOODLES WHILE THE PRAWNS ARE COOKING.

WINE SUGGESTION

TONI JOST RIESLING 'BACHARACHER HAAN,' MITTLERHEIN, GERMANY 2002

This dish calls for a rich, sweet wine, and the spicy Asian flavors always match well with semi-dry Rieslings from Germany.

1/2	TABLESPOON CANOLA OIL
2	TABLESPOONS MINCED YELLOW ONION
1	TABLESPOON MINCED CELERY
1/2	POUND DUNGENESS CRABMEAT, PICKED THROUGH FOR SHELLS AND SHREDDED
1/2	RED JALAPEÑO, SEEDED AND MINCED
1/2	GREEN JALAPEÑO, SEEDED AND MINCED
1/2	CUP CAYENNE MAYONNAISE (RECIPE FOLLOWS)
1	TABLESPOON CHOPPED FLAT-LEAF PARSLEY
	KOSHER SALT AND FRESHLY GROUND BLACK PEPPER
12	PRAWNS, PREFERABLY SPOT PRAWNS, PEELED WITH TAILS ON
	HOT-AND-SOUR SAUCE WITH CUCUMBER NOODLES (RECIPE FOLLOWS)
	ORANGE-JALAPEÑO HOLLANDAISE (RECIPE FOLLOWS)

PLACE THE CANOLA oil in a small sauté pan over medium-low heat. Add the onion and celery and sauté until soft but without color, about 2 to 3 minutes. Set aside to cool.

COMBINE THE CRABMEAT, red and green jalapeños, Cayenne Mayonnaise, parsley, and the cooled onion and celery. Season with salt and pepper. Fold the ingredients together to thoroughly combine. Cover and refrigerate while preparing the prawns.

PREHEAT THE OVEN to 400°F.

USING A SHARP knife, cut the prawns almost all the way through the underside curl of the body and open them flat to resemble a butterfly shape. Pack 1 tablespoon of the crab filling into the cavity of the prawns. Place the prawns tail side up on a baking dish and lightly season with salt and pepper. Add 2 tablespoons of water to the pan to create some steam. Transfer to the oven and bake until the prawns are firm and the stuffing begins to brown on the edges, 10 to 15 minutes.

TO ASSEMBLE AND serve: Divide the Cucumber Noodles among 4 plates, arranging them down the center. Set 3 prawns side by side on top of the cucumbers. Generously spoon the Hollandaise over the Stuffed Prawns, covering all of the stuffing. Spoon 2 tablespoons of the Hot-and-Sour Sauce around the prawns, making sure to get some of the scallion and red pepper in each spoonful.

CAYENNE MAYONNAISE

1	LARGE EGG YOLK
1	TABLESPOON FRESH LEMON JUICE
1	TABLESPOON WATER
1/2	TABLESPOON CAYENNE
1	TEASPOON DIJON MUSTARD
1	CUP CANOLA OIL
	KOSHER SALT AND FRESHLY GROUND BLACK PEPPER

PLACE THE YOLK, lemon juice, water, cayenne, and mustard in a blender or food processor and process to a smooth purée. With the motor running, add the oil in a thin steady stream until the mayonnaise is emulsified and thick. Season with salt and pepper. May be made up to a day in advance and stored, covered and refrigerated. The leftover mayonnaise is terrific on a roast beef or chicken sandwich.

ORANGE-JALAPEÑO HOLLANDAISE

MAKES 1 1/4 CUPS

1	CUP ORANGE JUICE, STRAINED
1	RED JALAPEÑO, STEMMED
1	GREEN JALAPEÑO, STEMMED
1	TABLESPOON CANOLA OIL
	KOSHER SALT
2	LARGE EGG YOLKS
1	CUP WARM CLARIFIED BUTTER (SEE PAGE 221)
1/2	TABLESPOON FINELY CHOPPED FRESH CILANTRO

PLACE THE ORANGE juice in a small saucepan over low heat and bring to a simmer. Cook until it reduces to a thick golden syrup, about 15 minutes. You should have about 3 tablespoons of reduced juice. Remove from the heat and allow to cool.

PREHEAT THE OVEN to 400°F.

PLACE THE JALAPEÑOS in a small baking pan and toss with the canola oil. Season lightly with salt. Transfer to the oven and roast until the skins begin to blister and the jalapeños soften, about 15 minutes. Remove from the oven and, when cool enough to handle, peel off the charred skins and scrape out the seeds. Finely mince the roasted chilies. Set aside.

COMBINE THE COOLED orange syrup with the egg yolks in a stainless steel bowl. Place the bowl over a saucepan containing barely simmering water (or use a double boiler); the water should not touch the bottom of the bowl. Whisk vigorously until the mixture forms yellow ribbons when lifted. If the eggs begin to scramble or the mixture gets too hot, remove the bowl from the heat and whisk to cool.

REMOVE THE BOWL from the pan and slowly drizzle in the Clarified Butter and continue to whisk until the hollandaise is thickened and doubled in volume, about 3 minutes. Stir in the jalapeños, cilantro, and a pinch of salt. Cover tightly with plastic wrap and place in a warm spot until ready to use. If the hollandaise gets too thick, whisk in a few drops of warm water to adjust the consistency so it is creamy and light.

HOT-AND-SOUR SAUCE WITH CUCUMBER NOODLES

MAKES 3/4 CUP

2	CUPS PINEAPPLE JUICE, STRAINED
2	CUPS FRESH ORANGE JUICE, STRAINED
1/2	CUP FRESH LEMON JUICE, STRAINED
1/4	CUP FRESH LIME JUICE, STRAINED
4	SCALLIONS, WHITE AND GREEN PARTS, CHOPPED
2	SHALLOTS, SLICED
3	CLOVES GARLIC, SMASHED
1-INCH	PIECE GINGER, SLICED
1/4	HABANERO CHILE, SEEDED
2	TABLESPOONS SUGAR
2	TABLESPOONS HONEY
1/3	CUP RICE VINEGAR
1	TEASPOON SOY SAUCE
2	TABLESPOONS SESAME OIL
1	ENGLISH CUCUMBER, PEELED, SEEDED, AND JULIENNED
1	SCALLION, GREEN PART ONLY, CUT ON A BIAS
1/2	RED BELL PEPPER, SEEDED, MEMBRANE REMOVED, AND MINCED

COMBINE THE PINEAPPLE, orange, lemon, and lime juices together in a bowl or pitcher. Set aside.

IN A LARGE saucepan, combine the chopped scallions, shallots, garlic, ginger, and habanero. Add the sugar, honey, and 2 tablespoons of the mixed juice. Place over medium-low heat and cook until the moisture evaporates from the vegetables and the sugar gets syrupy, about 5 minutes, stirring often to prevent scorching. Mix in the vinegar and soy sauce, and cook until the vegetables are soft and the flavor is balanced between hot and sour, another 3 minutes.

ADD THE REMAINING juice mixture and simmer until the liquid has reduced by about one-third and has body, about 30 minutes. The sauce should have thickened considerably due to all of the natural fruit sugars.

REMOVE FROM THE heat and pass the sauce through a fine-mesh strainer into a clean saucepan, discarding the solids. The sauce can be made in advance to this point and stored, covered and refrigerated, up to 3 days. Gently reheat before finishing the recipe.

WHEN READY TO serve, bring the sauce to a simmer over medium heat. Whisk in the sesame oil. Stir in the cucumber "noodles" and cook until they begin to soften like spaghetti but still remain crisp in the center, about 2 minutes. Using tongs, remove the cucumbers to a side plate, letting the excess sauce drip off. Remove the sauce from the heat and stir in the scallion greens and bell pepper.

MAINE LOBSTER POTPIE

MY WIFE AND I LOVE TO ENTERTAIN AT HOME ON SUNDAYS, MY DAY OFF. THIS IS WHEN I TRY OUT IDEAS THAT INEVITABLY BECOME ITEMS ON MY MENU. THE FIRST TIME I MADE THIS DISH WAS WHEN I HAD FRIENDS COMING OVER FOR A POOL PARTY. ORIGINALLY, I PREPARED A GIANT LOBSTER POTPIE TO FEED A CROWD AND SIMPLY REPLACED THE TRADITIONAL CHICKEN WITH SUCCULENT LOBSTER, AND EVERYBODY JUST DEVOURED IT.

WE WENT THROUGH SOME GROWING PAINS WITH THE EVOLUTION OF THE DISH TO REFINE IT ENOUGH FOR THE RESTAURANTS. I FINE-TUNED THE RECIPE BY COOKING THE LOBSTER IN THE SHELL TO PROTECT THE DELICATE MEAT FROM TOUGHENING. I NOW SERVE IT IN INDIVIDUAL COPPER POTS FOR A DRAMATIC TABLESIDE PRESENTATION. WHEN THE SERVER GRACEFULLY REMOVES THE FLAKY PASTRY CAP, STEAM FROM THE POTPIE RISES INTO THE AIR AND THE HEAVENLY SCENT FILLS THE DINING ROOM. CURIOUS ONLOOKERS OFTEN TAKE NOTICE AND ORDER SOME FOR THEMSELVES! WITHOUT QUESTION, THIS IS OUR MOST SOUGHT-AFTER RECIPE. YOU WILL NEED FOUR 1-QUART SOUFFLÉ DISHES TO COMPLETE THIS RECIPE. A GOOD TIP IS TO SOAK THE PEARL ONIONS IN WATER FOR 15 MINUTES TO SOFTEN THE SKINS SO THEY ARE EASIER TO PEEL. IF YOU ARE PRESSED FOR TIME, FROZEN PUFF PASTRY SHEETS MAY BE SUBSTITUTED FOR THE HOMEMADE DOUGH. THE VEGETABLES CAN ALSO BE ADJUSTED TO YOUR PERSONAL PREFERENCES AS WELL AS SEASONAL AVAILABILITY.

WINE SUGGESTION

AU BON CLIMAT CHARDONNAY 'SANFORD & BENEDICT,' SANTA YNEZ VALLEY 1998

This rich dish screams for a viscous and buttery wine, so a classic California Chardonnay is perfect. I selected an older Chardonnay from one of the greatest winemakers in America, Jim Clendenen. Another great pairing would be a ripe white Burgundy from a soft vintage.

SERVES 4 (MAKES 3 1/2 CUPS LOBSTER CREAM SAUCE)

1   RECIPE PÂTE BRISÉE/PIE DOUGH (PAGE 193)

LOBSTERS

4   LIVE MAINE LOBSTERS (1 1/2 POUNDS EACH)
1   TABLESPOON SEA SALT
   ICE BATH

LOBSTER CREAM SAUCE

4   TABLESPOONS VEGETABLE OIL
1   CUP BRANDY
2   STALKS CELERY, COARSELY CHOPPED
2   CLOVES GARLIC, SMASHED
1   YELLOW ONION, COARSELY CHOPPED
1   CARROT, COARSELY CHOPPED
1/2   BULB FENNEL, COARSELY CHOPPED
1/4   CUP TOMATO PASTE
1   CUP DRY WHITE WINE, SUCH AS SAUVIGNON BLANC
1   QUART HEAVY CREAM
3   SPRIGS FRESH THYME
1   BAY LEAF, PREFERABLY FRESH
1   TEASPOON WHOLE BLACK PEPPERCORNS
1   TEASPOON CORIANDER SEEDS
2   TABLESPOONS UNSALTED BUTTER
2   TABLESPOONS ALL-PURPOSE FLOUR
   KOSHER SALT AND FRESHLY GROUND BLACK PEPPER

VEGETABLE FILLING

1   TABLESPOON UNSALTED BUTTER
1/2   POUND ASSORTED WILD MUSHROOMS, SUCH AS CHANTERELLES
   AND OYSTER, WIPED OF GRIT AND HALVED IF LARGE
2   LARGE EGGS BEATEN WITH 2 TABLESPOONS WATER
   TO MAKE AN EGG WASH
12   WHITE PEARL ONIONS, PEELED AND HALVED LENGTHWISE
8   BABY CARROTS, GREEN TOPS TRIMMED, HALVED LENGTHWISE
3   FINGERLING POTATOES, SLICED
1/2   SMALL GREEN ZUCCHINI, SLICED IN HALF MOONS
1/2   SMALL YELLOW SQUASH, SLICED IN HALF MOONS
1/4   CUP ASSORTED CHOPPED FRESH HERBS, SUCH AS CHIVES,
   PARSLEY, THYME, AND CHERVIL
4   TEASPOONS WHITE TRUFFLE OIL (OPTIONAL)
1   FRESH TRUFFLE, SLICED PAPER-THIN (OPTIONAL)

PREPARE AND CHILL the Pie Dough as directed in the recipe.

TO COOK THE lobsters: Place the lobsters in the freezer for 20 to 30 minutes to numb them.

FILL A LARGE stockpot three-quarters full with cold water and add the sea salt. Bring to a rapid boil over medium-high heat.

TRANSFER THE IMMOBILE lobsters to a cutting board. Working with 1 lobster at a time, and holding the lobster securely with a kitchen towel to protect your hands, insert the tip of a chef's knife at the base of the head, parallel to the body, and swiftly cut completely through the head between the antennas.

USE A SIDEWAYS twist to break the claws, knuckles, and tails off of the lobsters. Reserve the bodies for making the sauce.

PLACE THE CLAWS and knuckles in the boiling water and boil for 1 minute. Add the lobster tails and continue to boil for an additional 4 minutes (the tails will be only cooked about halfway). Using a slotted spoon, transfer all the lobster pieces to the ice bath; let sit for at least 5 minutes to ensure the cooking process has stopped.

TO REMOVE THE meat from the claws, pull the "thumb" of the claws off and remove the inner cartilage. Lay the claws flat on a cutting board and carefully tap with the blade of a chef's knife to crack. Gently wiggle the meat out from the shell and place it in a large bowl.

USING KITCHEN SHEARS, cut open the knuckles and discard the shells. Add the lobster meat to the bowl.

LAY THE LOBSTER tails on a cutting board, shell side up, and hold with a kitchen towel to steady. Using a serrated knife, make 3 cuts crosswise between the joints so that you have 4 sections, including the tail fan. Add the lobster pieces to the bowl. Cover the bowl with plastic wrap and transfer to the refrigerator to chill until ready to use. The lobster may be prepared a day in advance.

WHEN CLEANING THE lobster bodies, it is best to wear kitchen gloves to protect your hands. Firmly pull the bodies and shells apart. When all of the bodies have been separated, use a tablespoon to scrape off the feathery gills and clean out the roe and innards from the underside of the shell. Coarsely chop the lobster shells and bodies.

TO MAKE THE sauce: Place a large stockpot over medium-high heat and coat with 2 tablespoons of the oil. When the oil gets hazy, add the cleaned lobster shells and bodies. Cook, stirring often, until the shells are well seared and bright red, about 3 to 5 minutes. Shells equal flavor.

TO KEEP THE alcohol from flaming, remove the pot from the heat and pour in the brandy. Carefully return the pot to the stove and cook until the brandy is almost totally evaporated. Push the shells to the sides of the pot and add the remaining 2 tablespoons of oil and the celery, garlic, onion, carrot, and fennel. Cook, stirring occasionally, until the vegetables are tender and begin to caramelize, 10 to 15 minutes. Stir in the tomato paste and cook for about 2 minutes until the color deepens. Add the wine and stir to deglaze the pot, scraping up the bits from the bottom with a wooden spoon. Continue cooking until all of the liquid is evaporated, about 1 minute.

ADD THE CREAM, thyme, bay leaf, peppercorns, and coriander. Reduce the heat to low and simmer until the sauce turns light orange and tastes like lobster, 15 to 20 minutes. Pass the sauce through a fine-mesh strainer into a clean saucepan to remove the solids, using a spoon or spatula to press out all the juice. Place over medium heat and bring the lobster cream to a simmer. Season lightly with salt and pepper. Remove from the heat and set aside.

IN A SMALL saucepan, slowly melt 1 tablespoon of the butter over low heat. Just as the foam subsides, sprinkle in the flour, stirring constantly with a wooden spoon to cook the starchy taste out of the flour. Cook for 1 minute, without allowing the flour to color.

SLOWLY WHISK THE roux into the lobster cream. Cook for 1 minute, stirring constantly to prevent lumps. The lobster cream should be thick enough to coat the back of a spoon. Remove from the heat. Cover to keep warm.

TO PREPARE THE filling: Place a sauté pan over medium-high heat. Add the butter and once it gets foamy, add the mushrooms. Season with salt and pepper and sauté until the mushrooms release their moisture and begin to brown, about 3 to 4 minutes. Remove from the heat.

PLACE AN EQUAL portion of the sautéed mushrooms, onions, carrots, potatoes, zucchini, and yellow squash evenly into each soufflé dish. Remove the lobster meat from the refrigerator and place the equivalent of 1 whole lobster into each dish. Ladle 1/2 cup of the warm lobster cream sauce into each dish, sprinkle with the chopped herbs, a drizzle of truffle oil, and a few slices of black truffle.

PREHEAT THE OVEN to 425°F.

TO ASSEMBLE: REMOVE the dough from the refrigerator and set it on the counter for 5 minutes to warm up and to make it easier to roll out. Sprinkle the counter and a rolling pin lightly with flour. Roll the dough out to a 1/4-inch thickness. Cut the dough into 4 circles, 1 inch larger than the diameter of the soufflé dishes (you need four 1-quart dishes). Using a pastry brush, lightly coat the outer edges of the pastry circles with the egg wash.

CAREFULLY CAP EACH dish with a pastry circle, egg wash side down, pressing the dough around the rim to form a tight seal. Brush the tops very lightly with egg wash and sprinkle with a little salt (preferably sea salt). Set the dishes on a baking sheet and transfer to the oven. Bake for 30 minutes, rotating halfway through cooking, until the potpie is puffed and golden.

TO SERVE: RUN a knife around the inside rims of the soufflé dishes. Using a fork and spoon, carefully remove the dome cap and place it in the center of a serving plate. For a great presentation, arrange the pieces of lobster on top of the pastry, scatter the vegetables decoratively all around, and drizzle the lobster cream sauce over everything.

PÂTE BRISÉE / PIE DOUGH

2 1/2	CUPS ALL-PURPOSE FLOUR, SIFTED, PLUS MORE FOR DUSTING
1	TEASPOON KOSHER SALT
1	CUP (2 STICKS) COLD UNSALTED BUTTER, CUT INTO CHUNKS
4	TO 6 TABLESPOONS ICE WATER

PLACE THE FLOUR and salt in the food processor and pulse to combine. Add the butter cubes, a few at a time, pulsing until the mixture looks like small peas. Slowly add the ice water, a little at a time, until the dough starts to come together without being too wet or sticky (you may not need all the water). Pinch a small amount together; if it is crumbly, add more ice water, 1 teaspoon at a time. Form the dough into a disk and wrap in plastic wrap. Transfer to the refrigerator and chill for at least 1 hour. The dough can be made 1 day in advance.

SALMON WELLINGTON WITH BRAISED
SAVOY CABBAGE AND FOIE GRAS EMULSION

I JUST LOVE THIS HEARTY WINTERTIME MEAL—IT IS COMFORT FOOD AT ITS FINEST. PEOPLE OFTEN ASK ME WHAT MY FAVORITE DISH IS AND SALMON WELLINGTON IS DEFINITELY IN THE TOP THREE. I HAVE ALWAYS BEEN A FAN OF TREATING FISH LIKE MEAT, WHICH I BELIEVE IS A BIG PART OF THE SUCCESS OF AQUA RESTAURANT. BEEF WELLINGTON HAS BEEN AROUND FOR YEARS AND THIS VARIATION TAKES THE CONCEPT TO THE NEXT LEVEL. AS A CHEF, I PLACE TREMENDOUS VALUE ON TECHNIQUE. THE PROCEDURE OF WRAPPING THE SALMON REQUIRES ACCURACY AND SKILL TO DO IT RIGHT; IF THE PASTRY IS TOO THICK, THE SALMON WILL OVERCOOK BEFORE THE DOUGH IS DONE. THE CABBAGE AND APPLES ADD RUSTICITY TO AN OTHERWISE ELEGANT DISH, WHILE THE BACON IMPARTS A SMOKY DEPTH. THE SILKY FOIE GRAS EMULSION PUSHES THE DISH OVER THE EDGE IN TERMS OF DECADENCE, BUT THE SALMON IS THE REAL STAR OF THE SHOW WITH ITS MELT-AWAY TEXTURE AND SUBLIME FLAVOR.

WINE SUGGESTION

HERMITAGE BLANC, RHONE, FRANCE 2002

This wine by J. L. Chave is a great Marsienne and Roussanne blend, with a baked apple and fennel-like flavor that adds spark to the rich foie gras emulsion. A light Pinot Noir would also be a good match.

2 FROZEN PUFF PASTRY SHEETS, THAWED
  ALL-PURPOSE FLOUR, FOR DUSTING
FOUR 6-OUNCE SKINLESS CENTER-CUT SALMON FILLETS,
  ABOUT 1/2 INCH THICK
  KOSHER SALT AND FRESHLY GROUND BLACK PEPPER
4 TEASPOONS TRUFFLE BUTTER, AT ROOM TEMPERATURE
  (SEE SOURCES)
8 SLICES FRESH BLACK TRUFFLE (OPTIONAL)
1 LARGE EGG BEATEN WITH 1 TABLESPOON WATER
  TO MAKE AN EGG WASH
  COARSE SEA SALT
  BRAISED SAVOY CABBAGE (RECIPE FOLLOWS)
  FOIE GRAS EMULSION (RECIPE FOLLOWS)
12 FRESH CHIVES, CUT INTO 1/2-INCH BATONS, FOR GARNISH

WORKING WITH 1 piece at a time, lay the puff pastry sheets on a lightly floured surface and, using a rolling pin, roll them out to a 12-inch square about 1/8 inch thick. Cut each square in half, to create four 12-by-6-inch pieces.

SLICE THE SALMON fillets in half horizontally to make two 3-ounce pieces. Season the fish well on all sides with salt and pepper. Coat the surface of the salmon with a bit of the truffle butter and lay 1 slice of truffle on top. Stack one salmon half on top of the other to create 4 even blocks, about 1 inch thick. Working with one piece at a time, place each block of salmon in the center of a piece of pastry, truffle side down. Using a paring knife, trim away the excess dough so you have even squares with about 2 1/2 inches remaining around the salmon. Cut out the 4 corners of the dough squares to form a cross (+) shape in order to limit the overlap of dough when you wrap the salmon. Using a pastry brush, lightly coat the dough flaps with the egg wash and fold them over the salmon to completely enclose. Press the pastry around the salmon to tightly seal. Flip the salmon over and place them, seam side down, on a platter. Cover and refrigerate while you prepare the Cabbage and Foie Gras Emulsion. (The salmon may be made up to 8 hours in advance.)

PREHEAT THE OVEN to 500°F. Coat a sheet pan with nonstick spray.

PLACE THE PASTRY-WRAPPED salmon on the prepared pan, leaving space around each so air can circulate during baking. Lightly brush the remaining egg wash on all sides of the pastry and season the tops with coarse sea salt. Bake until the pastry is golden brown and the salmon is medium-rare, 15 to 20 minutes.

REMOVE THE SALMON from the oven and place on a cutting board and allow to rest for 1 minute. Using a very sharp, thin-bladed knife, carefully slice each Salmon Wellington in half on the diagonal. Season the cut side of the salmon with salt and pepper.

TO ASSEMBLE AND serve: Mound a large spoonful of the Braised Cabbage in the center of each plate. Place 2 triangles of Salmon Wellington on top of the cabbage with the cut sides facing out. Spoon the Foie Gras Emulsion around and garnish with chives and any leftover truffle shavings.

BRAISED SAVOY CABBAGE

1/2 POUND APPLEWOOD SMOKED SLAB BACON, DICED
2 TABLESPOONS UNSALTED BUTTER
1 SMALL YELLOW ONION, CUT INTO MEDIUM DICE
1 HEAD SAVOY CABBAGE, HALVED LENGTHWISE,
  AND THEN CUT CROSSWISE INTO RIBBONS
  KOSHER SALT AND FRESHLY GROUND BLACK PEPPER
1/2 CUP APPLE JUICE, PREFERABLY FRESH
1 GRANNY SMITH APPLE, PEELED, CORED, AND DICED

LINE A PLATE with paper towels and set aside.

PLACE THE BACON in a large sauté pan over medium-low heat and fry until the fat is rendered and the bacon is crisp, about 5 minutes. Using a slotted spoon, transfer the bacon to the prepared plate to drain. Set aside. Leave all the fat in the pan and add the butter to it. Once the butter has melted, add the onion. Cook, stirring, until translucent, about 1 minute. Add the cabbage and turn it over with a wooden spoon to coat in the fat and slowly wilt. Season with salt and pepper. When the cabbage begins to soften, add the apple juice to keep the cabbage from browning. Cook until the liquid has evaporated, 1 to 2 minutes. Fold in the apple and reserved bacon, season lightly with salt and pepper, and give the cabbage another toss to combine. Remove from the heat and cover to keep warm.

FOIE GRAS EMULSION

MAKES 1 1/2 CUPS

2	CUPS CHICKEN STOCK (PAGE 222)
1/4	POUND GRADE B DUCK FOIE GRAS, CUT INTO CHUNKS
1/4	CUP (1/2 STICK) COLD UNSALTED BUTTER, CUT INTO CHUNKS
1/4	CUP PINOT NOIR REDUCTION (PAGE 221)
	KOSHER SALT AND FRESHLY GROUND BLACK PEPPER

PLACE THE CHICKEN Stock in a 2-quart saucepan over medium heat. Bring to a simmer and cook until reduced by half, 8 to 10 minutes. Add the foie gras and simmer gently until some of the fat has melted, about 5 minutes (you should still see chunks of foie).

POUR THE MIXTURE into a blender or food processor and process on medium speed to a smooth purée. With the motor running, add the butter, a tablespoon at a time, until the mixture thickens and becomes silky. Add the Pinot Noir Reduction and blend until foamy. Season lightly with salt and pepper.

WHOLE FRIED CHICKEN
WITH TRUFFLED MACARONI AND CHEESE
AND CARAMELIZED ONION SAUCE

THIS DISH REPRESENTS MY PASSION FOR MODERN AMERICAN-STYLE FOOD. TO ME, NOTHING IS BETTER THAN CHICKEN COOKED TO ORDER WITH MORSELS OF GOLDEN, CRISP SKIN AND PLUMP, JUICY MEAT.

AT MY RESTAURANTS, THE FRIED CHICKEN IS TREATED IN THE SAME MANNER AS CHINESE PEKING DUCK BY FIRST BEING RUBBED WITH A SALT CURE AND THEN HUNG INSIDE THE WALK-IN REFRIGERATOR OVERNIGHT WITH FANS BLOWING ON IT TO AIR-DRY. THIS TECHNIQUE TIGHTENS UP THE SKIN SO THAT IT WILL BE REALLY CRISPY WHEN FRIED. AT SERVICE, A CART IS WHEELED THROUGH THE DINING ROOM WHERE THE BIRD IS SECURED BY A SPIKED CUTTING BOARD AND EXPERTLY CARVED AT THE TABLE. WHILE UNCTUOUS DUCK FAT IMPARTS A DISTINCTIVE RICHNESS TO THE FRYING OIL, PEANUT OIL ALONE CAN BE USED. TRUFFLED MACARONI AND CHEESE HAS A FAIR AMOUNT OF CHICKEN MEAT IN IT AND CAN BE SERVED ON ITS OWN. PEAS AND CARROTS WITH CIPOLLINI ONIONS MAKE THE PERFECT SIDE DISH.

WINE SUGGESTION

AU BON CLIMAT PINOT NOIR 'KNOX ALEXANDER,' SANTA MARIA VALLEY 2001

Chicken can work with a number of different wines—Chardonnay, Pinot Noir, Gamay, and Dolcetto, to name a few. In this instance I recommend a perfumey Pinot Noir from the Santa Maria Valley. Although a red Burgundy could be used, I think an American wine is needed to work with the Truffled Macaroni and Cheese.

SERVES 4

	APPROXIMATELY 2 QUARTS PEANUT OIL
	(OR 1 GALLON IF NOT USING DUCK FAT)
	APPROXIMATELY 2 QUARTS RENDERED DUCK FAT
3	TABLESPOONS TRUFFLE BUTTER, AT ROOM TEMPERATURE
	(SEE SOURCES)
1	TEASPOON MINCED FRESH FLAT-LEAF PARSLEY
1	TEASPOON MINCED FRESH CHIVES
1	TEASPOON MINCED FRESH THYME LEAVES
ONE	2- TO 2 1/2-POUND WHOLE CHICKEN,
	PREFERABLY KOSHER OR FREE RANGE
1	FRESH TRUFFLE, SLICED PAPER-THIN
	KOSHER SALT AND FRESHLY GROUND BLACK PEPPER
	TRUFFLED MACARONI AND CHEESE (RECIPE FOLLOWS)
	CARAMELIZED ONION SAUCE (RECIPE FOLLOWS)

FILL A VERY large pot or deep fryer three-quarters full with the peanut oil and duck fat. Place over high heat and bring to 325°F on a frying thermometer attached to the side of the pot.

WHILE THE OIL is heating, mix the truffle butter, parsley, chives, and thyme in a small bowl. Set aside.

WORKING VERY GENTLY, lift up and peel back the skin from the chicken breast, taking care not to tear the skin. Slip the truffle slices under the skin without overlapping. Save any truffle scraps to garnish the serving plates. Heavily season both the exterior and the cavity of the chicken with salt and pepper.

PLACE THE CHICKEN in a fryer basket and carefully lower it into the hot oil and place a metal strainer on top to keep it submerged. The temperature of the oil will drop a bit, but should rise back up in a couple of minutes. It will take 20 to 25 minutes for a 2- to 2 1/2-pound chicken to cook through (about 10 minutes per pound). The chicken is done when the internal temperature reaches 165 to 170°F on an instant-read meat thermometer and the skin is light golden brown.

WHILE THE CHICKEN is cooking, prepare the Macaroni and Cheese and onion sauce.

CAREFULLY LIFT THE basket out of the hot oil. Transfer the chicken to a wire rack with a pan underneath to catch the oil that drains off. Be especially mindful to drain the oil that collects inside the cavity. Let the chicken rest for 5 to 10 minutes to let the juices settle.

USING A PASTRY brush, coat the exterior of the fried chicken with the truffle butter and herb mixture.

PLACE THE CHICKEN on a cutting board and pull the leg away from the body slightly in order to expose the joint. Using a sharp, thin-bladed knife, remove the legs at the thigh joint. You may want to separate the thigh from the drumstick also. Repeat the same process with the wings. Carefully cut along each side of the breastbone, following the contour of the bone down to remove all of the meat. Cut the breast meat into pieces and season the entire chicken with salt and pepper.

TRUFFLED MACARONI AND CHEESE

1/2	POUND ELBOW MACARONI
4	SKINLESS CHICKEN THIGHS
	KOSHER SALT AND FRESHLY GROUND BLACK PEPPER
4	TABLESPOONS CANOLA OIL
1	YELLOW ONION, SLICED
2	CLOVES GARLIC, SMASHED
10	SPRIGS FRESH THYME
1/2	TABLESPOON UNSALTED BUTTER
1	TABLESPOON ALL-PURPOSE FLOUR
2	CUPS CHICKEN STOCK (PAGE 222)
1	CUP HEAVY CREAM

1/4   POUND PARMIGIANO-REGGIANO OR ASIAGO CHEESE,
          COARSELY GRATED (1 1/2 CUPS)

1   TABLESPOON WHITE TRUFFLE OIL

1   TEASPOON CHOPPED FRESH THYME LEAVES

PLACE THE MACARONI in a saucepan of lightly salted boiling water and boil until tender but still firm, about 8 minutes. Drain well and set aside.

SEASON THE CHICKEN well with salt and pepper. Place the oil in a high-sided sauté pan over medium-low heat. When hot, add the chicken. Fry until brown, about 3 minutes, then turn the pieces over with tongs, and brown the other side for 3 minutes more (the chicken will not be fully cooked at this point). Transfer the chicken to a side platter. Keep the pan on the heat.

ADD THE ONION, garlic, and thyme sprigs to the chicken drippings. Sauté until the onions are transparent, about 5 minutes. Add the butter and flour, stirring to combine.

ADD THE CHICKEN Stock and bring to a simmer. When it begins to bubble, nestle the thighs into the liquid. Simmer gently until the chicken is fully cooked, 5 to 8 minutes. Using tongs, transfer the chicken to a side platter to cool slightly.

KEEPING THE PAN on the heat, whisk the cream into the sauce and gently simmer for 2 to 3 minutes. Pass the sauce through a fine-mesh strainer into a clean saucepan. Place over medium-low heat and add the cheese. Whisking constantly, cook until the cheese has completely melted. Remove from the heat and season lightly with salt and pepper.

WHEN THE CHICKEN is cool enough to handle, pull the meat off the bones, discarding any fat or gristle. Fold the shredded chicken into the cheese sauce. Add the cooked macaroni, stirring to combine. Before serving, mix in the truffle oil and chopped thyme.

CARAMELIZED ONION SAUCE

MAKES 1 CUP

2   TABLESPOONS CANOLA OIL

4   YELLOW ONIONS, SLICED

1   CUP DRY WHITE WINE, SUCH AS SAUVIGNON BLANC

5   SPRIGS FRESH THYME

1   BAY LEAF, PREFERABLY FRESH

1/4   TEASPOON WHOLE BLACK PEPPERCORNS

3   CUPS CHICKEN STOCK (PAGE 222)

2   TABLESPOONS VEAL DEMI-GLACE (PAGE 222 OR STORE-BOUGHT)

1/4   CUP (1/2 STICK) UNSALTED BUTTER

PLACE A LARGE saucepan over medium heat and coat with the oil. When the oil gets hazy, add the onions, stirring to coat. Sauté until the onions soften and reach a deep caramel color, about 15 minutes.

ADD THE WINE and deglaze the pan, scraping the bottom with a wooden spoon to loosen the brown bits. Simmer, stirring occasionally, until the wine has reduced and the liquid is almost totally evaporated, about 3 minutes.

ADD THE THYME, bay leaf, and peppercorns, stirring to blend. Add the Chicken Stock and Veal Demi-Glace and bring to a boil. Reduce the heat and simmer until the sauce has a deep onion flavor and is reduced by half, about 30 minutes.

REMOVE FROM THE heat and pass the sauce through a fine-mesh sieve into another small saucepan, pressing on the onions with a spatula to extract as much juice as possible. Discard the solids. Place the sauce over medium-low heat and stir in the butter. Lightly season with salt and pepper and keep warm over low heat.

TO ASSEMBLE AND serve: Mound an equal portion of the Truffled Macaroni and Cheese on each of 4 plates. Lay pieces of the fried chicken on top, and drizzle the Caramelized Onion Sauce all around. Garnish with any leftover truffle shavings.

MISO-GLAZED CHILEAN SEA BASS TAGINE
WITH PEPPER CRAB BROTH
AND ISRAELI COUSCOUS

THIS IS A SIGNATURE AT SEABLUE, ONE OF MY RESTAURANTS IN LAS VEGAS, WHERE NONE OF THE DISHES ON THE MENU, WITH THE EXCEPTION OF DESSERTS, CONTAINS BUTTER OR CREAM. THE REASON A MOROCCAN TAGINE (A CONICAL-SHAPED, EARTHENWARE COOKING VESSEL) WORKS SO WELL IS THAT THE GENTLE STEAM KEEPS THE FISH MOIST WITHOUT ADDING MUCH LIQUID BACK INTO IT; THIS CAPTURES ALL THE DELICATE FLAVOR AND AROMA OF THE FISH ITSELF. IF YOU DO NOT HAVE A TAGINE, A COVERED CASSEROLE DISH OR DUTCH OVEN IS AN ACCEPTABLE SUBSTITUTE. MY PRIMARY FOCUS IS TO PRODUCE CLEAN FLAVORS THAT BLEND WELL. I DON'T GET TOO HUNG UP ON STRICT PARAMETERS WHICH DICTATE THAT BECAUSE I LIKE COOKING WITH A MOROCCAN POT, THEN I MUST USE INGREDIENTS FROM THAT PART OF THE WORLD. I LOVE TO EXPERIMENT WITH ALL TYPES OF ETHNIC CUISINE. THE ASIAN ESSENCE IN THIS DISH IS THE RESULT OF A FOOD EVENT IN SINGAPORE. EVERY NIGHT AFTER SERVICE WE WOULD ALL GO OUT FOR PEPPERED CRABS. I COULD HARDLY WAIT FOR THE END OF THE DAY TO TASTE THEM; THIS NIGHTLY EXCURSION WAS A HIGHLIGHT OF MY TRIP. THE SPICY-SWEET FLAVOR OF PEPPERED CRABS IS IRRESISTIBLE, AND AS SOON AS I RETURNED TO THE STATES I HAD TO INCORPORATE IT INTO A DISH. THE TROUBLE IS, THE NATURE OF EATING PEPPERED CRABS IS SUCH THAT YOU UNAVOIDABLY MAKE A MESS, AND WHILE THAT IS PART OF THE FUN, IT JUST DOES NOT WORK FOR FINE DINING. I FOOLED AROUND WITH THE IDEA FOR A BIT AND CAME UP WITH THIS DISH. IF CHILEAN SEA BASS IS NOT AVAILABLE, ANY FIRM AND FATTY WHITE FISH WORKS REALLY WELL, SUCH AS BLACK COD.

WINE SUGGESTION

HEIDI SCHROCK MUSCAT, RUST, AUSTRIA 2004

After trying hundreds of wines, I found the perfect match for this dish. The earthy flavors of the pepper and the perfumelike Muscat work like magic. Other aromatic whites like Gewurtztraminer and Viognier could also be used.

MISO-GLAZED CHILEAN SEA BASS TAGINE

SERVES 4

MARINADE

1	CUP WHITE OR YELLOW MISO
1/3	CUP GRANULATED SUGAR
1/3	CUP DARK BROWN SUGAR, LOOSELY PACKED
3	TABLESPOONS MIRIN
3	TABLESPOONS DRY SAKE
2	TABLESPOONS WATER
1	TABLESPOON SOY SAUCE

FOUR	6-OUNCE SKINLESS CHILEAN SEA BASS FILLETS
8	BABY CARROTS, HALVED
4	CHINESE LONG BEANS, CUT INTO 2-INCH PIECES
4	OYSTER MUSHROOMS, WIPED OF GRIT AND HALVED
4	SMALL RADISHES, QUARTERED
1	SMALL RED JALAPEÑO, SLICED
1/4	CUP SHELLED SOYBEANS (EDAMAME)
2	OUNCES DUNGENESS CRABMEAT, PREFERABLY FROM THE LEG
	PEPPER CRAB BROTH (RECIPE FOLLOWS)
	ISRAELI COUSCOUS (RECIPE FOLLOWS)

TO MAKE THE marinade: Combine the miso, granulated and brown sugars, mirin, sake, water, and soy in a large bowl. Whisk to dissolve the miso and sugar (the marinade will be fairly thick).

PLACE THE FISH in a shallow baking dish and pour the marinade over it. Cover with plastic and refrigerate for at least 8 hours or up to 2 days.

PREPARE THE PEPPER Crab Broth and Couscous.

PREHEAT THE BROILER.

REMOVE THE FISH from the marinade, letting the excess drip off. Place the fish in a single layer on a broiler pan, making sure to leave space between the fillets. Broil until the fish is caramelized and slightly charred on top, 3 to 4 minutes.

PREHEAT THE OVEN to 425°F.

SCATTER THE CARROTS, beans, mushrooms, radishes, jalapeño, soybeans, and crabmeat in the tagine. Lay the fish on top of the vegetables, broiled side up. Pour 2 cups of the hot Pepper Crab Broth into the tagine. Cover and transfer to the oven.

BAKE FOR 15 to 20 minutes or until a knife pierces the fish without any resistance.

TO SERVE: PRESENT the dish in the tagine or transfer to a large bowl. Serve with the Israeli Couscous on the side.

MAKES ABOUT 1 QUART

4	TABLESPOONS CANOLA OIL
TWO	1 1/2-POUND LIVE DUNGENESS CRABS
2	CUPS DRY SHERRY
5	CLOVES GARLIC, SMASHED
2	BUNCHES SCALLIONS, WHITE AND GREEN PARTS, COARSELY CHOPPED
1	CARROT, COARSELY CHOPPED
1	STALK CELERY, COARSELY CHOPPED
1	YELLOW ONION, COARSELY CHOPPED
ONE	3-INCH PIECE OF GINGER, SLICED
1/2	CUP ASSORTED WHOLE PEPPERCORNS, SUCH AS BLACK, WHITE, PINK, AND GREEN
2	TABLESPOONS CORIANDER SEEDS
1	BUNCH FRESH CILANTRO, STEMS TRIMMED, COARSELY CHOPPED
1	QUART CHICKEN STOCK (SEE PAGE 222)
1	CUP CLAM JUICE
2	TABLESPOONS HONEY
2	TABLESPOONS SOY SAUCE
	KOSHER SALT AND FRESHLY GROUND BLACK PEPPER

PREPARE AN ICE bath. Set aside.

PLACE THE CRABS in a pot of boiling salted water and boil for 1 minute. Remove from the water and plunge them into the ice bath to cool quickly and stop the cooking process. Place the crabs top side up on a cutting board. Stick your thumb under the edge of the top shell and lift it up and off. Press your palm down on the shells to break them in half. Using a spoon, scrape out the feathery gills and soft insides of the crab and discard. Twist off the legs and claws and crack them with the flat side of a chef's knife or a mallet. Cut the crab into quarters.

PLACE A LARGE stockpot over medium-high heat and coat with 2 tablespoons of the oil. When the oil gets hazy, add the crab, including shells. Cook, stirring often with a wooden spoon until the shells are well seared, about 3 to 5 minutes.

TO KEEP THE alcohol from flaming up, remove the pot from the heat and add 1 cup of the sherry. Carefully return the pot to the stove and cook until the alcohol is almost totally evaporated, about 5 minutes. Push the crab to the sides of the pot and add the remaining 2 tablespoons oil. Add the garlic, scallions, carrot, celery, onion, ginger, peppercorns, and coriander, stirring so all the vegetables come in contact with the bottom heat. It may seem like a lot of vegetables, but they will cook down quickly. Reduce the heat to medium and continue cooking for 10 to 15 minutes until the vegetables begin to caramelize and their liquid has cooked out.

ADD THE REMAINING cup of sherry and deglaze the pan by scraping up the brown bits from the bottom with a wooden spoon. Continue cooking until all of the liquid has evaporated, about 1 minute.

ADD THE CILANTRO, Chicken Stock, clam juice, honey, and soy sauce. Reduce the heat to low and simmer until the sauce is reduced and tastes like crab, 25 to 30 minutes.

PASS THE SAUCE through a fine-mesh strainer into a clean saucepan, using a spoon or spatula to press out all the juice. Discard the solids. Season lightly with salt and pepper and keep warm over low heat.

ISRAELI COUSCOUS

MAKES 2 1/2 CUPS

2	CUPS CHICKEN STOCK (PAGE 222)
	KOSHER SALT AND FRESHLY GROUND BLACK PEPPER
1	CUP ISRAELI COUSCOUS (ALSO CALLED PEARL PASTA)
2	TABLESPOONS EXTRA-VIRGIN OLIVE OIL
2	BUNCHES FRESH BASIL LEAVES (ABOUT 3 CUPS)
1/2	CUP ICE WATER
1/2	POUND DUNGENESS CRABMEAT, PICKED THROUGH FOR SHELLS

PLACE THE CHICKEN Stock in a 2-quart saucepan and bring to a boil over medium heat. Season lightly with salt and pepper. Stir in the couscous and bring to a simmer. Cook until tender, 8 to 10 minutes. Transfer the couscous to a colander and drain well. When drained, place it in a large bowl, add the olive oil, and toss to coat. Set aside to cool.

PREPARE AN ICE bath. Set aside.

BRING A LARGE pot of water to a rolling boil and add 1/4 cup of salt. (When blanching, it is important that the water tastes as salty as the sea.) Once the water is at a full boil, add the basil, stirring the leaves into the water to immerse. Blanch until it resembles wilted spinach, about 2 minutes. Pour into a strainer and immediately plunge into the ice bath to stop the cooking process and lock in the vibrant green color. Remove the strainer from the ice water and, using your hands, squeeze the basil dry. Coarsely chop it and place in a blender or food processor. Add 1/2 cup of the ice water. Process to a completely smooth purée, about 1 minute. You should have about 2/3 cup of basil purée. It is important that the purée be kept cold to preserve the green color.

STIR 2 TABLESPOONS of the basil purée into the reserved couscous. It should be bright green. (The remaining purée can be used on pasta or in tuna salad.) Gently fold in the crabmeat and lightly season with salt and pepper. Serve immediately.

ROOT BEER FLOAT
WITH WARM CHOCOLATE CHIP COOKIES

MY ROOT BEER FLOAT IS AN UPDATED VERSION OF A CHILDHOOD SWEET DELIGHT. AT THE TIME I DEVISED IT, HAVING A ROOT BEER FLOAT ON THE MENU OF A FOUR-STAR RESTAURANT WAS REALLY PUSHING THE ENVELOPE. WHEN I TOLD MY STAFF ABOUT THE CONCEPT THEY THOUGHT I WAS NUTS, BUT AFTER THEY TASTED IT, THEY UNDERSTOOD THE METHOD TO MY MADNESS. I TOOK FLAVORS THAT PEOPLE LOVE AND LAYERED THEM INTO SOMETHING COMPLEX AND BOLD. THE SASSAFRAS ICE CREAM AND ROOT BEER SORBET REINFORCE AND INTENSIFY THE PRINCIPAL FLAVOR. MY YOUNG SONS, SAMMY AND ANTHONY, LIKE IT JUST BECAUSE IT TASTES GOOD.

SASSAFRAS EXTRACT AND OIL ARE AVAILABLE IN MANY CANDY-MAKING SUPPLY STORES AND ON THE INTERNET (SEE SOURCES, PAGE 242). ANOTHER CHOICE, OF COURSE, IS TO LEAVE THE EXTRACT OUT ALTOGETHER AND INCREASE THE VANILLA EXTRACT TO 1 TABLE-SPOON. THE LAST OPTION IS TO SIMPLY BUY SOME QUALITY VANILLA BEAN ICE CREAM. I RECOMMEND MAKING THE SORBET, THOUGH—IT IS UNIQUE AND VERY SIMPLE.

TO ME, CHOCOLATE CHIP COOKIES ARE NOT AS EASY TO MAKE AS ONE MIGHT THINK. I PAINSTAKINGLY RETOOLED THE DOUGH TO MAKE THE COOKIES INCREDIBLY MOIST AND RICH, CONTINUALLY ADJUSTING THE CAPACITY OF BUTTER AND CHOCOLATE TO STRETCH THE THRESHOLD. YOU HAVE TO HAVE A GLASS OF MILK WITH THESE!

WINE SUGGESTION
LUSTAU DEL TONEL OLOROSO SHERRY, SPAIN

ROOT BEER FLOAT

1	RECIPE ROOT BEER SORBET (RECIPE FOLLOWS)
1	RECIPE SASSAFRAS ICE CREAM (RECIPE FOLLOWS)
1	LITER OLD-FASHIONED ROOT BEER
	WARM CHOCOLATE CHIP COOKIES (RECIPE FOLLOWS)

PREPARE THE SORBET, ice cream, and cookies according to the directions in the recipes.

TO ASSEMBLE AND serve: Alternate scoops of Root Beer Sorbet and Sassafras Ice Cream in each of 4 chilled fountain glasses or big mugs. Set the glasses on small plates to catch any overflow, and fill with root beer. Serve the floats with straws and parfait spoons with the chocolate chip cookies on the side.

SERVES 4

ROOT BEER SORBET

MAKES 1 QUART

2	CUPS WATER
1	CUP COLD SIMPLE SYRUP (PAGE 225)
1	CUP ROOT BEER SYRUP, SUCH AS TORANI OR DA VINCI
1/2	TEASPOON FRESH SQUEEZED LEMON JUICE
1/2	TEASPOON SALT

COMBINE THE WATER, Simple Syrup, root beer syrup, lemon juice, and salt in a large bowl. Transfer to an ice-cream maker and process according to the manufacturer's directions. When done, the sorbet will have a creamy and stiff consistency. To fully harden the sorbet, transfer to a covered container and freeze until firm, at least 3 hours. The Root Beer Sorbet can be made 1 day ahead.

SASSAFRAS ICE CREAM

MAKES 1 QUART

2	CUPS HEAVY CREAM
1	CUP MILK
1/2	CUP SUGAR
	PINCH OF SALT
9	LARGE EGG YOLKS
1 1/2	TEASPOONS PURE VANILLA EXTRACT
1 1/2	TEASPOONS SASSAFRAS EXTRACT OR 1/4 TEASPOON SASSAFRAS OIL
1	LITER OLD-FASHIONED ROOT BEER, COLD
	WARM CHOCOLATE CHIP COOKIES (RECIPE FOLLOWS)

COMBINE THE CREAM, milk, sugar, and salt in a large saucepan over medium heat. Bring to a simmer and cook gently until the sugar is dissolved, 5 minutes. The temperature should reach 175°F (just scalding).

IN A LARGE mixing bowl, whisk the egg yolks until thickened. Using a ladle, very gradually add half the hot cream into the yolk mixture, whisking constantly (do not add too quickly or the eggs will scramble). Return the tempered eggs to the pan and whisk constantly over medium-low heat until the custard is thick enough to coat the back of a spoon and leaves a path when you run your finger across it, about 5 minutes.

PASS THE CUSTARD through a fine-mesh strainer into a large container. Place in a large bowl of ice water and chill completely, stirring occasionally. This should take about 5 minutes.

ADD THE VANILLA and sassafras extracts into the cold ice cream base, stirring to blend.

PLACE IN AN ice-cream maker and process according to the manufacturer's directions. When done, the ice cream will be the consistency of soft serve. To fully harden the ice cream, place in a covered plastic container and freeze for at least 2 hours.

WARM CHOCOLATE CHIP COOKIES

MAKES 2 1/2 DOZEN

1	CUP (2 STICKS) UNSALTED BUTTER, AT ROOM TEMPERATURE AND CUT INTO CHUNKS
3/4	CUP GRANULATED SUGAR
3/4	CUP DARK BROWN SUGAR, LIGHTLY PACKED
2	LARGE EGGS
1 1/2	TEASPOONS PURE VANILLA EXTRACT
2	CUPS ALL-PURPOSE FLOUR
1	TEASPOON BAKING SODA
1	TEASPOON SALT
1	POUND GOOD-QUALITY BITTERSWEET CHOCOLATE, SUCH AS VALRHÔNA OR SCHARFFEN BERGER, FINELY CHOPPED
1/2	POUND TOASTED PECANS OR WALNUTS, FINELY CHOPPED

COMBINE THE BUTTER and sugars in the bowl of a standing electric mixer fitted with a paddle attachment, or use a handheld electric beater. Beat on medium speed until fluffy and light, about 5 minutes. Using a spatula, scrape down the sides of the bowl from time to time. Add the eggs, 1 at a time, beating well to incorporate. Add the vanilla and continue to mix until combined. Turn off the mixer.

IN A SEPARATE bowl, combine the flour, baking soda, and salt. Turn the mixer to low speed and slowly add half the dry ingredients to the creamed mixture, beating just to combine. Beat in the remaining dry ingredients to just combine. Do not overmix or the cookie dough can become tough. Turn off the mixer and fold in the chopped chocolate and nuts with a large spoon or spatula, stirring until all the bits are incorporated into the batter.

PREHEAT THE OVEN to 350°F.

USING YOUR PALMS, roll the dough into 2-inch balls, about the size of a golf ball. Alternatively, you can use a small ice cream scoop. Place the balls on nonstick cookie sheets, about 2 inches apart. Bake until the cookies are just set on the edges but still fairly soft in the center, 15 to 20 minutes. Cool in the pan for 5 minutes. Serve warm. Once cool, the cookies may be stored in a covered plastic container.

BANANA TARTE TATIN
WITH MAPLE CRÈME ANGLAISE
AND MAPLE SUGAR ICE CREAM

AS A KID, I LOVED BANANA PANCAKES WITH MAPLE SYRUP AND USED TO EAT BANANAS DIPPED IN MAPLE SYRUP WITH VANILLA ICE CREAM. THIS DESSERT WAS BORN FROM THAT MEMORY. TARTE TATIN IS A CLASSIC FRENCH APPLE DESSERT. AT HOME I SOMETIMES PREPARE THIS TART WITH A COMBINATION OF SEASONAL FRUITS. YOU CAN USE ANY FRUIT YOU WISH; OF COURSE APPLES ARE TRADITIONAL, BUT ALSO PARTICULARLY DELICIOUS ARE PEARS OR PEACHES. THE EASE OF THIS RECIPE, ALONG WITH THE FACT THAT IT IS ELEGANT AND VERSATILE, MAKES IT A REAL WINNER.

WINE SUGGESTION
DISZNÓKÓ TOKAJI 5 PUTTONYOS, HUNGARY 1997

SERVES 8 — MAKES ONE 8 1/2-INCH TART

3/4	CUP SUGAR
2	TABLESPOONS WATER
2	TABLESPOONS UNSALTED BUTTER, CUT INTO CHUNKS
6	FIRM BANANAS
1	SHEET FROZEN PUFF PASTRY, THAWED
1	LARGE EGG PLUS 1 TABLESPOON WATER, BEATEN TOGETHER TO MAKE AN EGG WASH
1	RECIPE MAPLE SUGAR ICE CREAM (RECIPE FOLLOWS)

MAKE THE MAPLE Sugar Ice Cream and freeze.

TO MAKE TART: Combine the sugar and water in a 10-inch ovenproof sauté pan over medium heat; it should look like wet sand. Cook without stirring until the sugar melts and begins to caramelize into a syrup, about 3 minutes. Once the sugar starts to liquefy, stir with a wooden spoon so it doesn't burn. Continue to cook until the sugar begins to boil and takes on a medium amber color, about 2 minutes more. Remove from the heat and carefully add the butter, stirring to melt. Set the pan aside so the caramel firms up slightly.

PREHEAT THE OVEN to 475°F.

PEEL AND SLICE the bananas crosswise into coins. Lay the puff pastry sheet on a lightly floured surface and roll it out slightly so it covers the pan. Set a dinner plate on top of the pastry and cut around the outside rim to make a 10-inch circle.

PLACE THE BANANA slices over the caramel in tight, concentric circles to cover the entire bottom of the pan. Cover the bananas with the disk of puff pastry and make 3 slits in the top to let the steam escape. Using a pastry brush, coat the top with egg wash. Transfer to the oven and bake until the pastry is puffed and golden and the filling is bubbly, about 30 minutes.

REMOVE FROM THE oven and let the tart rest for 1 minute to settle. The pastry should have shrunken slightly and pulled away from the sides of the pan. Run a knife around the inside rim of the pan to make sure the tart will come out easily. Set a serving plate on top of the pan and quickly flip it over to invert the tart.

TO SERVE: Cut the Banana Tarte Tatin into wedges. Top each serving with a drizzle of the reserved Maple Crème Anglaise and a scoop of Maple Sugar Ice Cream.

MAPLE SUGAR ICE CREAM

MAKES 1 QUART

3 1/4	CUPS HEAVY CREAM
1 1/4	CUPS MILK
1	CUP MAPLE SUGAR
1/2	TEASPOON SALT
11	LARGE EGG YOLKS
1	TEASPOON PURE VANILLA EXTRACT

COMBINE THE CREAM, milk, maple sugar, and salt in a large saucepan over medium heat. Bring to a simmer, stirring to dissolve the sugar. Cook until the temperature reaches 175°F (just below scalding); this should take about 5 minutes.

IN A LARGE mixing bowl, whisk the egg yolks until thickened. Using a ladle, very gradually add half the hot cream into the yolk mixture, whisking constantly (do not add too quickly or the eggs will scramble). Return the tempered eggs to the pan and whisk constantly over medium-low heat until the custard is thick enough to coat the back of a spoon and leaves a path when you run your finger across it, about 5 minutes.

PASS THE CUSTARD through a fine-mesh strainer into a large container. Place in a large bowl of ice water and chill completely, stirring occasionally. This should take about 5 minutes. When cold, stir in the vanilla. Reserve 1/4 cup of the custard covered in the refrigerator to use as the Maple Crème Anglaise (basically liquid ice cream) for serving with the Banana Tarte Tatin.

PLACE IN AN ice-cream maker and process according to the manufacturer's directions. When done, the ice cream will be the consistency of soft serve. To fully harden the ice cream, place in a covered plastic container and freeze for at least 2 hours.

BONBONS

HAND-MOLDED CHOCOLATES HAVE BECOME POPULAR IN RESTAURANTS AS PETIT FOURS; I WANTED TO DO SOMETHING THAT WAS MORE PLAYFUL AND UNIQUE. SO, AS A DELICIOUS SURPRISE FROM THE KITCHEN, WE SEND OUT FROZEN BONBONS AT THE END OF THE MEAL. AFTER DINNER, PEOPLE ARE COMPLETELY STUFFED, YET THEY WILL STILL MAKE ROOM FOR THE BONBONS. EVERYBODY LOVES ICE CREAM DIPPED IN CHOCOLATE. THE BONBONS ARE SERVED ON A SILVER TRAY, COVERED BY A GLASS DOME TO PREVENT THEM FROM MELTING. THE TRAYS ARE ACTUALLY DESIGNED FOR ESCARGOT, BUT HERE THEY SERVE A DUAL PURPOSE AND FIT THE BONBONS REALLY WELL.

MAKES 1 DOZEN

1	RECIPE SASSAFRAS, MAPLE SUGAR, MASCARPONE, OR VANILLA ICE CREAM (PAGES 210, 214, 137, 155)
3/4	POUND CHOPPED GOOD-QUALITY CHOCOLATE, PREFERABLY DARK OR MILK CHOCOLATE
2	TABLESPOONS VEGETABLE OIL
	COOKIE CRUMBS, TOFFEE PIECES, OR GROUND NUTS (OPTIONAL)

LINE A SHEET pan with aluminum foil and place it in the freezer for several hours or preferably overnight.

WORKING QUICKLY WITH a melon baller, scoop the ice cream into twelve 1/2-inch round balls. Place the balls on the frozen sheet pan about 1 inch apart. If the ice cream gets too soft as you are working, return it to the freezer. Stick a sturdy toothpick in the center of each ice cream ball, making sure it stands up straight. Place the pan back in the freezer and freeze until very hard, preferably overnight.

MELT THE CHOCOLATE and oil in a microwave or in a metal bowl set over barely simmering water. Stir until the chocolate is completely smooth and shiny. Remove from the heat and pour into a small bowl. Let cool slightly.

USING THE TOOTHPICK as a handle, quickly dip the ice cream balls in the chocolate, turning to coat evenly. Let the excess chocolate drip back into the bowl. Set the bonbons on the sheet pan and return to the freezer until the chocolate shells harden, at least 5 minutes. If you wish, spread cookie crumbs (such as Oreos), toffee, or ground nuts on the sheet pan. This helps ensure the bonbons don't stick to the pan. Transfer the pan to the freezer until ready to serve. The bonbons can be made a day or two in advance.

03

THE BASICS

BEURRE BLANC/BEURRE ROUGE

It takes little more than butter to make a sauce. Add some aromatics, a little acid, and wham, a luxurious sauce. Beurre blanc is a French classic that has a multitude of applications and is not at all difficult to make. It has endless variations—your imagination is the only limit. The acid (the wine and vinegar) is what changes in the various versions of this recipe throughout the book. Use red wine and suddenly the sauce transforms to beurre rouge.

2	SHALLOTS, SLICED
3	SPRIGS FRESH THYME
2	SPRIGS FLAT-LEAF PARSLEY
1	BAY LEAF, PREFERABLY FRESH
1/2	TEASPOON WHOLE BLACK PEPPERCORNS
1/2	CUP WINE, SEE INDIVIDUAL RECIPES
1/4	CUP VINEGAR, SEE INDIVIDUAL RECIPES
1/4	CUP HEAVY CREAM
3/4	CUP (1 1/2 STICKS) COLD UNSALTED BUTTER, CUT INTO CHUNKS
	KOSHER SALT AND FRESHLY GROUND BLACK PEPPER

COMBINE THE SHALLOTS, thyme, parsley, bay leaf, peppercorns, wine, and vinegar in a 2-quart saucepan over medium heat. Bring to a simmer and cook until the liquid is reduced to a little more than 1 tablespoon, 5 to 8 minutes. (This is called *au sec*, the French phrase meaning to cook ingredients until dry.)

STIR IN THE cream and continue to simmer until reduced slightly, 1 minute.

REDUCE THE HEAT to low and slowly whisk in the butter, 1 or 2 chunks at a time. Continue whisking until all of the butter has been incorporated, producing a creamy emulsified sauce. Season with salt and pepper.

STRAIN THE SAUCE through a fine-mesh sieve, discarding the solids. Cover and keep warm.

BEURRE MONTÉ

Heating butter above 160 degrees will cause it to break or separate into its different parts. A beurre monté is a way of keeping melted butter in an emulsified state between 160 and 190 degrees, which is perfect for poaching fish or vegetables.

TO MAKE BEURRE Monté: Bring 2 tablespoons of water to a simmer in a small saucepan over medium-low heat. Whisk chunks of cold butter into the water, 1 or 2 pieces at a time, until the mixture is emulsified and thick. You can add as much as a pound of butter to this little bit of water. Hold over gentle heat to maintain the temperature and do not allow the sauce to boil or it will break.

CLARIFIED BUTTER

Butter is composed of butterfat, water, and milk solids. By clarifying the butter, you are able to separate the different components, evaporate the water, and strain out the milk solids that can burn easily. What is left is a clear, golden butterfat. While clarified butter has less flavor than whole butter, it does have a higher smoke point. This means you can pan-fry meats and fish at a higher temperature than you can with regular butter. One quarter of the original volume is lost during the clarifying process. Clarified butter will keep covered in the refrigerator for about 1 month. This recipe may be doubled or tripled.

MAKES 1 1/2 CUPS

2   CUPS (4 STICKS) UNSALTED BUTTER, CUT INTO CHUNKS

PLACE THE BUTTER in a heavy saucepan over low heat to slowly melt. Occasionally swirl the pan to ensure that the butter does not sizzle or brown. Cook, without stirring, until the milk solids have separated and sunk to the bottom of the pan, about 10 minutes. Remove from the heat and let stand for a minute. Skim the foam off the top with a spoon.

PASS THE CLARIFIED butter through a fine-mesh strainer lined with several layers of cheesecloth into a clean container, leaving behind the browned milk solids. The clarified butter should be perfectly clear and golden yellow. Store, covered and refrigerated.

PINOT NOIR REDUCTION

This robust wine sauce is a natural accompaniment to grilled steak as well as fish, such as meaty tuna.

MAKES 2 1/2 CUPS

1/4	CUP CANOLA OIL
1	POUND CREMINI OR BUTTON MUSHROOMS, WIPED OF GRIT, COARSELY CHOPPED
6	SHALLOTS, SLICED
2	BAY LEAVES, PREFERABLY FRESH
1/2	BUNCH FRESH THYME
1	TABLESPOON WHOLE BLACK PEPPERCORNS
1/2	TABLESPOON CORIANDER SEEDS
1/4	CUP SUGAR
1/2	CUP RED WINE VINEGAR
1	(750 ML) BOTTLE PINOT NOIR
1	QUART VEAL DEMI-GLACE (PAGE 222 OR STORE-BOUGHT)

PLACE A LARGE saucepan over medium-high heat and coat with the oil. When hot, add the mushrooms, shallots, bay leaves, thyme, peppercorns, and coriander. Cook, stirring, until the natural moisture from the shallots and mushrooms is released and they begin to brown, about 10 to 15 minutes.

SPRINKLE IN THE sugar, stirring to dissolve. Add the vinegar to deglaze the pan, scraping up the bits in the bottom with a wooden spoon. Add the wine and simmer, stirring occasionally, until the mushrooms are deep purple and the wine is almost totally cooked out, about 40 minutes.

ADD THE VEAL Demi-Glace and continue to simmer until the liquid is reduced by half, about 30 to 40 minutes.

STRAIN THE SAUCE into a clean saucepan or container and discard the solids. Serve hot.

CHICKEN STOCK

Chicken stock is an indispensable commodity in a restaurant kitchen. It is good to always have it on hand for use as a base for soups and sauces.

MAKES ABOUT 1 GALLON

- 5 POUNDS CHICKEN BACKS, NECKS, AND BONES
- 2 YELLOW ONIONS, UNPEELED AND HALVED
- 2 STALKS CELERY, HALVED
- 2 CARROTS, HALVED
- 4 SPRIGS FLAT-LEAF PARSLEY
- 2 SPRIGS FRESH THYME
- 1 BAY LEAF, PREFERABLY FRESH
- 1 TABLESPOON WHOLE BLACK PEPPERCORNS
- 1 TEASPOON CORIANDER SEEDS

RINSE THE CHICKEN bones under cold running water to remove any blood, which would cloud the stock. Place the bones in a stockpot and add just enough cold water to cover by 2 inches, about 1 gallon.

PLACE THE POT over medium-low heat and slowly bring to a simmer, uncovered, skimming any foam and impurities that rise to the surface. Add the onions, celery, carrots, parsley, thyme, bay leaf, peppercorns, and coriander. Reduce the heat and simmer gently for about 2 hours, skimming occasionally to keep the stock clear.

REMOVE FROM THE heat and pass through a fine-mesh strainer into a large container, discarding the solids.

IF NOT USING the stock immediately, place the container in a sink full of ice water and stir frequently to cool the stock. When cold, remove any fat that has solidified on the surface. Cover and refrigerate for up to 1 week or freeze for up to 1 month.

VEAL STOCK

In this stock, the veal bones and vegetables are roasted to create a more pronounced flavor and deep color. The gelatin in the bones adds viscosity to the stock.

MAKES ABOUT 3 QUARTS

- 2 TABLESPOONS CANOLA OIL
- 5 POUNDS VEAL BONES, PREFERABLY MEATY LEG BONES, CUT INTO 2-INCH CHUNKS
- 3 STALKS CELERY, COARSELY CHOPPED
- 2 YELLOW ONIONS, COARSELY CHOPPED
- 1 CARROT, COARSELY CHOPPED
- 1 HEAD OF GARLIC, HALVED
- 1/4 CUP TOMATO PASTE
- 2 CUPS DRY RED WINE, SUCH AS MERLOT
- 5 SPRIGS FLAT-LEAF PARSLEY
- 5 SPRIGS FRESH THYME
- 2 BAY LEAVES, PREFERABLY FRESH
- 1 TABLESPOON WHOLE BLACK PEPPERCORNS
- 1 TEASPOON CORIANDER SEEDS

PREHEAT THE OVEN to 425°F. Place a large roasting pan in the oven to preheat. When hot, coat the pan with the oil and heat in the oven for 2 minutes.

REMOVE THE PAN from the oven and arrange the veal bones in a single layer. Return to the oven and roast for 1 hour, turning the bones once or twice, until they are evenly brown on all sides. Add the celery, onions, carrot, garlic, and tomato paste, stirring to mix well. Return to the oven and roast for an additional 15 minutes.

CAREFULLY REMOVE FROM the oven and pour in the wine to deglaze the pan, stirring with a wooden spoon to release any caramelized bits that have stuck to the bottom. Transfer everything to a large stockpot and fill with enough water to cover the ingredients by 1 inch (about 1 gallon).

PLACE THE STOCKPOT over high heat and bring to a boil. Reduce the heat to low and gently simmer, uncovered, for 30 minutes, diligently skimming any impurities that rise to the surface. Add the parsley, thyme, bay leaves, peppercorns, and coriander. Continue to simmer gently for 3 to 4 hours, skimming occasionally and adding water as needed to keep the bones and vegetables covered.

REMOVE FROM THE heat and strain through a fine-mesh sieve into a large container, discarding the solids. Place the saucepan in a sink full of ice water and stir to cool the stock down quickly or let it sit and slowly come to room temperature. Remove any fat that has solidified on the surface. When cool, cover and refrigerate for up to 1 week or freeze for up to 1 month.

TO MAKE DEMI-GLACE:

PLACE 1 QUART of veal stock in a 2-quart saucepan over medium heat and gently simmer until the liquid is reduced by half (about 2 cups); this takes about 30 minutes. Demi-Glace should have deep brown color and be thick enough to coat the back of a spoon. When it is cold, it looks like chocolate Jell-O.

LOBSTER STOCK

MAKES ABOUT 1 QUART

4	LOBSTER BODIES
4	TABLESPOONS VEGETABLE OIL
1	CUP BRANDY
1	YELLOW ONION, COARSELY CHOPPED
1/2	BULB FENNEL, COARSELY CHOPPED
1	CARROT, COARSELY CHOPPED
2	STALKS CELERY, COARSELY CHOPPED
2	CLOVES GARLIC, SMASHED
1/4	CUP TOMATO PASTE
1	CUP DRY WHITE WINE, SUCH AS SAUVIGNON BLANC
3	SPRIGS FRESH THYME
1	BAY LEAF, PREFERABLY FRESH
1	TEASPOON WHOLE BLACK PEPPERCORNS
1	TEASPOON CORIANDER SEEDS

WHEN CLEANING THE lobster bodies, it's best to wear kitchen gloves to protect your hands. Firmly pull the bodies and shells apart. When all of the bodies have been separated, use a tablespoon to scrape off the feathery gills and clean out the roe and innards from the underside of the shell and discard. Coarsely chop the lobster shells and bodies.

HEAT A LARGE stockpot over medium-high heat and coat with 2 tablespoons of the oil. When the oil gets hazy, add the lobster shells and bodies. Stir often until the shells are well seared and bright red, 3 to 5 minutes. Shells equal flavor.

TO KEEP THE alcohol from flaming, remove the pot from the heat and add the brandy. Carefully return the pot to the stove and cook out the brandy until it is almost totally evaporated. Push the shells to the sides of the pot and add the remaining 2 tablespoons of oil and the onion, fennel, carrot, celery, and garlic. Cook and stir until the vegetables are tender and begin to caramelize, 10 to 15 minutes. Stir in the tomato paste and cook until the color deepens, about 2 minutes. Pour in the wine and deglaze by scraping up the browned bits from the bottom of the pot with a wooden spoon. Continue cooking until all of the liquid is evaporated, about 1 minute.

POUR IN JUST enough cold water to cover by 2 inches, about 1 gallon. Slowly bring to a boil, uncovered, skimming any foam and impurities that rise to the surface. Add the thyme, bay leaf, peppercorns, and coriander. Reduce the heat to low and simmer gently for about 1 hour, skimming occasionally to keep the stock clear. Strain the stock through a fine-mesh sieve into another pot or large container. Discard the solids.

USE THE STOCK immediately or if you plan on storing it, place the pot in a sink full of ice water and stir to cool it down rapidly. Once cold, remove any solidified fat from surface of the stock. Cover and refrigerate for up to 1 week or store in the freezer for 1 month.

TOMATO WATER

This unassuming, almost clear liquid has a clean tomato flavor that often surprises people. Oddly enough, the color is closer to yellow than red. Because it is not heated, the resulting tomato water infuses very naturally with other flavors. Tomato water makes a great base for a consommé or jelly; we also frequently use it in the restaurant for vinaigrettes.

MAKES 3 1/2 CUPS

10   RIPE ROMA OR HEIRLOOM TOMATOES, CORED AND HALVED
1   TABLESPOON KOSHER SALT

JUICE THE TOMATOES in an electric juicer. If you do not have a juicer, process the tomatoes in a blender or food processor with 1/4 cup of water until the mixture is liquid.

LINE A FINE-MESH strainer with a tea towel or double layer of cheesecloth and set over a bowl. Pour the tomato juice (or liquid) into the sieve and sprinkle with the salt. Transfer to the refrigerator and allow the tomato water to slowly drip out. This will take a few hours or up to overnight. Tomato water can be stored, covered and refrigerated, for up to 1 week.

SIMPLE SYRUP

Simple syrup is nothing more than a mixture of sugar and water heated until it is clear. It is used in many recipes throughout the book or to sweeten mixed or iced drinks.

MAKES ABOUT 2 CUPS

1   CUP SUGAR

2   CUPS WATER

COMBINE THE SUGAR and water in a saucepan over medium heat. Bring to a boil and, swirling the pan over the heat, cook at a bare boil until the sugar is totally dissolved and the liquid becomes clear, about 2 minutes. Do not allow the syrup to boil or it will darken. Remove from the heat and cool completely before using. Simple Syrup can be stored indefinitely, covered and refrigerated.

SEGMENTING CITRUS

This technique is utilized several times throughout the book. Follow this procedure for any type of citrus fruit, be it oranges, lemons, limes, tangerines, or grapefruit.

TO SEGMENT CITRUS, first trim off the top and bottom flat so the fruit stands steady on a work surface; cut deep enough so you see the meat of the fruit. Using a paring knife, cut off the skin and bitter white pith of the fruit, following the natural round shape and turning the citrus as you do so. Trim off any white pith that remains. Hold the fruit over a bowl to catch the juices. Carefully cut along the membrane, on both sides of each segment, to free the pulp. Let the segments drop into the bowl as you cut. Squeeze the remaining fruit into the bowl to extract any remaining juice.

TRIOS VISUAL REFERENCE

FIRST COURSE TRIOS

SEARED DIVER SCALLOPS

PAGE 08

SESAME-CRUSTED SOFT-SHELL CRAB WITH DUNGENESS CRAB FALAFEL

PAGE 17

TRIOS VISUAL REFERENCE

FIRST COURSE TRIOS

TORCHON OF FOIE GRAS WITH FOIE GRAS GASTRIQUE

PAGE 27

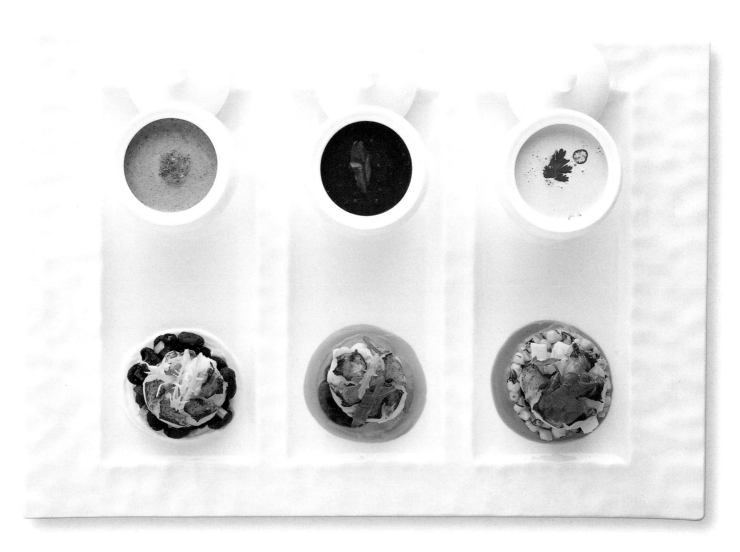

LOBSTER SOUP AND SALAD

PAGE 37

TRIOS VISUAL REFERENCE

FISH ENTRÉE TRIOS

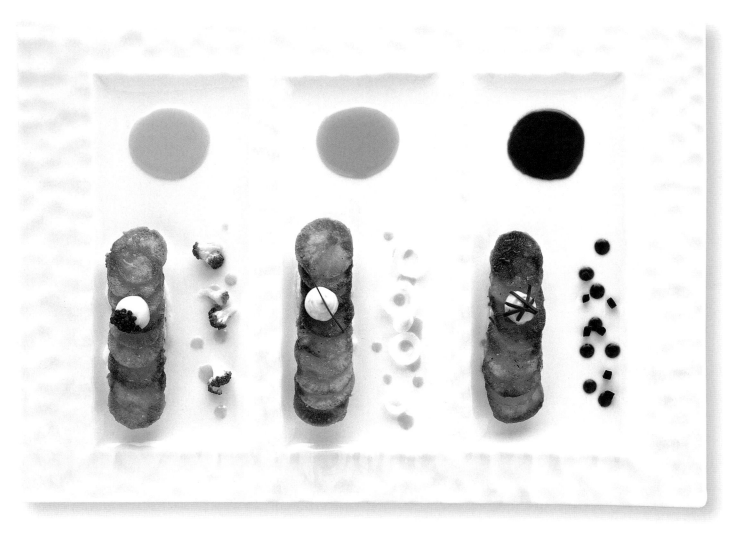

POTATO-CRUSTED DOVER SOLE

PAGE 48

SEARED BLACK BASS, CRISPY PORK BELLY, AND CITRUS CONFIT

PAGE 57

TRIOS VISUAL REFERENCE

FISH ENTRÉE TRIOS

SAUTÉED ABALONE, FRESH FETTUCINE, AND BROWN BUTTER SAUCE

PAGE 67

TAPIOCA-CRUSTED RED SNAPPER

PAGE 7 8

BUTTER-POACHED KOBE BEEF RIB EYE WITH PINOT NOIR REDUCTION

PAGE 90

OLIVE OIL—POACHED RACK OF LAMB

PAGE 98

TRIOS VISUAL REFERENCE

MEAT ENTRÉE TRIOS

SEARED SQUAB BREAST, SQUAB LEG CONFIT, SQUAB STOCK, AND DEMI-GLACE

PAGE 109

CRISPY LOIN OF KUROBUTA PORK, PULLED PORK

PAGE 120

TRIOS VISUAL REFERENCE

DESSERT TRIOS

SUMMER BERRY COBBLER, BERRY SUNDAE WITH MASCARPONE ICE CREAM

PAGE 134

STONE FRUIT PAIN PERDU, CRÈME FRAÎCHE SHERBET

PAGE 143

TRIOS VISUAL REFERENCE

DESSERT TRIOS

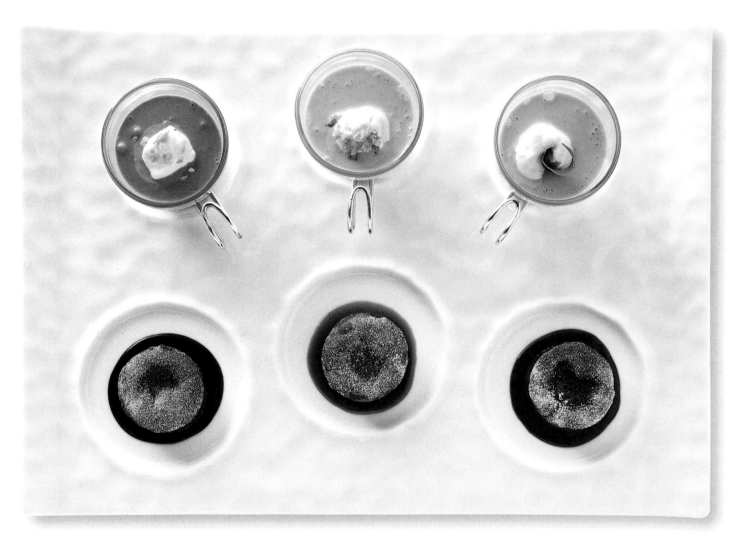

WARM CHOCOLATE PUDDING CAKE WITH MILK SHAKE

PAGE 152

APPLE *FINANCIER*, SPICED HOLIDAY DRINKS

PAGE 160

M

SOURCES

CANE AND REED
caneandreed.com
800.227.8498
Old Hickory sassafras extract

CHEF'S RESOURCE
chefsresource.com
866.765.CHEF (2433)
White soy sauce, saffron

D'ARTAGNAN
dartagnan.com
800.DARTAGN (327.8246)
Foie gras, duck fat, demi-glace, squab, gourmet mushrooms,
fresh truffles, and truffle butter

FROG HOLLOW FARM
froghollow.com
888.779.4511
Stone fruit

HUDSON VALLEY FOIE GRAS
hudsonvalleyfoiegras.com
845.292.2500
All things duck, including foie gras and rendered duck fat

KALUSTYANS
kalustyans.com
800.352.3451 and 212.685.3451
Sel rose, tapioca starch, white soy sauce, lentils

KING ARTHUR FLOUR
www.kingarthurflour.com or www.bakerscatalogue.com
800.827.6836
Almond flour, praline paste, Valrhôna and Scharffen Berger chocolate

LORANN OILS
lorannoils.com
888.4LORANN (456.7266)
Sassafras oil

MONTEREY ABALONE
montereyabalone.com
831.646.0350
Abalone

PLANTIN
plantin.com
201.867.4590
Truffles, truffle vinegar, truffle oil, truffle butter

SAUSALITO SPRINGS
sausalitosprings.com
415.331.5906
Watercress (2 pound minimum order)

SNAKE RIVER FARMS
snakeriverfarms.com
800.657.6305
Kobe-style beef and Kurobuta pork

SURFAS
surfasonline.com
310.559.4770
Gelatin sheets, fennel pollen, fish sauce, black forbidden rice, caviar

VERDURE FARMS
415.990.4749
Heirloom tomatoes (1 case minimum order, 10-15 pounds)

ACKNOWLEDGMENTS

When my partnership with Aqua ended in 2002, I founded Mina Group with tennis legend Andre Agassi as my partner. Being affiliated with a man as driven and dedicated as Andre has been a life-changing experience for me. His penchant for physical conditioning and his persistence and determination set him apart. I look at Andre's accomplishments and am constantly inspired. Ethically, he is one of the finest individuals I've ever met. His charitable foundation assists underprivileged children with recreational and educational opportunities. It has been a deep privilege to partner with a person who is not only one of the greatest athletes of our time but also a deeply caring human being. Being associated with Agassi Enterprises has allowed me to be united with two of the most intelligent and business-savvy men on the planet, Perry Rogers and Todd Wilson. They have guided me and put me on the right road to a successful business. I owe special thanks to these men from whom I have learned so much.

Any degree of achievement calls for two indispensable things—hard work and good people. Restaurants don't just invent themselves; the real story is about the people who create and run them. For me, it has been important to forge a strong infrastructure of colleagues who share my culinary philosophy. Part of my job is to mentor and guide aspiring young chefs, and I have been extremely fortunate to work with some extraordinary people. Chris L'Hommedieu, Jeffrey Lloyd, Mark LoRusso, Michelle Retallack, and Jay Wetzel were my core team at Aqua. Some of them are still with me and others have gone on, but these were the ones who supported me and enabled me to grow, expand, and open multiple restaurants. A new addition to the team is Anthony Carron, who has opened several restaurants with me and shares the same solid vision.

In the front of the house, I've hired an incredible management team, many of whom have crossed the line from professional contact to friend and all of whom have been there for me when I needed them. Patric Yumul, who is vice president of operations, ensures the service standards for all of my properties. He is a key figure in my company and I can't imagine my life without him. Chuck Kelley and Paula Kaduce are the core of Mina Group and have been with me from the beginning. Their administrative expertise is the reason I have been able to hold it all together. Rajat Parr, aka "the genius," not only wrote the wine pairing notes for this book but also develops and manages the wine programs at each of my restaurants. Raj is a sommelier extraordinaire with intense passion and wisdom. Kristin Koca McLarty's vast knowledge of public relations and marketing is a vital part of my success. Stacey Morrone's development and coordination skills help bring it all together seamlessly. Nancy Zammit not only is an able manager but also never fails to let us all know what we are doing wrong! Viki Card, my faithful assistant for eight years, keeps me organized on a daily basis. Bryan Philon, one of my dearest lifelong friends and general manager of MICHAEL MINA San Francisco, has the insight and enthusiasm to make it all run smoothly. Jorge Pagani and Ari Kastrati—general managers of MICHAEL MINA Bellagio and Nobhill respectively—are my lifelines in Las Vegas.

Every restaurant that I have in Las Vegas came about because of the trust and belief given to me by Gamal Aziz, the forward-thinking president of the MGM Grand. I owe so much to this man and count him as one of the most influential and significant forces of my career. I am proud to call him friend. The people at MGM Grand have been fantastic business partners with a keen ability to take the vision to its most complete fulfillment.

I would like to thank the chefs I've had the privilege of working with over the years. At the top of the list is George Morrone, whom I trained under the longest and thus has had the most profound influence on my career. Thank you, George, for your mentoring and for your brotherly love. To Charlie Palmer, Don Pintabona, and Gerry Hayden, I am forever appreciative for your encouragement, guidance, and friendship. I would also like to acknowledge the late Jean-Louis Palladin, one of the greatest chefs of all time. He was a true master of his craft, known for his passion and commitment to the very best. I was extremely fortunate to work alongside Jean-Louis at several culinary events and considered it a great honor to become friends with him. His spirit is irreplaceable and his memory is one I will always cherish. This book could not have been possible without the collective energy of several individuals to whom I am grateful. A million thanks to JoAnn Cianciulli, for her infectious enthusiasm and dedication to the almost impossible task of writing this book with me. She moved to San Francisco in order to write the book properly and learn our culture—her commitment is unsurpassed. She is one of the most talented writers I know and I couldn't have chosen anyone better. Jojo, you are part of our family now. Thanks to my brilliant photographer Karl Petzke for effectively capturing the essence and imagery of this book. You grabbed hold of the challenge and ran with it. Enormous thanks to the legendary Michael Vanderbyl for his expert efforts in designing such a beautiful book and for saying yes in the first place. You are a class act and one of the most creative people I have ever encountered. Thanks to Erica Wilcott at Vanderbyl Design for her hard work. An additional thank-you to my executive sous chef Michelle Retallack for her concerted efforts with recipe testing and food styling. Thanks to Mickey Choate for connecting me with Bulfinch Press and to Karen Murgolo and her tremendous staff, including editor Karyn Gerhard and production coordinator Pamela Schechter, for believing in this book and for supporting me graciously throughout the process.

On a personal note, I would like to thank my parents, Ezzat and Minerva, who sacrificed everything to bring our family to the United States. You have both given me more than I can put into words. Thanks to my brother, Magid, and my sister, Mennell, for their lifelong support. Last, but certainly not least, a huge thank-you to my wife, Diane, whose love, patience, sense of humor, and confidence continue to inspire me, and for giving me the two most incredible sons in the world, Sammy and Anthony, who keep me smiling and balanced.

INDEX